Madness and Crime

Madness and Crime

Philip Bean

WILLAN
PUBLISHING

BP53

Published by

Willan Publishing
Culmcott House
Mill Street, Uffculme
Cullompton, Devon
EX15 3AT, UK
Tel: +44(0)1884 840337
Fax: +44(0)1884 840251
info@willanpublishing.co.uk
www.willanpublishing.co.uk

Published simultaneously in the USA and Canada by

Willan Publishing
c/o ISBS, 920 NE 58th Ave, Suite 300
Portland, Oregon 97213-3786, USA
Tel: +001(0)503 287 3093
Fax: +001(0)503 280 8832
e-mail: info@isbs.com
website: www.isbs.com

First published 2008

Hardback
ISBN 978-1-84392-297-1

British Library Cataloguing-in-Publication Data

A catalogue record for this book is available from the British Library

Project management by Deer Park Productions, Tavistock, Devon
Typeset by GCS, Leighton Buzzard, Beds
Printed and bound by T.J. International, Padstow, Cornwall

8/2/10

For Teresa

Contents

Preface   *ix*

Part 1 Some thoughts on the nature of madness   **1**
Introduction and overview   1
Madness and the disease model   4
An empirical theory of madness   10
Empirical, statistical and emotional theories compared   25
An assessment of empiricist theories of madness   35

**Part 2 Madness as genius, and madness as an aid
to creativity**   **47**

**Part 3 Restraining the mad: justifications for
compulsory detention**   **61**
Detaining the mad   61
De jure and *de facto* detentions   68
A note on liberty   77
Mental health law and formal law   82
Typical legal justifications and their limitations   86
The impact of compulsion   93
Who does the detaining?   96
Paternalism v. autonomy   105
Summary and conclusion   108

Part 4 Madness and crime   **123**
Some methodological problems in the madness and
    crime nexus   123

An overview of the problem 127
Psychiatric services in the penal system: an overview 131
A model for examining the links between madness
(mental disorder) and crime 139
Comments on future research 174
Summary and conclusion 177

Subject Index 185
Author Index 189

Preface

I have divided these essays into four unequal parts: on the nature of madness; on madness as genius, on the detention of the mad, and finally on the links between madness and crime. These essays are about selected features of madness, or rather aspects that have relevance to contemporary society. I have selected these topics out of personal interest, but I hope of interest to others also, with the slant towards the criminological, except perhaps in the section on genius. The aim is not to provide a comprehensive review of the literature, or a definitive statement about where we stand, but to reflect on a field that continues to perplex and challenge. I hope the book will be seen in these terms.

My own interest in madness goes back to the late 1970s as a result of a research study on compulsion under the then 1959 Mental Health Act. I was puzzled about the world these mentally disordered patients inhabited, and that sense of curiosity remained. This book is an attempt to dip into some of those questions; 'dipping' is the best one can hope for, since resolution of such an immense subject is neither feasible nor possible. Given its complexity I can do little more than raise points of interest, hoping they may spark others to take things further. Sceptics may doubt whether more needs to be said about madness, believing too much has been said already, at least until the mystery of consciousness is unearthed. And that may never be. They could be right, but I hope to show that there is no harm trying.

In Part 1 the question is about madness itself; what is it, and what are some of the main considerations given to it. I have tried to answer these questions by reference to an empirical model. It is surprising how little attention has been given to these matters. There are ample high-quality historical-sociological studies tracing the development of the madhouses, and of psychiatry, alongside accounts of nineteenth-century thinking. In all this, however, there is little to guide us on ways of thinking about madness itself. Nor have philosophers done much to help. Anthony Quinton opened his chapter on 'Madness' with the observation that madness is a subject that ought to interest philosophers, but they have had surprisingly little to say about it. His contribution will be acknowledged throughout. In Part 2 I have indulged in a short discussion on madness, genius and creativity.

Part 3 is about compulsion, a topic on which I have written before but never given it full consideration. Nowadays, with rare exceptions, it is not part of the public debate. Sociologically one can see why: I suspect the rights of mental patients have become of less significance than hitherto; perceptions have changed, and the mad have moved from victim to violator. Yet the problem remains, or should remain, if only because it raises those age-old questions about liberty, power and the nature of deviant identities. How to justify compulsory detention, and who should undertake the process? These questions have numerous sociological, ethical and jurisprudential elements, and cannot be resolved by reference to medical authorities. I hope this section revitalises a debate about the detention, treatment and discharge of the mentally disordered, and will help produce more rational mental health legislation. At the time of writing (March 2007) the Mental Health Bill 2006 was still before Parliament. I have made reference to this where appropriate and assume from what the Department of Health says that the final version will not differ greatly.

Part 4 is about the links with crime. It is a straightforward criminological study, avoiding that interesting but for these purposes less relevant debate about criminal responsibility, and its various defences. Such matters have been dealt with by numerous lawyers more capable than I in the ways of the legal world. My interests are about the madness–crime nexus; what are the links with crime, and which particular crimes are linked to which types of disorder. I am not concerned with sentencing practices or how these offenders are dealt with in the penal system. There is an imbalance in the literature, with a profusion linking madness to violence, but much less linking it to other crimes.

I have used terms such as 'schizophrenic' and 'depressive', thereby turning adjectives into nouns. Some may see this as disrespectful, but that is not intended. I prefer this to using the more long-winded approach such as 'people with schizophrenia' or 'those with a depressive condition'. It is a convenient shorthand way of dealing with complex terminology.

I am grateful to all those who have indulged my interest in the topic, to the point where, almost always, they have found ordinary conversations directed towards some feature contained in the book. My particular thanks go to Louis Blom-Cooper, Leo and Mary Goodman, Georg Hoyer, Teresa Nemitz, Jill Peay, Herschel Prins, and John Weston who read the drafts and made valuable comments, often too valuable to be ignored. Of course the format and the content remains my responsibility.

Philip Bean

Part I

Some thoughts on the nature of madness

Introduction and overview

I read somewhere, I've long since forgotten where, that most of us can expect to have at least one period of madness in our lifetime. It may not be severe, it may not last long, but it will certainly be unpleasant. It might act as a beacon from which to judge or measure our subsequent sanity, or it might be forgotten, buried and never reconsidered. Whatever its legacy, madness is not a benign condition; it is not one of those slight quirks which the labelling theorists were wont to dismiss as a minor deviance (see Roth and Kroll 1986: 88). Nor is it simply the product of those who enforce the label, as if the rule enforcers decide on the basis of some manufactured evidence, or conspiracy, that some were mad and others not – surely one of the greatest pieces of inhuman theorising of our age, and a disservice to the mad. It ignores their suffering. Madness is painful; if acute, it can be debilitating, and if chronic it can ruin one's life.

I want to look a little more closely at what constitutes madness, and to do so by concentrating on the empirical model, sometimes called the cognitive. I have selected this because I think it offers a promising solution to some of the more intractable problems associated with insanity. If madness is 'something', painful though that may be, how best can it be described?

There is no shortage of material from which to draw. We know a great deal about how the mad were dealt with, whether by alienists or in the early asylums (see Scull 1979; Porter 1991; Foucault 1977). Historians, and in particular some psychiatric historians, have put their own slant on the subject, as we all do, some interpreting the history of psychiatry and treatment as progressive, adding their hopes for the future. Others offer a different interpretation. Nonetheless, all these historical accounts remind us of the complexities of the subject matter and the dangers of making simple generalisations. Alongside these are the interpretations of the treatment by professionals, lawyers and others who have managed, treated and written about them. Together these add to a burgeoning and impressive literature, although this has produced rather less emphasis on the nature of madness itself. It means, in Roy Porter's terms, that we know *about* them, but almost nothing *of* them (Porter 1985: 64; Scull 1979).

This failing, if it is a failing, is often offset through the writings of the mad, but these too can be slanted, aimed at providing an excuse or apology for their shortcomings, or blaming those who detained them. Countless autobiographies and biographies have described what it is like to be mad, sometimes the authors insisting that they, or others, were wrongly accused, or if not then madness was the tunnel through which they gained enlightenment. In their writings madness appears to shade into sanity, or *vice versa*. There seems to be no clear dividing line. It is part of the great mystery that this is so. Their writings also show the pain and the extravagance of maniacal fury or the sinking into despondence and melancholy (Porter 1991: 4–8, 12–13). If anyone doubts this the accounts by Kay Jamison of her life with a bipolar condition (Jamison 1996) or by Peter Chadwick, suffering from schizophrenia, should dispel any illusions (Chadwick 1997).

There is also a rich classical literature on which to draw. Various types and aetiologies of madness are displayed in fiction, ranging from bereavement, a lost love, intense personal pressure, or simply being in love. King Lear talks of the pain of madness (Act IV scene 7: 45) and compares the sane to being 'a soul in bliss' for his world was 'bound Upon a wheel of fire, that mine own tears Do scald like molten lead.' Lear's madness was speeded up by self-pity. He pleads with his daughters to remember, 'Your kind old father whose frank heart gave all', then rebukes himself for 'O that way madness lies! Let me shun that; No more of that' (Act 3 scene 4: 20).[1] Self-pity distorts the truth of relationships. Lear's associate the Duke of Gloucester blamed his condition on the failings of his son: 'The grief hath crazed my wits' (Act 3 scene 4: 164). Grief unhinges the mind. Gloucester's madness occurred when 'thoughts are sever'd from griefs', that is, split from each other, or separated (broken) from the conscious world.

Lear's madness moved him to another level of consciousness, but when sanity returned he was restored to an earlier mental state. His madness provided insights that are often the prerogative of those who have gone beyond us to reach new points of reflection. 'When we are born we cry that we are come To this great stage of fools' (Act 4 scene 6: 180). That is more than recognition of old age, but a sad, realistic recognition of existence. For this *is* a stage of fools, with some actors more foolish than others. Dr Johnson saw it less in theatrical terms and more as capable of producing suffering: 'Every man will readily confess that his own condition discontents him', and 'The general lot of mankind is misery' (quoted in Porter 1985: 69). Madness is stark, there is no way of hiding it; the mad give themselves away by their appearance, by the way they look, walk, and talk. Everyone knows who they are, what Porter calls 'behaving crazy, looking crazy and talking crazy' (Porter 1987a: 35). There are no special skills needed to identify them.

This slight digression into classical literature reveals more than the quality of its poetry; it suggests there remain numerous aetiologies embedded deep within our consciousness. We assume, and often know, that some angry people will become mad, as will some who are grief-stricken. But then others may not, for not all fit the scheme of things.[2] Sometimes madness or the cause of it is easily explained, common knowledge perhaps, yet sometimes we are puzzled why it should occur.

Nor is normality any easier to understand. While normality may be the converse of madness, as reason is to unreason, with the latter a parody on the former, normality does not mean a perfect state; it can in certain circumstances include a measure or degree of disorder or instability. Indeed the idea that everyone is a little mad, and craziness a way of the world is not uncommon. The young Charles Darwin said that his father thought there was a perfect gradation between the sane and insane, but that everybody was insane at some stage of their lives (quoted in Porter 1987a: 1). Others, however, were convinced that there was a clearer divide. John Haslam (1764–1844), a British psychiatrist, argued early in his career that reason and madness, or sanity and insanity, were as distinct as black and white; as clear as straight and crooked. However, in old age he confessed that he knew no one who was in their right mind except perhaps the Almighty, and of this, incidentally, he had been reassured on the authority of eminent Church of England divines (quoted in Porter 1991: 2).

Finally, there is an equally extensive and rich literature on the aetiology of madness going back at least to Plato and Aristotle. In the late seventeenth century John Locke distinguished between those who were born witless and those who fell out of their wits, the mad being the latter. Locke saw a difference between madmen and idiots, the former having too many ideas, the latter too few; while Voltaire, anticipating modern psychiatric thinking, saw it as a disease of the brain: 'A lunatic is a sick man whose brain is in bad health.' He then adds somewhat pessimistically, and rather worryingly for modern psychiatrists, 'Doctors will never understand why a brain has regulated and consistent ideas. They will believe themselves to be wise and they will be as mad as the lunatic'. (quoted in Porter 1987a: 17). In 1810 the London physician William Black tabulated the causes of insanity among admissions to Bedlam. Of the 800 or so patients over 200 were there due to 'Disappointments, Grief, and Troubles'. The next largest group, over 100, were due to 'Family and Hereditary Matters', closely followed by 'Fevers', then 'Religion and Methodism'. 'Love', 'Drink, Intoxication', and 'Fright' all figured prominently (Porter 1987a: 33). So too did 'Study'; the idea that too much learning turns one's head was a providential threat found in the New Testament. And just as there was no shortage of aetiologies in the early nineteenth century, nor would there be today. It would not be difficult to compile a similarly lengthy list, which might not tally with that of William Black but would have many 'causes' in common.

To ignore these sources is to miss out on numerous insights that direct attention towards a more eclectic view of madness, or rather towards one that emphasises multiple causes and myriad responses. I am not suggesting that all these views be considered, but I want to show that the current fashionable modern view, which concentrates on psychosis as a disease, is not the only one, nor is it necessarily the sole path to the truth. In fact I suggest such a view has serious shortcomings.

Madness and the disease model

Madness can be seen as arising from different origins; a socio-psychological model, to be called multi dimensional, and a disease model, to be called quasi dimensional, the latter an extension of the clinical. These different models have produced schisms in the research programmes and given rise to different conclusions. (Claridge 2001: 95). The aim here is to emphasise the multi dimensional, that is to see madness as arising from a set of socio-psychological dimensions.

In essence this means madness lies at one extreme of a continuum, with sanity at the other, and with personality traits of a more or less severe kind in between. Claridge (2001: 96) calls these 'personality variations,' i.e. they represent individual differences.

A multi-dimensional view opens up numerous opportunities, one of which is to break from traditional medical terminology – more specifically, to use the term 'madness' in preference to 'psychosis' or other such medical terms. It would, of course, be possible to stick to established terminology found in standard psychiatric textbooks, but to do so would be to accept the psychiatric paradigms and become more attuned to matters of diagnosis and treatments than I would wish. It would tie the debate into the world of medicine, and the disease model of psychiatry, and that would not do.

There is another reason: using the term madness does more than create distance from the clinicians; madness is an evocative word, poetic and able to encapsulate the depth of the subject matter. When King Lear recognised the turmoil devouring him and said to his Fool: 'O Fool! I shall go mad', he feared the onset of an overpowering presence. Would he have said the same had he thought he was becoming psychotic or mentally ill? I think not. King Lear was 'mad'. That says more than he was 'mentally ill', 'psychotic', or 'mentally disordered'. Madness also conveys the richest resonances in everyday parlance. It can be widely applied to all manner of abnormalities and extremes, such as being madly in love, or being mad at someone who has upset us (Porter 1991: xi). It encapsulates terms like 'crazy', 'loopy', and numerous others, all of which suggest variations in mad behaviour.[3] Yet it is not just the language and the poetry that makes things different, 'madness' reflects a different way of looking at the world.

Of course, it is not without its problems. Like all such concepts definitional problems abound. What, for example, are its borders and boundaries? Where does the Visionary, the Religious Prophet or the Eccentric fit in? (Porter 1991: xiv). Or, how does it differ from other terms, such as insanity? But, following Polonius, no definition seems able to answer the question, for what is it 'To define true madness' except to say, 'is't to be nothing else but mad'.

The impression might be conveyed that there is something afoot here that is anti-psychiatry, or a relic of the anti-psychiatry movement of the 1960s. Quite the reverse. The stance is not confrontational, extensive use will be made of the psychiatric literature, and of the insights gained. Yet there are differences; the aim is not to classify patients, or diagnose their condition, or suggest treatments.

5

Psychiatry takes that stance; it is also interested in the neuroses, the personality and psychopathic disorders. I do not regard the latter as falling within the compass of the debate, the former are but milder forms of disorder, although sometimes as painful, and for the latter, I am persuaded these conditions have little or nothing to do with madness. Leaving aside the psychopath means ignoring many of the real difficulties faced by the criminal justice system, and the countless issues that have held up the new Mental Health Act, but to include that condition opens up too many avenues to be handled in a work of this length. (Personality disorders and psychopathic disorders are, however, dealt with more fully in Part 4). It has not been possible to eschew all psychiatric terms; modern research uses these terminologies, and clinicians likewise.

The disease model offers one approach but not an entirely satisfactory one, and its weaknesses are becoming increasingly apparent. I admit to being unconvinced by it, although in saying this I am not giving support to the Szaszian view that madness is nothing more than 'a problem of living'. Eschewing the former does not mean support for the latter. Madness is more than a problem of living, it is a special condition, unique in its way. It requires special attention, but that does not make it an illness. Nor am I impressed by the constant search for a physiological basis for those mental disorders such as schizophrenia or depression, a view incidentally increasingly shared by others (Clarke 2001; Read 2004). And even if an underlying physiological condition were to be identified there remains a basic logical problem that attempts to deduce a causal relationship from a correlation. Is the mental state a product of or cause of the physiological change? And how to tell? Assume a correlation, then what? Is it anything more than a connection to the 'person's way of life', with all its physical and psychological dimensions? (Ingleby 1981: 37). And how is a correlation to be interpreted? High levels of adrenalin clearly accompany anger or excitement; but no one seriously suggests that adrenalin causes the anger – nor incidentally, as a treatment for anger that patients should have their adrenalin levels adjusted or reduced by neuro-physiology.

For convenience we can call the quasi-dimensional the disease model – not the medical model, for as Tyrer and Steinberg (1998) say, the medical model is a generic term; the disease model is more specific. The disease model regards mental malfunction as a consequence of physical and chemical changes, primarily in the brain but sometimes in other parts of the body (Tyrer and Steinberg 1998: 9). This model asserts that psychoses are clearly identifiable disease syndromes with a distinct biological and genetic substrate, a view that was given a boost by the development from the 1950s of neuroleptic medication, which provided marked symptom relief (Clarke 2001). Typical of many modern psychiatrists, Tyrer and Steinberg recognise that knowledge of mental illnesses is incomplete, but do not want to abandon the disease model; i.e. they make the assumption that there exists an underlying recognised disease condition and operate *as if* this were so. The hope is that the elusive physical pathology will one day be found, confirming all suspicions that at last psychiatric illnesses are explicable in terms of physical illness. That would allow psychiatry to take its place at the medico-scientific table.

The disease model offers a materialist conception of madness and encapsulates the mind-brain theory. It leaves no problem about explaining how the mind and brain interact, or about whether mental states are able to provide a causal explanation of behaviour (Glover 1980: 8). So for each piece of behaviour there is some reaction in the brain, and all behaviour is reducible in that form. Psychosis (madness) is explained by defects or changes in the brain.

But things are never that simple. Attractive though it may be there remains the same age-old problems of Cartesian dualism; that is, what is the relationship that is supposed to exist between the brain and the mental states it produces? And if they are identical, as some have suggested, do they have the same or different properties, such as those observed by neurosurgeons and those accessible by introspection, i.e. through consciousness. This intriguing question was asked by Jonathan Glover: what would happen if future work provided all the answers the materialist ever wanted, where every mental state would be claimed to be identified as a so-called brain state (1980: 9)? And the answer, he says, is that we are no further forward, for the Cartesian dualist would simply claim that all the neuro-physiologists have done is to show correlations between two different kinds of states (1980: 9). It is the old mind-body problem all over again; Descartes would recognise it immediately. (Descartes implied that consciousness was rational, and if so insanity must be a consequence of some precarious connection to the brain (Carter 1983).) So, the mind-brain materialist offers a variation on an old Cartesian theme.

There has been, at least since the 1960s, an incessant demand to have the disease model accepted by patients and public alike. Whatever its strengths, and there are many, in my view the model has been overplayed. It has been promoted and accepted by clever marketing, that is by linking it to the idea of a progressive enlightened psychiatry where rejection is to return to dark, unsympathetic days. Its acceptance has also been assisted by the law of repetition: if assertions are made with sufficient regularity, and by people of high status, eventually they will become accepted. And so it has proved. This is in spite of some weak and curious arguments by those making the assertions; for example, as Tyrer and Steinberg say, 'the fact that we cannot identify a part of the brain that is pathological at the present state of our knowledge does not mean that no such change exists' (1998: 29).[4] Well yes, but that argument could apply to any social problem, or any other piece of behaviour that one cared to name. Second, it is often asserted that there must be a disease condition, as treatment, through the medium of chemical therapy, cures or alleviates it. The trouble with this is that one cannot assume that the condition is that which the chemicals change, or which tranquillisers tranquillise. Tranquillisers may block or simply change matters that have little or nothing to do with the so-called disease.

Doubtless the search for a disease or neuro-physiological base will continue; there is too much at stake to do otherwise. In part research is driven by a laudable and honest desire to see psychiatry recognised as a scientific discipline. But there are other deeper, self-seeking reasons afoot; for example, modern psychiatric research is often propelled by drug companies eager to find that elusive physiological base for their product. Conveniently, commercial considerations can fit easily into that disease paradigm.

That may well be so, and if identified may produce benefits. But they will not answer the basic question, and may turn out to be a chimera. The philosopher David Chalmers, draws a distinction between the 'hard' and 'easy' problems of consciousness. 'Easy' problems are the stuff of neuroscience. They concern the objective study of the brain, such as where and how are certain psychological functions (perception, memory, language, and so on) distributed across different brain systems. The 'hard' nut to crack, he says, is the problem of phenomenal consciousness, that is, awareness. Objective science can tell us about the functions of pain, for example, how it can be avoided, and the associated patterns of neuro-physiological activity, but not why and how much does it hurt. Or what does it mean to be in pain, and how does pain hurt? It is a problem with an extensive pedigree (Paul Broks reporting in *The Sunday Times*, 15 June 2003).

Clearly improvements have been made within psychiatry, making it a stronger scientific discipline; yet systemic weaknesses remain. In a swingeing assessment Hunter and Macalpine, gurus of modern psychiatry, talk of aetiology remaining speculative, pathogenesis symptomatic and hence arbitrary, and possibly ephemeral. They say it all stems from an inherent weakness in a lack of an objective method of describing and communicating clinical findings without a subjective interpretation (Hunter and Macalpine, quoted in Porter 2002: 3–4). Modern psychiatric classifications remain beset by traditional defects; problems of definition and of boundaries, and a mixture of moral judgements interspersed with unsupported generalisations, plus an ever-changing nomenclature.[5] Physical medicine, according to Bolton and Hill (1996), operates on the categorical model, that is, each illness or condition is defined in a sufficiently distinctive way that it can be logically distinguished from other concepts. There is an assumption that the subject either has the condition or does not, most clearly so where there is a definable pathology with a clear cause (Bolton and Hill 1996: 279). But psychiatric conditions are rarely like this. Bolton and Hill suggest that most psychiatric conditions are best characterised by scores on a dimension such as depression, anxiety or aggression, making their definition additionally problematic.[6]

Worse than that, existing foundations may turn out to be based on shifting sands, unable to sustain even the current direction or flow. Many major psychiatric conditions such as schizophrenia and depression are heterogeneous: while they bring into play physiological factors, they operate with and alongside the genetic, environmental and sociological.[7] Of course, so do some medical conditions, but much less so than in psychiatry. There is no better example than the psychopath, the personification of inadequate social learning, for lacking in conscience he/she learns how to manipulate the environment to advantage. The psychopath's aim is to operate according to his/her set of rules, oblivious to any ethical or moral considerations that may intervene. I find it difficult to see how this becomes a psychiatric problem; it is certainly a sociological, psychological and criminological problem but not the province of psychiatry as a medical specialism. Depression too. Feelings of inadequacy linked to a sense of blameworthiness are moral matters about one's sense of worth and not simply about the patient's physiology. This puts it within reach of other disciplines.

I have spent time on a critique of the disease model not simply because of its inherent defects, but because I want to emphasise the heterogeneous nature of many psychiatric conditions; while they bring into play the physiological, they operate alongside the environmental and sociological. Psychiatry has always been recognised as multifaceted, but more recently it has promoted a uni-dimensional view and in so doing it lost something on the way. In its eagerness to appear scientific it threw out something deeply evocative. What was once a liberating instrument for modern society, has unwittingly become a tight and ironically strangling noose (Krim (1968) quoted by Porter 1991: 507). No doubt all was done for the best, but this is not the point; that noose was designed in the interests of medicine rather than anything else. Things are changing, however, with the 'straitjacket' being challenged. These are straws in the wind perhaps, but straws that ought not easily be dismissed. Richard Bentall (2003), for example, emphasises the 'environmental'. He notes that such views are likely to be seen as controversial having been successfully censored or airbrushed from the psychiatric literature (2003: 484). He recognises the strength of what he calls 'the biological time bomb' hypothesis, that is, there are within us defects in the brain that explode into illnesses when a person reaches maturity; but he thinks this misses out on other matters, including what he calls 'the trials of life' (2003: 438 and chapter 18). These trials are those that beset us all to some degree – family upbringing, adult relationships, etc. – but bear down more heavily on some less fortunate.

I do not want to promote a 'trial of life' model, interesting though this may be, but I do want to promote a view of madness that is distinct from biology and genetics. As to likely accusations that this might be a return to a less scientific age, well, madness never was scientific in that sense. Madness *inter alia* implies beliefs, intentions and actions that cannot be reduced to a nomological form. That has always placed madness outside the realm of a deterministic system, and set it apart from the world of physics, and thereby of science. Some events are scientific (for example the impact of drugs on bodily changes) but others imply intention and thinking, and lie outside a deterministic structure (see Davidson 1980 for a discussion on this). Insanity is a personal condition, a disorder perhaps, a problem of living certainly, but interpreted through a mixture of signs and meanings and consequently through social science methods. It is not the sole province or purview of neuroscience; it is also about how mad people manage their condition, and consequentially about human reactions and intentions. I want to identify those features that are common, and that help determine what is meant by being mad.

An empirical theory of madness

To begin with a basic proposition. A common feature of madness is its unreason; or, put in a different way, madness is defined as systematic unreasonable beliefs. Madness is about losing one's reason or losing one's mind. It is not about a defect of emotions, or a statistical rarity based on unusual and infrequent actions but, to quote John Locke, is about the way we join up ideas wrongly. This of course puts it at odds with any physiological or genetic theory, as the definition used here places it within an empirical cognitive tradition – the terms can be used interchangeably although I prefer empirical. It certainly places madness within the 'environmental' nexus as defined by Bentall (2003).

We can begin with John Locke who asked two essential questions: How does the mind work? And why does it frequently misfire? He saw the newborn as *tabula rasa* – an idea now largely rejected. Yet to Locke, the mind was built as a result of sensation and perception; the latter he called the internal sense, which is the operation of each individual mind. Sensations and perceptions develop into conceptions and ideas, and finally emerge through chains of thought. This makes man a self-creation, as opposed to a divine creation, or even a mixture of both (Locke 1690; see also Yolton 1956).

Locke's thesis promotes the view that the madman is flawed by his grasp on reality. That flaw did not come from original sin or through some elemental strife between reason and appetites, but through his consciousness, which was intricate and dynamic, albeit liable to erroneous as well as true beliefs. Locke saw the human psyche as being a product of his experience. The sane person's psyche was filled with normal ideas and normal judgements, but with the mad it was different, for the mad were cognitively disoriented. What, then, created the one rather than the other, the sane rather than the mad? Well, nothing was for certain, it all depended on personal experiences (Porter 1987a: 188). So, following from Locke, madness encompasses false beliefs, unjustified and inappropriate to the circumstances in which the person finds himself.

How then does madness arise? Locke likened the human mind to a closet that lets in shafts of light through a small opening. The light produces pictures that fall to the floor, but not always in an orderly manner. They might fall in ways that are disorderly, and so are ill forged at the outset, or orderly at first but might be disturbed later. In doing so 'they would very much resemble the understanding of a man in reference to all objects of sight and the ideas of them' (Locke, quoted in Porter 1987a: 191). So the key to insanity was not found in the way reason was overthrown by the passions, for the passions had their own histories and were not necessarily blind or wilful. Insanity was to be found in reasoning itself, the way the mad were in error, that is, as someone who draws a just inference from false principles; this was in contrast to the then accepted view that madness was either original sin or a slave to passions and appetites. To Locke madness arose because the mad joined together some ideas wrongly, which he said they mistake for truths and accordingly err, as humans do, from wrong principles.

Locke, unlike the Scholastics (read 'the Church'), did not believe that people were born with innate ideas or principles. In a famous passage he said,

> Let us suppose a mind to be as we say white paper void of all characters, without any ideas; how comes it to be furnished? Whence comes it by that vast store, which is the busy and boundless fancy of man has painted on it, with an almost endless variety? Whence has it all the materials of reason and knowledge? To this I answer in one word, from experience; in that all our knowledge is founded, and from that it ultimately derives itself. (Locke 1690: book 11, chapter 1, section 2)

He also distinguished between those who 'were born witless' as opposed to those who 'fell out of their wits' – the former being the mentally impaired, the latter corresponding to the psychotic. The difference, said Locke, was that:

> There are degrees of madness as of folly, the disorderly jumbling of ideas together is in some more, and some less. In short herein lies the difference between idiots and madmen. That madmen put wrong ideas together and so make wrong propositions, but argue and reason right from them; but idiots make very few or no propositions but argue or reason scarce at all. (Locke 1690)

Locke's theory of knowledge provided a break from the past, and release from the baggage of the Scholastics; anyone who believes man is born with an innate moral sense, or a set of moral God-given rules, will not see it as baggage, but they will be hard put to say what those rules and moral precepts are, and how they might differ one to another. Yet modern thinking dismisses out of hand the idea of a *tabula rasa*, mainly under the weight of genetics, biology and neurophysiology. Nonetheless, Locke demands of those wanting to bring on board some other baggage, from genetics or otherwise, that they should be certain about its content. Geneticists may be able to provide evidence of a disposition to believe or act in a certain way, but they are not yet able to say from whence come our ideas. Moving from genetics, neuro-physiology or whatever to consciousness remains as yet an unchartered path. We may have a physiological predisposition to behave in certain ways, that biological time bomb of Bentall (2003), but that does not explain our sensations, the origin of our sensations, or our perceptions. For Locke asked the question that genetics still has to answer: where do our thoughts and ideas come from? And the answer must be from our experiences. He also asked why the mind frequently misfired, and why it produced error, questions that dominated much of the eighteenth century and beyond. His answer was, again, according to our experiences.

The Scholastics, in ways not dissimilar to modern geneticists, saw the mind as having within it sensations and perceptions placed there by some form of divine or genetic intervention: human beings were, after all, God's specially selected creatures, granted with a higher moral sense than other animals and given by divine intervention moral capabilities that were unique. The Scholastics held that the mind knew all sorts of things *a priori*. Locke, generally thought of as the founder of empiricism – the doctrine that says all our knowledge is derived from experience – challenged this. Not surprisingly, given the power of the Church at the time, this was seen as dangerous; he fled to and spent much time in Holland. Locke said that our ideas come from our sensations and perceptions, the latter being the operation of our own mind. To quote Bertrand Russell, 'since we can only think by means of ideas, and since all ideas come from experience, it is evident that none of our knowledge can antedate experience' (Russell 1946: 634). Perception, said Locke, was the first step and degree towards knowledge and the inlet of all the materials of it (1946: 634).

Yet, and to quote Bertrand Russell again; empiricism is faced with a problem to which so far philosophy has found no satisfactory solution. This is the problem of showing how we have knowledge of other things than ourself and the operations of our own mind. Locke thought that certain mental occurrences, which he called sensations, have causes outside themselves, and that these causes resemble the sensations that are their effects. But, says Russell, how, consistent with the principles of empiricism, is this to be known? We experience the sensations, but not their causes; our experience will be exactly the same if our sensations arise spontaneously. The belief that sensations have causes, and that they resemble the causes, is one which if maintained must be maintained on grounds wholly independent of experience (Russell 1946: 636). This difficulty has troubled empiricism down to the present. But Russell assures us that no one has succeeded in inventing a philosophy at once credible and self-consistent. Locke aimed at credibility and achieved it at the expense of consistency (1946: 637).

It is difficult to appreciate Locke's influence, and equally difficult to tease out his impact on the treatment of the mad over the last 300 years. I do not want to attempt a historical review, nor suggest that there is a direct seamless thread, or a simple linear progression to link Locke with modern thinking. There has been no single path, no single ideology, and changes, such as there were, have been erratic, sometimes as much swayed by fashion as by sound thinking and research. Often one or two exceptional persons, by their idiosyncratic nature or the force of their personality, have changed the face of psychiatry, and produced new ways of thinking (for instance, Pinel, Connelly). They have done so by innovation in one sphere, yet paradoxically often remained desperately conservative in almost all else. Change, when it occurred, was much more erratic, more vertiginous, more uneven. While Locke's empiricism required a new way of looking at the mad, his views were dismissed by others. Those following Kant believed it impossible to penetrate the madman's world; Kant thought the mad were locked into their delusions and could not be reached by, or through others. Who can reason with the unreasonable? Or, who can get the mad to understand when they are unable or unwilling to examine themselves?

There are, however, some strands, a few stronger than others, showing how Locke's thinking has survived. One of the strongest comes in the life of Dr Samuel Johnson, a classical empiricist albeit a life-long sufferer from depression who was preoccupied with thoughts of madness. It was the evil he most dreaded, and the object of his most dismal apprehension (Boswell 1992: 35). That he suffered from a state of mind 'unsettled and perplexed' is obvious from the following, it being as clear a description of depression as one gets: 'When I survey my past life, I discover nothing but a barren waste of time with some disorders of body and disturbances of the mind very close to madness'. Dr Johnson hoped 'that He who made me will suffer to extenuate many faults and excuse many deficiencies' (Boswell 1992: 695). To Johnson the supreme enjoyment was through the exercise of reason; he saw madness as its antithesis, it was the great divide, it separated reason from unreason and the reasonable from the unreasonable.

Johnson believed madness to be a common condition, if rarely known; what nowadays we would call 'under-reported'. He gave an example of how a man in certain instances goes through life without having his madness perceived, whereas another exhibiting a similar condition is immediately identified. Consider, he said, the case where madness has seized a person supposing himself obliged literally to pray continually; had the madness turned the opposite way, and the person thought it a crime *ever* to pray, it may, not improbably, have continued unobserved (Boswell 1992: 959). Madness was an indulgence of the imagination (1992: 1081), which required it to be managed (1992: 607). 'To have management of the mind is a great art' (1992: 607). But how best to achieve it? According to Dr Johnson by constant occupation of mind, accompanied by a great deal of exercise, moderation in eating and drinking and, he added somewhat archly, avoiding drinking at night. Melancholy people, said Dr Johnson, were apt to fly to intemperance for relief, and that was a mistake. Boswell says his devotions were eminently fervent, and he was comforted by intervals of quiet composure and gladness (1992: 695). Nowhere did he view his condition as being medical, yet he seems to have swallowed more than his share of pills and potions for his numerous physical conditions.

Much to Boswell's annoyance, Dr Johnson insisted on joining melancholy with madness. Boswell wanted to distinguish between a disorder that affects the imagination and the spirits, and that by which the judgement is impaired (1992: 35). Boswell also spoke of madness as a disease (1992: 35). Yet to Johnson, melancholy was a gradation of madness; the source was the same, the effect might differ. Roy Porter claims that Johnson's insight was that madness was not unequivocal, but an existential hazard of living in the world of opinion (1985: 63). By that he means madness occurs within the experiences of human existence, whether brought on as in biblical terms through 'oppression' or through 'much learning' but in any case through the interactions of social life. (The former is found in Ecclesiastes 7: 7, which though attributed by tradition to Solomon is in the Hebrew text referred to as the work of the Preacher (*Qoholet* in Hebrew). The latter is from Acts of the Apostles 26.24 and is an exclamation by Festus.) Johnson believed that we are what we are because of our learned experiences and we are mad because those experiences make us so.

If managing madness was the key, then how to do it? One way was to contain our wishes. Boswell saw madness as 'affecting the imagination and spirit', that is, mixing the emotional with the cognitive, whereas Dr Johnson saw it as through the world of opinions.

Dr Johnson would assert that it is our social and intellectual world that makes us mad, with madness occurring because some are unable to cope with that world of knowledge and experiences. We wish for too much. Johnson thus dreaded that his mind would be corrupted with the inveterate disease of 'wishing' and that he would eventually pay the price and go mad. In Roy Porter's eloquent phrase, the sleep of reason left imagination free to spawn monsters (1987a: 60). So, madness could be explained as a normal distribution in a population. In the same way that many of our physical and cognitive skills are normally distributed (statistically) so too would be our abilities to hold madness at bay. Some at one end would succumb, others at the other end would not. Dr Johnson feared that he would one day be unable to manage it, his experiences would be too heavy, and his thoughts too burdensome; these were the source of his strengths but also of his failings.

Another signpost of Locke's influence is found in the rise of moral treatment, albeit more than a century later. From its inception, moral treatment was hailed as a break from the ancient traditions surrounding the demonology of madness, and its location within the blood or bile. Moral treatment was not a cognitive theory, the Tukes in the Retreat at York (one of the first modern asylums, opened in the 1790s) were no theoreticians; they were not even physicians, but practising Quakers eager to re-establish 'Reason' in the patients. In this they acknowledged their debt to Locke. Certainly, strands of a cognitive theory can be found in the comments from Benjamin Rush, the great American psychiatrist and guru of moral treatment. He saw it as 'bringing the patients' shattered and crooked thoughts into their original and natural order' (quoted in Donnelly 1983: 47).

In practice this meant listening to the mad – a revolutionary idea, for if what the mad said was of interest it meant that they no longer rambled or were incoherent. But who was to interpret those thoughts? The key person in any moral treatment programme was the governor of the asylum; in the case of York it was governor of the Retreat. The ideal governor was a paternal figure with noble and philanthropic qualities who nonetheless had exclusive direction over his patients' minds. For if madness was learned so it could be unlearned, and moral treatment offered the obvious facility for that unlearning. Its supporters claimed that it established an atmosphere of confinement appropriate to that new age of Enlightenment. In so doing moral treatment was an exercise in social learning, a form of re-education 'like the upbringing of a child', where patients were treated as children in order to relearn experiences and avoid past mistakes. There was something almost Freudian in the way it took the patient back to childhood, while displaying many features of cognitive theory as it emphasised learning new beliefs.

A much later signpost came during and after the First World War in one of the treatments for 'shell shock'. Those being treated received a mixture of cognitive therapy and 'ergotherapy', that is, cure by functioning – in effect, work. Patients worked in teaching posts in local schools, or as farmhands, or even joined study groups in sociology and were taught 'to open their eyes and the ears … to the social deprivation and inequalities in the home front society' (Webb 2006: 344). Their treatment was about unlearning or modifying earlier experiences, allowing the patient to come to terms with those experiences. It was about relearning how to see the world.

Of course, these are strands in a 300-year history of psychiatry and I want to make nothing more of them than that, although Locke's theory had its supporters and his influence remained in some form throughout the eighteenth and early nineteenth centuries (see Porter 1985). There was no single path to enlightenment, to modern psychiatry. It was more a troubled history where those involved had to struggle with a condition that had defied so many. The decision was always whether to contain, detain, let alone or cope. And moral treatment was subject to as much severe criticism as any other. An early critic, Francis Willis, grandson of the Lincolnshire physician *cum divine* who had treated George III's madness, had no time for anything other than a medical disease model. 'Insanity has been considered by some to be merely and exclusively a mental disease, curable without the aid of medicine by what are termed moral remedies, such as travelling, and various kinds of amusements.' Of this he clearly disapproved.

Yet in spite of all the changes, the new theorising and the effort put into modern theories, Locke's thinking has been amazingly resilient. We find in Anthony Quinton a modern approach to an empirical theory of madness that is not a world away from Locke. Quinton sees madness as a systematic breakdown in the belief-forming mechanism or capacity of the mind (Quinton 1985: 18). Dismissing an emotional theory, which he says, fails because the emotions of the mad are not in themselves indicators of madness, he asserts that the main indicators are unreasonable beliefs. So, consider schizophrenia: there is nothing in the emotional state of the schizophrenic that is unusual, such as fear, coldness, anger. Or take the depressive patient. Again, nothing unusual there: a wide range of moods and emotional states characterise the depressive patient but so do they with others who are not depressed. It is the patient's beliefs about their unworthiness that are the key. For that which separates the mad from the sane is the primacy of those false beliefs, says Quinton. The mad may have emotions embedded within their madness, but it is their false beliefs that set them apart. The schizophrenic falsely believes he is being persecuted, and the depressive falsely believes he is of neither value nor use. Quinton sees those beliefs as the determining factor – beliefs that are unjustified (Quinton 1985: 22). It is not so much that they are wrong – we all have false beliefs – but that they remain inappropriate to the circumstances in which the patient finds himself.[8] And in spite of himself the madman cannot and will not change them – at least until change occurs through treatment or as a result of spontaneous recovery or as a result of mind management.

Quinton adds two qualifications. The first is that the unreasonable beliefs of the madman are systematic, that is, these unreasonable beliefs are neither short-lived nor localised. Nor do they leave room for other beliefs. Unreasonable beliefs dominate in such a way as to exclude that mass of other held beliefs that might provide a contrast, or a standpoint from which unreasonable ones can be criticised. Quinton distinguishes between the unreasonable beliefs of the neurotic, the obsessive, or the phobic and those of the psychotic, whose unreasonable beliefs dominate. The former, says Quinton, are not mad; the latter are. However, the point I shall make later is that this distinction is neither necessary nor feasible. Madness can be seen on a continuum where the neurotic occupies a place somewhere between sanity and madness, but nearer to sanity than otherwise.

Second, Quinton says that the unreasonable belief system of the madman must be practical; it must concern, or be central to his everyday life. It must dominate his existence in the way the severely depressed person is dominated by the belief in the awfulness of his life and the world around him, or in the way the paranoid schizophrenic avoids all situations likely to lead to danger, those situations being both dominating and extensive. So:

> The psychotic is a danger to himself and a danger to others in the same way as a retarded person but for different reasons. The retardate does not know what to do or how to do it; the psychotic does not realise because of his delusions that things he knows perfectly well how to do ought to be done. (Quinton 1985: 26)

Quinton, one of the few modern philosophers to have interested himself in such matters, suggests that unreasonableness may occur in the manic depressive who has delusions of his own abilities, whether in the manic stage, where there are delusions of power, importance or intellectual brilliance, or of failings; or within the awfulness of his world when depressed. Or in the schizophrenic, whose whole system of thought demonstrates cognitive impairment. However, delusions and hallucinations are not confined to the mad; they occur in sleep deprivation or can be induced by other means, and need not be about unreasonableness (Quinton 1985: 17, 34). They are, however, symptomatic of madness when they preoccupy a person's life and dominate existence.

What of the religious fundamentalist, and the political ideologue? Do not these resemble the mad in that they hold an unreasonable belief system, which is both systematic and practical? After all, their faith protects them from rational investigation, and the greater their faith the more devout they appear. Quinton considers this but sloughs it off by saying that religious fundamentalists and political ideologues take the world to be real in the same way that it is conceived by everyday reasonable belief (1985: 27). He means, presumably, that they live in a measure of harmony with others and go about their business in unremarkable ways, except, that is, when it comes to matters dear to them: their faith and/or ideology. But if so, then their grasp on the world is hardly different from the neurotics who cope well with almost everything except, say, a fear of enclosed spaces, open spaces, or whatever. That still makes them slightly mad, slightly out of touch with the reality experienced by the rest of us, and with their unreasonable beliefs on board. But then, how unreasonable is unreasonable? It is worthwhile noting that many people have religious experiences that are akin to madness, and some claim to have revelations and visions of God or the gods. Erasmus (quoted by Screech 1985), writing in 1511 in the Praise of Folly, wrote that Christianity at its best is nothing other than a kind of madness. Enraptured Christians were seen as demented, deprived of their *mens*, their mind. They enjoyed an experience very like what we call dementedness, and saw it good to be condemned by the hostile standards of this transitory life (Screech 1985: 26–7). Political ideologues display similar traits.

Clearly, many walk that thin line between madness and sanity. Perhaps the solution is a pragmatic one. It all depends on the level of intensity and severity. Given we are all odd in some way, each with our fair share of strange beliefs and prejudices, including religious and political, yet managing nonetheless to stumble along reasonably well, then how close do these approximate to madness? The answer, it seems, is that in spite of everything we manage somehow to struggle through. Sanity is not a clear-cut condition; it is not one that we either have or don't have, but one that occasionally slips away from us when we lose our grip on reality, but more often than not we regain it as readily. Sanity involves retaining belief systems, which are best served if kept under control, even if we may harbour some that are extreme and appear to others to be unjustified or unreasonable. And those beliefs might be religious or political.

It also depends on the social situations in which the beliefs are expressed. Most religious and political believers work within prescribed and proscribed settings; their liturgy, doctrine and beliefs are set out publicly and their belief systems able to be challenged. This is a world away from the psychotic patient who often inhabits a solitary world unable to set out his beliefs for comment, let alone examination. Of course, the more secretive the religious and political sect, and the more it eschews public scrutiny, the more its members approximate to insanity. For there are some political ideologues and religious fundamentalists who are so dominated by their belief systems, and so intolerant of any who disagree with them that their actions are akin to our definition of madness. In the old days it was called religious mania. Such beliefs can and often do lead to justifications, for political or religious reasons, to kill others for their peculiar political or religious gain. They may not be fully mad according to the definition provided here, but they come mightily close to it. That their unreasonable beliefs have so dominated their lives that they are prepared to kill others, and sometimes kill themselves, must be included within this definition of madness. The rest of us, whose full-time lives include but do not wholly embrace a number of unreasonable beliefs, must still be judged by the same criteria, perhaps on more secular grounds, but essentially whether those beliefs are the dominant force in our lives.

When Locke says that madness is about producing just inference from false principles, and Quinton that madness is the acceptance of unreasonable beliefs, they are not far apart in their thinking. Both emphasise the importance of beliefs in a definition of madness. The search for a common factor in madness has led both to see the belief system as central to any theory. There are differences, of course: Locke was concerned to formulate a theory of knowledge, Quinton is more restricted, confining his attention to madness rather than develop his own theory of knowledge based on empiricism. Yet both, in vastly different times, challenge existing orthodoxies, Locke more so than Quinton. Focusing on beliefs provided a different emphasis, a break with existing thinking and a challenge to traditional thinking. Contemporary psychiatric textbooks tend not to place empirical theories within mainstream psychiatric thinking, because they undermine the orthodoxy. Yet Locke and Quinton clearly have something important to say, for in one sense it is glaringly obvious that erroneous beliefs feature heavily in madness. The question is, are they pivotal and are they the key to unlocking a particularly obdurate door? I think they are and that a resurrection of the empirical model might well be of value.

Having said that, I want also to acknowledge the influence and impact of cognitive behavioural therapy (CBT), itself another strand in the empirical tradition, even if not acknowledged as such. For in spite of all that has been said above about the tight grip displayed by the disease model, CBT is further testimony that things may be changing. CBT may not be in the form Locke would have wanted, but it is emerging as a potent force, aided perhaps by a reaction against those psychiatric treatments that include heavy tranquillisers. The modern version, said to have its origins in the 1970s, is defined in the idioms of behaviourism, although technically speaking there remain important differences between behaviourist theorists and their empiricist counterparts (Clarke 2001: 11–14). I do not want to enter this debate, except to point out two differences. As I understand it, behaviourists argue that we acquire behaviour through the association of stimuli with responses, whereas empiricist theorists retain the original Lockean view that we learn through the association of memories, ideas and expectations. Also, behaviourists insist that learning takes place through trial and error, while empiricists say that it takes place through experience and problem-solving. The dispute can get bloody.

These disagreements apart, behaviourists and empiricists seem to work in some measure of harmony, and I do not want to emphasise differences; indeed, some influential psychiatric texts draw no distinctions (Gelder *et al.* 2006). They accept the dominance of behaviourism, or rather, merge it into a generic term and call it cognitive theory, and I shall follow that lead. Behaviourism is about translating behaviour into different forms, emphasising abnormal or dysfunctional aspects. Behaviour therapists will take on psychotic patients, but prefer those whose conditions are more amenable to their techniques, such as phobic disorders or anxiety disorders. This is not a crude swipe at behaviourism – the floridly mad are not the easiest patients to treat, being rarely responsive to therapy. Psychotic patients do not take easily to techniques where the patient is an active partner in treatment, has homework assigned, where patients practise new behaviours between sessions, and are asked to record thoughts associated with their behaviour (Gelder *et al.* 2006: 589). With the floridly mad some adjustments are required – and, to be fair to behaviourists they have tried to make those adjustments (Morison 2004).

NICE, the National Institute for Health and Clinical Excellence, defines Cognitive Behavioural Therapy (CBT) as a generic term that refers to the pragmatic combination of concepts and techniques derived from cognitive and behavioural therapy (February 2006). These structured approaches are based on the assumption that prior learning is currently having maladaptive consequences. According to NICE the purpose of this type of therapy is to reduce distress or unwanted behaviour by undoing existing learning, and by providing new, more adaptive learning experiences. CBT is based on the patient's needs; phobic patients require something different from those with eating disorders, and from the depressed and the schizophrenic. NICE claims overall effectiveness of CBT, saying that it is supported by evidence from randomised controlled trials. It claims that important improvements have been obtained for many diagnostic groups in approximately 50 per cent of individuals with depression, these results are similar to outcomes achieved with antidepressant drugs. NICE is clearly a fan and supporter of cognitive behavioural therapy, and one can see why; if it is successful it is also cheaper and with fewer side effects than drug treatment. Currently support is running high and CBT is assuming cult status.

Not surprisingly, in view of such powerful recommendations CBT is presented in the psychiatric literature as new and exciting, young, thriving and having far to go (Tyrer and Steinberg 1998: 75–85). Similarly, others see it as having made great strides since its inception in the 1970s (see Gelder *et al.* 2006). Gelder *et al.* classify it as a form of psychological treatment, which can be used for many conditions, albeit mainly for the neuroses, especially eating disorders, anxiety disorders and phobias; but again, also effective in severe depression and schizophrenia. Lauded and applauded it may be, it is certainly not young, or new, though it may be exciting and thriving. The differences between behaviourism and a cognitive theory have been suggested above; the point to make here is that behaviourism itself is a relatively recent phenomenon. Locke's influence can be seen again: Tyrer and Steinberg say that the cognitive therapist operates on the basis that the patient's thoughts are wrong and correct ones are needed. To achieve success, they believe the therapist needs a more indirect and subtle approach than simply meeting the errors head on, or challenging beliefs. It involves working within the delusions, realigning the patient's thinking, and analysing the patient's thoughts in a rational manner. Unfortunately, NICE gives no recognition to Locke or what he has to say about madness, or acknowledges any indebtedness to him, or that period.

On the other hand what Locke would have made of modern behaviourist thinking is difficult to say. Having cleared away the baggage of Scholasticism, doubtless he would be puzzled to see it replaced by the behavioural idioms of modern cognitive therapy, with its orgy of psychological/therapeutic speak, its jargon and techniques – some of which display common sense, others being unintelligible. We have terms such as 'laddering', 'modelling', and 'ABC techniques' to cope with. The first is common sense, and involves asking a series of connected questions, the answer to one leading to the next question and so on. A patient with an eating disorder might be asked what would happen if she gained weight (it is usually a 'she'), to which the reply might be that she would lose friends; this is then followed by the question 'why?', and the reply to that might be that only thin people are attractive and popular. But 'modelling' seems quite unintelligible. It is described as where 'the therapist demonstrates the necessary exposure himself', and I have no idea what that means. ABC stands for antecedents, behaviour and consequences, or factors that precede the disorder, provoke or maintain it (see Gelder *et al.* 2006: 588–99 for details of CBT). ABC seems not too far away from taking a social history. In spite of all this, CBT is trying to do something eminently worthwhile: that is, treating the mad as having something intelligible to say, and not in need of heavy doses of tranquillisers to get better.

CBT has numerous critics. Some speak of the failings of cognitive behavioural therapy as similar to those of psychoanalysis: short on success rates – in spite of what NICE believes – yet selective about its patients. They say that only the most reflective and articulate are selected, especially middle-class patients with phobic or eating disorders – likely candidates for success anyway. (It was always said that psychoanalysts, given their fees, only took rewarding patients!) Critics view many of the techniques as being of little use with the floridly mad; nor, it seems, were they designed to be, for behaviourism has always been for patients of a certain disposition, as with alarm techniques for enuresis, response prevention for obsessive rituals and so on. For the floridly mad different techniques must apply; treatment follows a standard approach aimed at offsetting the patient's negative thoughts, beliefs and assumptions, and errors of logic (Gelder *et al.* 2006: 596). For schizophrenia, CBT emphasises the importance of coping with stress by challenging delusions (2006: 598). As such CBT follows traditional empiricist thinking.

Of course, it is not necessary to be an out-and-out cognitive behaviourist to recognise some merit in empiricist thinking. Peter Chadwick, himself a 'recovered schizophrenic', talks of the value of finding an interpretation of evidence that can 'genuinely eat away and destroy a psychotic delusion', a process he calls cognitive replacement (Chadwick 1997: 157–58). Mental health workers' refusals to listen to deluded talk is to Chadwick 'utterly useless and even pathogenic and mentally weakening therapeutic manoeuvres' (1997: 157). He is part of that group of psychologists who are enlarging the boundaries of a disease model to incorporate many of the features of cognitive therapy without calling it that.

Aside from the therapies, empiricist strands can be found in modern law and criminology. Cognitive views of madness have held legal sway and lawyers are clearly supportive. Move away from the cognitive, they say, and the law gets messy and unclear. The M'Naughton Rules (dating from the mid-nineteenth century) have a strong cognitive component, with a clear privilege towards cognition, although whether formulated according to a Lockean view is unclear – I have not seen the argument put that way. These rules have withstood criticism, mostly but not entirely from psychiatrists who argue that they do not contain a sufficient concern for extreme emotions. Those in favour, judges included, argue that in spite of the many psychiatric critics the rules provide clarity, albeit a stern test of insanity. They have been weakened but not overthrown by the introduction of 'diminished responsibility' under the 1957 Homicide Act, which stemmed from Scottish law. This offers a defence where those suffering from such conditions, although not rendered legally insane, nonetheless are affected in their powers of understanding or self-control. The legal fear is that the law becomes impossibly muddy once we move away from a cognitive towards an emotional route. Emotions are more difficult to handle legally because it is not clear how much weight should be given to them.

In criminological theory Edwin Sutherland's theory of 'differential association' is a straightforward empirical model. Crime, said Sutherland, is learned, in interaction with others, in intimate social groups, and that form of learning is no different from the way other forms of learning occur. Sutherland talked of 'definitions' for which read 'attitudes', the person being criminal or not depending on the number of definitions favourable to violation of law over those unfavourable. It wasn't simply a matter of counting; the intensity, priority and duration of definitions was more important. Probation officers did not become criminal because they mixed with criminals, the intensity and priority of those relationships being less than with parental figures who presumably gave them non-criminal definitions. Differential association has had a chequered history, being at various times in and out of favour; in favour because it offers a common-sense approach of the impact of family values and other key figures in a person's life, out of favour because it has been too difficult – almost impossible – to identify and measure the various definitions, including the important ones. Some research has yielded interesting and useful results: a study of dishonest lawyers, for example, found that the distinguishing feature that separated them from the honest was the duration, intensity and priority of earlier criminal definitions. Other research on the professional thief came to similar conclusions. Sutherland's criminals were qualitatively different; they had learned to be criminals, and differed from the non-criminals who had learned to be upright citizens. It is reason from unreason all over again.

Criminologists have searched for that elusive feature in the criminal's background (or personality) that separates him from the non-criminal. Sutherland's theory was a major step forward in that search. It was later used to develop subcultural theory, and then to include other areas of learning, as with Akers' theory of 'differential reinforcement', which includes learning through the environment, or with Bernard's theory involving the structural conditions generating cultural beliefs, where chronically aroused people engage in violent responses. Bernard goes so far as to suggest that the legal defences to crime, such as self-defence and insanity, turn out to be definitions favourable to violation of law because they offer excuses. This is legal theory turned on its head (see Vold *et al.* 1998: chapter 12 for a discussion on social learning theories generally). But taken all in all, this form of empiricism has offered useful insights into the 'causes' of crime. And if for crime, then why not madness?

Empirical, statistical and emotional theories compared

The statistical theory

How does an empirical theory compare with more traditional theories, such as the statistical or emotional? We can begin with the statistical, much favoured by Hobbes and Voltaire, although both mixed it with other theories: Hobbes with the emotional, Voltaire with the cognitive. Hobbes saw the madman as 'having stronger and more vehement passions for anything than is ordinarily seen in others' (Hobbes 1996: 48–9), while Voltaire defined madness as 'that disease of the organs of the brain which inevitably prevents a man thinking and acting like others' (quoted in Porter 2002: 18). For both, madness exists because of its unusual nature – it is excessive or statistically unusual; Hobbes includes an emotional theory, that is, it is 'still more than is ordinarily' seen, and Voltaire adds a disease theory but retains a statistical input in that it 'prevents a man acting like others'. Voltaire sees madness as a disease of the organs of the brain, and in this he anticipates much contemporary thinking.

Madness is thus defined as a statistical abnormality. As such it fits into an earlier tradition, which defines physical illnesses in the same vein; illnesses (or diseases) are abnormal conditions of the body, producing biological disadvantage, where 'abnormal' is defined as being rare or less common, and a biological disadvantage may include *inter alia* a failure to conceive or have children.[9] In one sense, of course, all illnesses produce biological disadvantages, and mental illnesses are no different. Physical and mental ill health disrupt family life, and reduce employment prospects – that is obvious and well known. Yet why should that lead to any profound conclusions? There are many features of human existence that are disruptive and rare, and may even produce biological disadvantage, but so what? All it means is that they occur infrequently and may not be welcomed. And anyway, I am not sure that diseases are always statistically abnormal – what of epidemics? And as to biological disadvantage, I am not sure that means very much either. The range of human behaviour is so wide and varied that to see illnesses, including mental illnesses, as being at the extremes includes too much and too little. Too much in that many extreme behaviours are not mad, and too little in that it does not identify those that are. Madness disrupts roles, and changes role ascriptions and expectations. It is presumptively bad for the sufferer, often reducing the sufferer to a dependent role. That seems of greater significance than biological disadvantages.

More often than not, and put simply, a single statistical theory boils down to one assertion: that the behaviour in question is so odd, so unusual, that the person responsible must be mad. It is a way of interpreting extreme behaviour through exasperation, about having a sense of bewilderment that certain actions are more than unusual, they are simply out of this world. It is about being aghast at actions that are so incredulous that madness becomes the only credible explanation. The action is beyond comprehension, and as madness is also beyond comprehension the one explains the other. As reason explains reason, so unreason explains unreason. There may be other considerations – the perpetrator may have acted under provocation, or had some defect in his upbringing – but all are trumped by the incredulity surrounding what has been done. No one in their right mind could do such a thing.

The perpetrator 'must be mad' is the oft-heard lament in particularly brutal cases, especially those involving children, or in sexual activities that commonly involve perversions. Being unusual or bizarre the action surpasses belief: it is beyond normal imagination. Criminals often behave in ways that to the rest of us are bizarre: paedophiles, and extremely violent offenders – alongside petty criminals whose behaviour is so persistent, so non-utilitarian that they never seem to learn from their mistakes. Implied within a statistical model is that the actions or crimes are 'motiveless'. For if there is no motive, no reason to commit them (at least none that are apparent), then madness is easily presumed. Mentally healthy normal people are presumed to act from motives, which may not always be rational but are at least understandable – again, intelligible. So judged by this criterion anyone who acts without such motives must be mentally sick. Motives may be revealed later, in which case the offender is no longer 'mad', and if once mad and not responsible for his actions, when sanity is restored then so is responsibility. Revealing motives is not a haphazard matter, it relies on more than new knowledge and new attitudes, but on ascribed expertise, preferably by those with high status able to claim a unique understanding and operating according to cultural assumptions about what is acceptable behaviour. These interpretive specialists provide acceptable or unacceptable motives, sane or mad ones: sane being where a persistent thief 'gets a kick' from stealing, or has to support a drug habit, or where a child abductor is desperate for a child; mad where the thief is already rich, or the abductor already a parent.

Donald Cressey concludes that the economic status of the expert is of great importance in deciding motives, such as determining whether a person is a thief or a compulsive shoplifter. He believes that if all psychiatrists were poverty-stricken the proportion of thieves would drop and compulsive shoplifters increase (quoted in Wootton 1967: 234). In a similar vein Barbara Wootton says:

A well to do person who can buy anything that he desires, has no socially recognised motive for stealing, must therefore be judged to be mentally sick if he is guilty of dishonesty. The stealing of the poor by contrast must be criminal because it is rational, except in cases where the poor also engage in repetitive stealing of useless objects. (1967: 234)

Or again, quoting Donald Cressey, who suggests that a physician was not behaving neurotically when he stole medical books, only when he stole porcelain figures that were of no value (1967: 234). With sex offences different factors operate, and with, say, rape, incredulity is suggested by reporting the offender as 'married with two children.' The implication is that an abundance of freely available goods and services help define 'motiveless' offences. Not always; paedophiles are exceptions, but then their crimes are 'motiveless' if only because they are so malevolent.

Statistical theories of madness are based on the presumption that human behaviour occurs within well-defined boundaries – a normal distribution, as it were – where at the extremes something beyond the 5 per cent confidence levels of abnormality exists. Statistical theories have a number of advantages, not the least that they offer something eminently plausible. They set out the field of study, and in Quinton's words do so in an 'irresistibly objective and uncontroversial way' (Quinton 1985: 35), although I am not sure that I see them as objective.

They also need the support of a strong normative component. Suppose I am extremely interested in the life of my great-aunt Julie, a woman who led a very unremarkable life. No one else is interested. Does my interest make me mad? Clearly not. Or, suppose I am interested in the life cycle of an obscure butterfly, and as in the case of my aunt Julie I spend a great deal of time and money on my pastime. Am I mad? Again, clearly not. I may be odd, eccentric even, but not mad. And the reason I am not mad, statistically, is not because of my interests *per se* but because those interests are not harmful to myself or others. I would, however, be mad if I spent all my money on that research and devoted my whole life to it to the detriment of my welfare and that of my family; or, worse still, I was interested in a form of activity that led to physical injury or death of myself or my aunt Julie. Statistical rarity is not enough; the actions in question must be regarded as morally reprehensible.

Two examples of a statistical theory illustrate the point. The first is from a journalist (*The Sunday Times*, 19 March 2006) who reported on a rare event and a horrific crime – it was a particularly violent sadistic killing by a serial killer. The offender was seen by a specialist (psychiatrist) who concluded that he was not mentally ill, but was cunningly fabricating the symptoms of mental illness; the jury thought so too. 'Personally,' said the journalist, 'I should have thought that it was evidence itself of madness – of diminished responsibility – to break into a stranger's house and kill them horribly just for the buzz of it; sane people don't do that.' In the second example a lawyer was commenting on the case of a man who had brutally killed his wife after she had tormented him with her sexual exploits. The lawyer was explaining how the courts might react to this offence. He believed that an ordinary murderer, to use such a phrase – my term not his – stood little chance of claiming diminished responsibility, but 'if the defendant has a history of mental trouble ... then the more horrible the killing the more likely diminished responsibility will be established because the further removed from normal behaviour the behaviour of the defendant, the more he appears to be mentally ill, or so the submission runs' (quoted in Prins 1995: 33).

These strands give clues to the way the statistical theory remains in our thinking, rarely appearing as a full-blooded statement, more likely as an adjunct, or an aside to something else. All societies find ways of ostracising and explaining their most extreme behaviour and a statistical theory of madness is a way of achieving that. It offers no theory of treatment, but detention is the first priority, community safety being paramount. The fear of reoffending is high, the assumption being that the statistically mad are also unpredictable. Rare and unusual crimes often require lengthy sentences.

A statistical theory does more than provide an avenue for our revulsions, it offers an explanation and provides credulity in areas of uncertainty. It takes away doubt by providing an explanation, appearing to show that such levels of behaviour are beyond all forms of reason, but which is itself a reason. I take a less charitable view of the statistical theory than Barbara Wootton, who sees it as providing criteria for distinguishing the normal from abnormal, thereby avoiding the circularity of many arguments where abnormality is inferred from the behaviour. Here abnormality is inferred from the motives – in this case lack of them (Wootton 1967: 235). That may be so but within statistical theory there is always the danger of an unhealthy popularism that demands offenders receive disproportionate sentences in order to fit public revulsion. It smacks of lashing out at what we cannot understand – and a common reaction to madness.

Assessing the merits and relevance of a statistical theory is difficult. It often appears more an exclamation than a theory. It becomes most potent when tied to other theories, or it adds acuity to their arguments, for example as in Hobbes' definition of madness as involving 'stronger passions than are ordinarily seen in others' Quinton's criticisms are sound; the statistical theory pretends to give a scientific account of the field but in fact lets in more than it ought (Quinton 1985: 35). Yet there remains something permanent about it, irresistible perhaps, for it offers an explanation when there is only incredulity. Unreason is explained by unreason, and that seems to be its legacy.

The emotional theory

There has long been an intense and detailed debate on the emotions, especially their biological origin (see Damasio 1994 for a neurological account of the emotions). Yet even an out-and-out neurologist such as Damasio has to acknowledge that 'to understand ... the brain that fabricates human mind and human behaviour it is necessary to take account of its social and cultural context' (1994: 260). While neurological explanations offer an account of how the emotions are linked to the brain's circuitry they tell us only about the link, not the content. Yet the content is important.

Whereas the statistical theory appeals to a common-sense view of madness, the emotional theory has a more professional pedigree. The idea that madness is a slave to the passions has a long distinguished history. Most psychiatric textbooks include within their definitions of psychotic conditions strong reference to the patient's emotional state. Take, for example, the article by P.T. Liddle in an influential textbook of psychiatry (Liddle 2000). In his description of schizophrenia he says that 'an extensive range of disorders of emotion occur in schizophrenia. Blunted and inappropriate affect are the most characteristic and also tend to be the most persistent but transient excitation, irritability, lability, and depression also occur.' He adds that there is also a cognitive component in that 'during the chronic phase of illness many schizophrenic patients exhibit persistent cognitive impairments' – a mixed theoretical position. Nonetheless, this definition is in accord with traditional views that show the mad as being sensual, full of emotional immaturity, having a lack of emotional intelligence, and needing to develop more appropriate emotional responses. Here, emotions are often separated from the intellect with the oft-heard comment about some intelligent people not being able to operate emotionally at the same high intellectual level. Psychoanalytic theory also stressed the importance of having emotions under control, the id being the source of dark, hidden emotions and the super ego of excessive controls, leading to irrationality and neurosis. A solution: a strong ego able to provide sufficient insight into one's behaviour to control aberrant emotions; for if not, neurosis was the expected outcome.

Modern psychiatry has often favoured an emotional theory of madness, pointing to the distorted emotions in depression, or those in schizophrenia, especially the paranoid version. Madness is thus about emotional instability, about emotions being out of control, about the intense sadness of the depressive accompanied with feelings of deep unworthiness. Or about the coldness of the schizophrenic whose level of detachment leaves him isolated and lonely, and whose emotional response is inappropriate. True, there is also a disorder of thought but the emotional theorist will emphasise the schizophrenic's world as inhabited by the squeak and gibber of ghosts, and their emotional world as a desperately unhappy place.

An emotional theory of madness has an extensive pedigree; Thomas Hobbes in *Leviathan* (1996, Book 1, Chapter 8: 48–9) distinguishes between madness caused by the passions and that caused by demons, those possessed of spirits. The passions, he says, come partly from the different constitution of the body, and, anticipating Locke, partly from differences in education. The passions that most cause differences in wit – 'wit' being reason – are the desire for power, riches, knowledge and honour; but now anticipating modern sociology, Hobbes says that all may be reduced to the desire for power (linking class, status and power, as Max Weber did). For riches, knowledge and honour are but several sorts of power. Thoughts become desires, and to be without desires is to be dead. So too with passions. To have weak passions is dullness, and to have indifferent passions is to be distracted, but when the passions are stronger and more vehement, that way madness lies.

Tied into Hobbes' emotional theory is a statistical component, for these passions in the insane are greater 'than is ordinarily seen in others'. Later he again incorporates a statistical theory when he says that in sum, all passions that produce strange and unusual behaviour are called by the general name madness. The major features of madness are domineering, unguided passions. Hobbes says that rage and melancholy are those passions that also make madness: pride leading to rage, and dejection leading to melancholy (1996: 48–9, paras 14–20). Passions unguided are for the most part the major determinants. Individual passions, however, lead to different behaviour, 'some of them raging, others loving, others laughing, all extravagantly, but according to their several domineering passions' (1996: 50, para. 37). Madness is similar to drunkenness, said Hobbes, 'for the variety of behaviour in men that have drunk too much, is the same with that of madmen' (1996: 20).

Hobbes, one of the few great philosophers favouring an emotional theory of madness, sees the passions of the mad as more extreme, or they often appear to be. Modern definitions fit easily into that view. Take depression as defined in ICD-10 (from the World Health Organisation's *International Classification of Mental and Behavioural Disorders*), 'as a depressed mood, loss of interest, and enjoyment and increased fatiguability being regarded as the most typical symptoms of depression' (WHO 1992: 121). Or ICD-10 for schizophrenia, defined as having 'characteristic distortions of thinking, perception and by inappropriate or blunted affect' (1992: 86) – notice 'blunted affect' there alongside 'cognitive distortions'; if not always extreme, then certainly prominent according to the ICD definition.

But it is doubtful if the passions in the mad are always extreme. Some schizophrenics appear to be distant, cold and detached, but have less extreme emotions than those experienced by the sane. Nor is it that all who experience extreme emotions are mad, for many of us have extreme fears, experience extreme sadness and extreme isolation, but that does not make us mad. Death of a child or very dear loved one can, and often does produce extreme sadness, but again, that does not mean madness. Many experience extreme fear, soldiers in combat say they are terrified, but no one suggests this is madness. It would be if the fear became dominating and existed away from the combat area as with 'shell shock' in the First World War.

So, what part do the emotions play? The answer is that emotions embody beliefs. (Quinton 1985: 23) That means emotions cannot of themselves explain madness. The schizophrenic patient may experience a coldness, an aloofness perhaps, even a sense of detachment. He may exclaim inappropriate responses, but those experiences and responses need not be extensive. The depressive or manic patient may experience deep uncontrollable sadness but so does the bereaved, and the manic a belief in his indomitable, impregnable, invincibility, but then so do others whose confidence is supreme. The emotions experienced by the mad are not therefore exclusive to madness. Some people are cold, aloof, react inappropriately, are sad, think themselves unworthy etc. but are clearly not mad. They are able to lead reasonably ordered lives. We may call them shallow, unfeeling, melancholy or whatever, but they are not mad.

Second, to say that emotions contain within them beliefs means that we do not just hate, we hate someone or something. We are not just frightened, we are frightened of someone or something. And we do not just love, we love somebody or something. (I am aware that Freud talked of free-floating anxiety – anxiety apparently without a cause or reason – but he thought that this was unconscious anxiety and best eased by attaching it to someone or something. And anyway it is sufficiently rare or unusual not to affect the main argument.) What characterises the emotions of the mad is that their beliefs are false: the schizophrenic falsely believes his imagined world is real, the depressive that his prospects and the world generally is dreadful, the manic that only he has the answers, and the paranoid that this person or others are against him (Quinton 1985: 23). Were any of those beliefs to turn out to be factually correct then there is no possibility of deeming the person mad, and in this respect his emotions are correspondingly of little or no consequence. It is the beliefs that give the game away; the emotions attached to the beliefs simply follow the beliefs.

One forceful objection to this way of thinking is that there is more to madness than emotions and beliefs. The depressive stupor and the intense activity of the manic cannot be discounted in the overall scheme of things. How do these fit into the equation? Or when the language of the schizophrenic is jumbled, incoherent, making little sense? This is more than unreasonable beliefs, it is as if the person cannot produce simple sentence structures, being unable to display basic ideas that are meaningful. It is almost an expression of broken consciousness. But it still boils down to beliefs. What is the point of doing anything if the world is so awful, why bother to care for oneself if death is to be preferred? If the manic believes that humankind can be saved, that his idea for wealth creation is the best ever, then why not get on with things? And if the language of the schizophrenic is jumbled and incoherent then this is because his beliefs are jumbled and incoherent. This is not, of course, always the case; sometimes they are incredibly clear, well worked out, and with clear conclusions, even if starting from a premise that is wildly wrong. But the beliefs are what matter, and the falseness of the beliefs is the critical variable.

Turning away from the nature of emotions and madness towards more practical matters, it is interesting that the common law tradition in England and Wales has never easily embraced an emotional theory of madness – unlike, say, France, where irresistible impulse has figured large in a plea of insanity, especially involving a *crime passionelle* – defined as a disorder of emotion. Why should this be so? I suggest because the emotional theory is itself too woolly, too difficult to pin down and too abstract for the common law. It is not, however, completely absent. Provocation has been accepted as a defence; the offender must show that at the time of committing the offence he/she was under such provocation that his/her emotions were sufficiently distorted as to no longer be in control. This is not madness but a mad moment, and allows the court to say he/she is not guilty of a crime. The offender does not require treatment, as with the insanity defence under M'Naughton. However, can provocation be used as a defence when, for instance, an abused wife kills her abusive husband while he is asleep? On the face of it this appears to be a case of unlawful killing, there being no current provocation, and the emotions are not distorted, but the courts have permitted it nonetheless. Presumably the argument is that while not under current provocation the backlog as such is sufficient to claim a residue of emotional disturbance.

Consider also the Infanticide Act of 1938. This gave statutory recognition to a specific state of mind in a woman who has caused the death of her child (the child has to be under 12 months old), as a result of having given birth to that child, or by reason of the effect of lactation consequent upon giving birth. She cannot claim the infanticide defence if she kills another of her children; it has to be the child born in the last 12 months, and her defence is the emotional disorder arising from that birth. Criticisms abound: some say there was no need for a special defence, there are only a few cases each year, the defence is difficult to apply and is an anomaly standing in contrast to other defences. All true, but the Act was a response to psychiatric persuasion that the mother's disturbed emotions ought to be a defence by acknowledging the dangers of *post partum* depression as a consequence of childbirth, while circumventing the usual existing defences. It emphasised a disorder of the emotions, and their primacy, but it did not, nor could it specify which emotions should be considered as having caused the killing. If it is presumed that depression was the key, then we return to the problem as before: was it cognitive or emotional? That is, were the mother's belief systems to blame or her emotions? The answer depends on which model of madness is seen as most valid.

To stay on this for the moment, Brenda Hoggett with her usual clarity points out the dangers of this type of emotionally led legislation.

The Infanticide Act was justified on the basis of the emotional stress on the mothers of the newborn, but Hoggett asks why this should amount to an excuse at all, and if it should, why not also apply it to the father? Or to other people driven to killing by the intolerable pressures of their lives? (Hoggett 1984: 160; see also Prins 1995). The Infanticide Act was a good example of the medicalisation of the criminal justice system – the belief that women's hormones can drive them out of control – but may reflect a different and passing age. The modern approach is to tidy up legislation on homicide, putting all under one rubric – infanticide, death by dangerous driving – thereby demoting these defences to mitigation. Were this to happen it would be a further rebuttal of the emotional theory of madness, at least as far as the law is concerned.

This is not to say that an emotional theory has been completely discounted. Emotional distress may not be a legal defence but it can be and often is used in mitigation. Probation and psychiatric reports are full of accounts of the way offenders find themselves in varying degrees of emotional distress – marital, financial or otherwise. Social work and probation practice have long centred around failings in the emotions of their clients, and this is reflected in their reports. (I have never seen a report that emphasises cognitive failings but many that link criminality to stress, unhappiness or inappropriate reactions.) Offenders were often placed on probation or sent for psychiatric treatment because of their emotional problems; the probation order itself, with the early requirement of 'advise, assist and befriend', was directed towards this end. Theories of criminality become woven into theories of madness when in psychiatric reports crime, emotional disorder and madness are entwined into a single set of explanations and a recommendation for sentence.

An assessment of empiricist theories of madness

Empiricism is more than an interesting argument, it has a persuasive practical appeal. Madness is about unreasonable beliefs, it is not a disease. Empiricist theory stresses the unifying feature of madness that can be assessed objectively; at one extreme is madness (psychosis), having gradations into less extreme forms (neurosis) and finally into sanity. Yet empiricist theory offers hope because it suggests the possibility of retraining the mad into new ways of thinking. If our beliefs are wrong, then it is possible to produce new beliefs, often through forms of moral and social training. The type of training used, from moral treatment in the eighteenth and nineteenth centuries to modern behaviourism nowadays, is a testimony to the enduring quality of a cognitive approach.

Another strength of an empiricist theory is that it is more precise than the emotional, and paradoxically more so than the statistical. Also, it offers a more objective view; an emotional theory is more dependent on acceptable cultural views, with the statistical theory suffering similar defects. Another strength is that it allows distinctions between the mad person and the social deviant, often blurred elsewhere – the disease theory, for example, uneasily includes personality disorder and psychopaths within its framework. Social deviants are not mad; they may be wicked, do undesirable things, may even set new fashions, but they are not mad. Hitler and Stalin behaved in ways utterly deplorable and reprehensible but they were not mad; their unreasonable beliefs were too much under control for that.

Above all, a cognitive theory puts sanity and madness on a continuum, where gradations of madness are related to the nature of unreasonable beliefs. That avoids entering that orgy of classifications so beloved of ICD – the number of conditions seem to increase daily, now including psychiatric conditions in remission. Instead of identifying phobias, anxiety conditions, obsessive disorders, eating disorders, mild forms of depression and the like, and calling them neurotic psychiatric conditions, why not see them as steps on the continuum of insanity? That is, they represent various stages of the strength and dominance of unreasonable beliefs, reaching the highest point, the apotheosis as it were, with schizophrenia and manic-depressive psychosis. Points on the continuum become marked by the intensity of those unreasonable beliefs; the obsessive are likely to be more intense than, say, the neurotically depressed, but all are on that continuum. Cognitive theory provides a different way of looking at madness, seeking to establish the existence of unreasonable beliefs, then to determine their point on the continuum, and if treatment is required to develop it accordingly. Whether or not the treatment is CBT is not important, so long as the aim is to return unreason to reason. It differs also from trying to cure a disease.

A great strength of Locke's position is to associate madness with ideas. Roy Porter's study of Dr Johnson confirms a cultural role for, 'Dr Johnson suffered his afflictions in the idioms of the day perceiving derangement through the Lockean lens that located madness in the mind, the deluge of delusion invading the realm of reason' (Porter

1985: 79–80). Whatever Dr Johnson was, he saw himself as being a person only because of the strength of his mind, but he always feared the uncertain continuance of reason. Empiricism emphasises nurture not nature; it is about the way human beings live and develop. It is sociologically based, which gives little account of a biological inheritance. It requires an understanding of madness as beliefs, not as an emotional response or as a statistic. Of course, no one has the monopoly of right answers in such a complex field, for what is not known is how to explain why one person's unreasonable beliefs develop in one way and another's quite differently. Or, in modern psychiatric terminology, why one person becomes depressed, another manic, and a third schizophrenic? That and a host of other questions remain, whether about treatment, individual responses to madness or whatever. And always there is the question about how best to deal with those whose unreasonable beliefs are so severe as to make them pained, incapacitated or a danger to themselves and others.

I accept that an empiricist theory of madness will not suit everyone. Porter sees the implications of Locke's philosophy as 'Janus faced' (1985a: 192). It was emancipatory in that it humanised madness by taking it away from the divine. But just as Locke's philosophy could provoke sympathy, so could it raise a sinister potential, for if wrong thinking was madness then all in error must be mad. Foucault was certainly critical of the Tukes and the Retreat, viewing moral treatment as a new form of imprisonment – treating the mad as children – but he ignores the obvious benefits that moral treatment introduced (Foucault 1977). But being 'Janus faced' is not the prerogative of empiricism; all theories offering explanations of madness that suggest that the mad are different – whether genetically, socially or physiologically – emphasise the differences. What can be more destructive than to be told that the causes are genetic, or physiological, and therefore outside one's ability to make amends? Are not these 'Janus faced' too?

It will certainly not suit those supporting the psychoanalysts, the anti-psychiatrists, or others intent on seeing madness as a political statement. It will be challenged also by those enduring sceptics who view the sane as mad, and the mad as sane. Erasmus thought the entire world crazy and reason was unreasonable. These uncompromising sceptics object to the mad being defined as such by a Mental Health Act enforced by a medical group of experts. Yet madness has always been the peroration of those experts, to be defined by them, and they assert their superiority accordingly. All societies claim that there is a group who are disturbed and need control by representatives of the majority.

Nor will it suit those supporting the traditional disease model of psychiatry. The disease model was reiterated in the mid-nineteenth century and in truculent form by William Lawrence, the newly appointed surgeon at Bethlem. 'Arguments, syllogisms, discourses, sermons, have never yet restored any patient; the moral pharmacopoeia is quite inefficient, and no real benefit can be conferred without vigorous medical treatment which is as efficacious in these affections, as in the disease of any other organ' (quoted in Porter 1985: xxii–xxiii). Much later the twentieth-century doyens of psychiatry Hunter and Macalpine also asserted a disease model and were dismissive of the cognitive. 'You don't crack mental illness by decoding what the mad say for mental disease has a biological base' (quoted in Porter 2002: 157). They may accept that psychiatric disorders have a cognitive component but view cognitive changes as occurring as a result of physiological changes or chemical therapy – treatment was by way of antidepressants for the depressed, and so on. That is to say, cognitive change occurs as the mood improves. Accordingly they say that there is no point listening to what the mad are saying, for the mad are ill, or diseased. On that basis the psychiatrist must first diagnose the patient as mad, or ill, probably deluded, and from a diagnosis proceed with treatment, usually of a chemical kind. If Hunter and Macalpine are to be believed, listening to or understanding the content of those delusions is not the way forward.

Nonetheless, there is merit in the empiricist argument. It may not satisfy everyone but that was to be expected, especially as Bentall argues that all arguments likely to compete with the disease model are airbrushed out of the system (Bentall 2003: 484). At least it might avoid one of the outcrops of current thinking that the disease model helps proliferate: those numerous therapies, many that are if not directly attributable to Freud then borrow its language and methods. They help promote and expand many of so-called psychiatric 'illnesses'.[10] This and the millions of prescriptions given out annually for antidepressants, along with pills to cure sexual inadequacy, to relieve anxiety, to reduce stress and perhaps even to banish boredom. All seeking a solution from what they perceive as medical conditions – assisted by psychologists and others who seem endlessly keen to identify these new syndromes.

Psychiatrists may not be popular but their pills and potions are. Can we really believe that all these conditions are 'illnesses'? A young man's girlfriend leaves him and he gets antidepressive pills from his GP; is this a depression and an illness? Was it not one of the greatest follies to call these pills 'anti-depressants', and these problems 'illnesses'? It might have been better to be truthful and upfront and call them 'anti-unhappiness' or 'avoiding problems of living' pills? For is not the young man seeking relief, *via* an antidepressant from one of the oldest problems of living, to use one of Thomas Szasz' favourite phrases? Are the millions of antidepressant pills taken today really for an illness? Or have we got ourselves into a corner where all impertinent psychological pain becomes an illness and has to be removed by medical treatment, alongside those endless therapies that allow us to luxuriate in paying for other people's attention? Roy Porter asked, is Folly jingling its bells once again? Well, perhaps yes. And whose fault is that?

Notes

1   The most poignant speech from *King Lear* occurs after his madness has abated. He recognises his predicament and the fear of being laughed at, and at his shortcomings.

Pray do not mock me,
I am a very foolish fond old man,
Fourscore and upward, not an hour more or less;
And to deal plainly, I fear I am not in my perfect mind.

2   And from *A Midsummer Night's Dream* (Act 5 Scene 3) we get a different set of aetiologies, where madmen are compared to poets and lovers. Theseus says, 'Lovers and madmen have such seething brains. Such shaping fantasies, that apprehend More than cool reason ever comprehends. The lunatic, the lover, and the poet Are of imagination all compact.' But there is a world of difference in experiences. The madman's world is more painful. 'One sees more devils than vast hell can hold; That is the madman.' The poet and lover enjoy a more constructive existence, for although the 'lover is frantic', and the poet's eye is in a 'fine frenzy', these are to be preferred.

3   There are, of course, organisations such as SANE with their own social and political agenda who will object, as they did in 2003 when popular boxer Frank Bruno was committed under the 1983 Mental Health Act. 'It is both an insult to Mr Bruno and damaging to the many thousands of people who endure mental illness to label him as "bonkers" or "a nutter" and having to be put in a mental home.' This was in response to a headline in the *Sun* newspaper, 'Bonkers Bruno' (*The Times*, 24 September 2003, Supplement: 22).

4   One of the problems for psychiatry is that the sociological/environmental dimension that envelops psychiatric definitions of disease or illness may not shrink or whither away but remain stubbornly relevant. Psychiatrists

have accordingly spent considerable effort looking for those physical agents that provide psychiatry with its biological base. I suggest that search is proving elusive, so that psychiatry remains obstinately dependent on sociology. From the perspective of the sufferer it may turn out to be more socially acceptable to see his/her disorder as an 'illness', and it may appear that the depressed mood, the schizophrenic hallucinations, etc. are illnesses in which he/she is the passive recipient of a state that has intruded inexplicably into his/her life (Bolton and Hill 1996: 281). However comforting that may be, at least at one level, it can only be a short-term solution. In the ominous words of Bolton and Hill, if there is no reduction of mental process to a neuro-scientific state, psychiatry is stranded without a causal story (1996: 274).

5   That point is ably illustrated by reference to the ICD-10 *International Classification of Mental and Behavioural Disorders*, the latter it defines as 'a repetition of persistent patterns of dissocial aggressive or defiant conduct … more severe than ordinary childish mischief or adolescent rebelliousness' (F91) (WHO 1992: 266). There are numerous subdivisions of these conduct disorders, some more problematic than others. Take, for example, the 'Dependent Personality Disorder' (F60.7). It has two facets. The first is encouraging or allowing others to make most of one's important life decisions, and second is a preoccupation with fears of being abandoned by a person with whom one has a close relationship, as of being left to care for oneself. Then, of course, there is homosexuality. In the 1950s it was regarded as a psychiatric disease. Fifty years later homophobia, the dislike of homosexuality, is the disease. The ICD-10 classification also lists a 'Dependence Syndrome Currently Abstinent' (F1.21). One wonders how that can be a disorder if one does not have it? It remains a puzzle. I can find no reference in a standard medical text to a disease that the patient no longer has!

6   To pursue this point a little further. In the psychiatric field one thing merges into another. There is often comorbidity between symptoms. Depression and panic disorders are common (Bolton and Hill 1996). So too do schizophrenic conditions occur with depression. Endless psychiatric debates occur surrounding this: 'is it a schizophrenic condition with an underlying depression or *vice versa?'* (Bean 1980). Bolton and Hill ask whether one confers vulnerability on the other, or is there a lack of distinctiveness? In physical medicine we are all anatomically much the same, at least within a moderate range of shapes and sizes, and according to age, and sex (Bolton and Hill 1996: 36). If our body temperature rises or falls above or below a narrow range there is cause for concern; similarly if the level of physical exertion is restricted below that which should be expected for our age and sex there is equal cause for concern. That is to say, we remain fairly anatomically homogeneous. This is much less so for mental conditions. The range of tolerable behaviours, even within

one culture or social class, may be fairly wide. Families adopt different standards and family members may differ markedly. Many of us act and think in ways that others might believe are strange. For example, there may be those with a dominating interest in Shakespeare's plays or the Stock Exchange, and those interests become an abiding passion. That should not lead us to believe that such passions signify mental disorders.

7 Take depression, for example. There is no agreed psychiatric definition; definitions differ from one textbook to another, in terms of symptoms, duration and intensity. They include a multitude of feelings including sadness, dejection and despondency, alongside stupor, associated with severe suicidal tendencies. Ultimately, it seems, the diagnosis depends on the interpretations of the clinician. The *International Classification of Mental and Behavioural Disorders* (ICD-10, F30–F39) puts it thus: 'It seems that psychiatrists will continue to disagree about the classification of disorders of mood until methods of dividing the clinical syndromes are developed that rely at least in part upon physiological or bio-chemical measurements rather than being limited as at present to clinical descriptions of emotions and behaviour' (WHO 1992: 13).

The most typical symptoms of depression appear to be a loss of interests and enjoyment, and increased fatigability (1992: 121) while a severe depressive episode involves 'delusions, hallucinations or depressive stupors … Delusions usually involve ideas of sin, poverty, imminent disasters the responsibility for which may be assumed by the patient. Auditory or olfactory hallucinations are usually of defamatory or accusatory voices, or of rotting filth or decomposing flesh. Severe psychomotor retardation may progress to stupor' (1992: 121). Few of these terms are scientific in the sense that they are morally neutral; most are descriptions of moral states, merging into states of feeling regarded as unpleasant.

The other major disorder, schizophrenia, fares little better, containing its own brand of subjective feeling states. The ICD-10 classification defines it as a group of disorders having 'characteristic distortions of thinking and perception and by inappropriate or blunted affect … The disturbance involves the most basic functions that give the normal person a feeling of individuality, uniqueness and self direction. The most intimate thoughts feelings and actions are often felt to be known to or shared by others and explanatory delusions may develop to the effect that natural or supernatural forces are at work to influence the affected individual's thoughts and actions that are often bizarre' (1992: 86).

8 The following quotations from Shakespeare add to the view that madness is about loss of reason, about systematic unreasonable beliefs, while sanity is about keeping one's reason intact: knowing who one is and being able to go about one's daily business, i.e. having systematic reasonable beliefs. Sebastian in *Twelfth Night* (Act 4 scene 3: 16–20) dismisses the suggestion that Olivia is mad.

> Or else the lady's mad; yet if't were so,
> She could not sway her house, command her followers,
> Take and give back affairs and their despatch
> With such a smooth, discreet, and subtle bearing
> As I perceive she does.

And from *King John* (Act 3 scene 4: 20–60), Constance welcomes death ('Death, death; O amiable lovely death … Come, grin on me, and I will think thou smil'st, And buss me as thy wife. Misery's love, O come to me!') but is told she is mad to do so. Her response to Cardinal Pandulph, the Pope's legate, is swift. She cannot be mad, she says, when she can reason and be in control of her thoughts.

> Thou are not holy to belie me so.
> I am not mad; this hair I tear is mine;
> My name is Constance; I was Geoffrey's wife;
> Young Arthur is my son, and he is lost.
> I am not mad – I would to heaven I were;
> For then 'tis like I should forget myself.
> O, if I could what grief should I forget;
> Preach, some philosophy to make me mad,
> And though shalt be canoniz'd, Cardinal;
> For, being not mad, but sensible of grief,
> My reasonable part produces reason
> How I may be deliver'd of these woes,
> And teaches me to kill or hang myself.
> If I were mad I should forget my son,
> Or madly think a babe of clouts were he.
> I am not mad; too well, too well I feel
> The different plague of each calamity.

Finally, for dementia Polixenes asks his son in *The Winter's Tale*.

> Is not your father grown incapable
> Of reasonable affairs? Is he not stupid
> With age and altering rheums? can he speak? hear?
> Know man from man? Dispute his own estate?
> Lies he not bed-rid? And again does nothing
> But what he did being childish?

9 While a disease might be a rare occurrence, and produce a biological disadvantage, and therefore be of statistical interest, this definition conflicts with a Benthamite Utilitarian position, that diseases produce pain and unhappiness (i.e. a dis-ease). It was typical of Bentham, but wrong, that he should define disease in line with his 'greatest happiness' principle – we may be unaware we have some diseases – but he was right to emphasise that they are presumptively bad for the sufferers. A

further merit of the Utilitarian definition is that it can easily encompass a social role where diseases are judged according to the role of the sufferer. Diseases are flexible; for example at a certain age my stamina is such that I cannot be a fast bowler at cricket. This does not make me ill, but it would if at the age of 20 and being already a fast bowler I am unable to perform that task. Or consider a watchmaker with extremely keen vision. Assume that his vision deteriorates to be in line with the rest of us. Is his vision diseased? Not in terms of any biological abnormality, but it is in terms of what is presumptively bad for him, and of his role as a watchmaker.

10 'Factitious disorder' – the deliberate distortion of information to mislead others – is now said to be a 'meaningful psychiatric diagnosis'. Most of us, however, would simply call this telling lies. Bass and Halligan (2007) describe this as another example of 'diagnostic creep'. They say the time has come to review and confront the conceptual blurring and diagnostic overreach that continues to impede meaningful discussion of illnesses which involve deception. This is correct but is, I think, part of a much wider problem for us all.

References

Bass, C. and Halligan, P.W. (2007) 'Illness related deception: Social or psychiatric problem', *Journal of the Royal Society of Medicine*, 100(2) (Feb): 81–4.

Bentall, R.P. (2003) *Madness Explained*. London: Penguin.

Bolton, D. and Hill, J. (1996) *Mind, Meaning and Mental Disorder: The Nature of Causal Explanation in Psychology and Psychiatry*. Oxford: Oxford University Press.

Boswell, J. (1992) *The Life of Samuel Johnson*. London: Everyman Library.

Bynum, W.F., Porter, R. and Shepherd, M. (1985) *The Anatomy of Madness*, Vol. 1. London: Tavistock.

Carter, R.B. (1983) *Descartes' Medical Philosophy*. Baltimore/London: Johns Hopkins University Press.

Chadwick, P.K. (1997) *Schizophrenia: The Positive Perspective*. London: Routledge.

Claridge, G. (2001) 'Spiritual Experience: Healthy Psychoticism', in I. Clarke (ed.) *Psychosis and Spirituality*. London/Philadelphia: Whurr Publishers, 90–106.

Clarke, I. (2001) 'Cognitive Behaviour Therapy for Psychosis', in I. Clarke (ed.) *Psychosis and Spirituality*. London/Philadelphia: Whurr Publishers, 11–14.

Damasio, A.R. (1994) *Descartes' Error: Emotion, Reason and the Human Brain*. New York: G.P. Putnam.

Davidson, D. (1980) 'Psychology as Philosophy', in J. Glover (ed.) *The Philosophy of Mind*. Oxford: Oxford University Press.

Donnelly, M. (1983) *Managing the Mind*. London: Tavistock.

Foucault, M. (1977) *Discipline and Punish*. London: Allen Lane.

Gelder, M., Harrison, P. and Cowen, P. (2006) *Shorter Oxford Textbook of Psychiatry*. Oxford: Oxford University Press.

Glover, J. (1980) 'Introduction', in J. Glover (ed.) *The Philosophy of Mind*. Oxford: Oxford University Press.

Hobbes, T. (1996) *Leviathan* (Oxford World Classics). Oxford: Oxford University Press.

Hoggett, B. (1984) *Mental Health Law*. London: Sweet and Maxwell.

Ingleby, D. (1981) 'Understanding Mental Illness', in D. Ingleby (ed.) *Critical Psychiatry*. London: Pelican.

Jamison, K.R. (1996) *An Unquiet Mind: A Memoir of Moods and Madness*. London: Picador.

Liddle, P.T. (2000) 'Descriptive Clinical Features of Schizophrenia', in M.C. Gelder, J. Lopez-Ibor and N. Andreason (eds) *New Oxford Textbook of Psychiatry*, Vol. 1. Oxford: Oxford University Press, 571–4.

Locke, J. (1690) *An Essay Concerning Human Understanding* (ed. J. Yolton). London: Everyman Library, 1961.

Morison, A.P. (2004) 'Cognitive Therapy for People with Psychosis', in J. Read, L. Mosher and R. Bentall (eds) *Models of Madness*. London: Brunner Routledge, 291–306.

Porter, R. (1985) '"The Hunger of Imagination": Samuel Johnson's Melancholy', in W.F. Bynum, R. Porter and M. Shepherd (eds) *The Anatomy of Madness*, Vol. 1. London: Tavistock, 63–88.

Porter, R. (1987a) *Mind Forged Manacles*. London: Athlone Press.

Porter, R. (1987b) *A Social History of Madness*. London: Weidenfeld and Nicolson.

Porter, R. (1991) *The Faber Book of Madness*. London: Faber and Faber.

Porter, R. (2002) *Madness: A Brief History*. Oxford: Oxford University Press.

Prins, H. (1995) *Offenders, Deviants or Patients?* London: Routledge.

Quinton, A. (1985) 'Madness', in A. Phillips Griffiths (ed.) *Philosophy and Practice*. London: Royal Institute of Philosophy.

Read, J. (2004) 'Biological Psychiatry's Lost Cause,' in J. Read, L. Mosher and R. Bentall (eds) *Models of Madness*. London: Brunner Routledge, 57–65.

Read, J., Mosher, L. and Bentall, R. (2004) (eds) *Models of Madness*. London: Brunner Routledge.

Roth, J. and Kroll, J. (1986) *The Reality of Mental Illness*. Cambridge: Cambridge University Press.

Russell, B. (1946) *History of Western Philosophy*. London: George Allen and Unwin.

Screech, M.A. (1985) 'Good Madness in Christendom', in W.F. Bynum, R. Porter and M. Shepherd (eds) *The Anatomy of Madness*, Vol. 1. London: Tavistock, 25–40.

Scull, A. (1979) *Museums of Madness*. London: Allen Lane.

Scull, A. (ed.) (1981) *Madhouses, Mad Doctors and Madmen*. London: Athlone Press.

Scull, A. (ed.) (1991) *The Asylum as Utopia*. London: Routledge.

Tyrer, P. and Steinberg, D. (1998) *Models for Mental Disorder*, 3rd edn. Chichester: John Wiley.

Vold, G.B., Bernard, T.J. and Snipes, J.F. (1998) *Theoretical Criminology*, 4th edn. Oxford: Oxford University Press.

Webb, T.E. (2006) '"Dottyville" – Craiglockhart War Hospital and the shell shock treatment in the First World War', *Journal of the Royal Society of Medicine*, 90: 342–6.

WHO (World Health Organisation) (1992) *International Classification of Mental and Behavioural Disorders*. Geneva: WHO.

Wootton, B. (1967) *Social Science and Social Pathology*. London: George Allen and Unwin.

Yolton, J.W. (1956) *John Locke and the Way of Ideas*. Oxford: Oxford University Press.

Part 2

Madness as genius, and madness as an aid to creativity

One feature of madness that has retained its fascination is the link with genius and creativity. It has preoccupied many, some since antiquity. It concerned the Greeks, and more recently a host of thinkers in the seventeenth, eighteenth and nineteenth centuries including Locke (1690), Maudsley (1873) and Lombroso (1891). In his anthology of madness Roy Porter (1991) begins his chapter on 'Madness as Genius' with the observation that the mad are different; and so too are artists, writers, scientists and other so-called 'pointy-headed' intellectuals. The result is that over the centuries they have been yoked together (Porter 1991: 490). All have been inspired, consumed even, by that divine fire, or conversely perhaps by Aristotle's notion of the 'black bile', the humour of melancholy that is common among people of achievement. In Renaissance times that association served to enhance the status of artists, for artists were uniquely inspired by some divine *furore*. Later, criminologists such as Lombroso (1891) regarded the geniuses as 'undesirables' due to their unconventional lifestyle, calling them 'sociopaths' and 'moral cripples'.

Two different views of madness as genius are neatly encapsulated in the Aristotelian and Platonic traditions. They do not differ widely but have led to different paths. Aristotle viewed melancholy as a disease, but from which genius might spring, whereas Plato saw that sanity was to be cherished, but only up to a point, for he thought that the greatest blessings come from the gods and appear through charismatic manias. Plato's theories depend on man being a compound creature; earthbound through his body, heaven seeking through his soul (Screech 1985: 28). Aristotle's view leads through many twists and turns to Freud, who was deeply suspicious of genius, seeing it as taking the same route as neurosis, that is, a failure to negotiate the traumas of infancy. Plato's thought emerges in the Romantics, as a supporter of creative madness, for art exacts its toll on mental as well as physical health, leading inexorably to great visions, and in many cases towards madness.

It was the Romantics, and particularly those at the end of the nineteenth century, who sought to develop the link between creativity, genius and madness. Their influence remains. The proximity of art to madness retains its hold, as witnessed in the use of art as a therapeutic tool used to assist diagnosis, or as a means of releasing emotions, or assist with communication between patient and therapist. That apart, the Romantics saw great art, alongside other forms of creativity, as an expression of the self, but forged on the anvil of suffering created by a tension produced within the tortured soul. This, they believed, was the genesis of great poetry, literature and painting. The sane, of which the bourgeoisie were the most evident, did not experience that level of feeling; they were either too stable, too adjusted or simply too dull, being unable to reach that level of sublimity reserved for those who knew despair, suffering and madness. The Parisian artists of the day remained unshaken in their belief that the sane, sensible and (thankfully) commercially minded on which they were dependent were by definition only fit to finance their creative powers. To some, such as Virginia Woolf, Freud and his psychoanalysis were dangerous, she being fearful of its designs (Porter 2002: 82). For if psychoanalysis released internal tensions, then that was the end of great art.

Nowadays the term 'genius' is used liberally and applied to a host of public entertainers, where anyone with a taste for publicity can be hailed as a genius, or perhaps, having special talents. Yet Dr Johnson believed a genius to be someone with superior intellectual powers; genius should be a term reserved for those who have achieved enormous eminence, a select group of people of letters, composers, scientists, all of special note. In that way the term becomes more manageable. Of those that have been called geniuses, some have been floridly insane; others have been severely depressed, and others had hallucinations and displayed numerous idiosyncratic characteristics of insanity. Nisbet (1900) includes Swift, Johnson, Cowper, Southey, Shelley, Byron, Campbell, Goldsmith, Lamb, Walter Savage Landor, Rousseau, Pascal and Edgar Allen Poe in his list of geniuses, and suggests that they all were mad, drawing heavily on Dryden for support. 'Great wits are sure to madness near allied, And thin partitions do their bounds divide' (Nisbet 1900: 81–108 and 513). Nisbet seems rather overgenerous in his listing, using what I consider to be a less than rigorous definition. And this, of course, is the problem; it is a definitional one, whether for 'genius' or 'madness'.

It ought to be possible to explain any such link between genius and insanity using a similar model to that in Part 4, that is, condition A (madness) leads to condition B (genius), or condition B leads to condition A, or, that the two conditions, A and B, have no relationship. Unfortunately, we cannot be that specific, for the data are not available. We can get some answers, however, if the questions are posed in a different, more general form.

1 What is the link, if any, between genius and madness?
2 Is there anything in the background of the genius that could help explain that condition?
3 What is creativity and what link, if any, is there with madness?

In the first question what sort of link between genius and madness has been suggested? A number have been promoted, some less satisfactory than others. One of the least satisfactory has been to ascribe the mad – all of them – as being specially gifted, able to offer special insights, if not at the level of genius then certainly greater than the rest of us. These insights may have been providential, or secular, but they are special nonetheless. For example, the anti-psychiatrist David Cooper said, 'All delusion is a political statement … and all madmen are political dissidents'. Madness, in his eyes, is a process towards political autonomy, while psychiatry, with its powers of compulsion, attempts to return the mad to controlled 'family modelled institutions' (Cooper, quoted in Porter 1991: 498). Just how much credence we should give to this is difficult to say. Most mad people I have met say that they experience something different; they often recognise that things are not what they should be, and see their condition as painful, even accusing others of treachery and deceit. I do not see this as a political statement, but that may be my failing by not appreciating the deeper political significance contained therein.

Many, however, have noted a direct link with insanity and genius. Henry Maudsley (1873), who according to Roy Porter was himself a gloomy genius, believed the insane temperament to be compatible with, if not seldom coexisting with, considerable genius. He noted too that many with insane temperaments exhibit remarkable special talents and aptitudes, such as an extraordinary talent for music, for calculation, or a prodigious memory for detail 'when they be little better than imbeciles in other things' (1873: 64). Maudsley believed that the insane temperament came in different forms, ranging from its mildest to actual idiocy; one of these forms incidentally he thought occurred in a distinct and incurable criminal class, members of which had no pretentions to be a genius, let alone being talented, having 'peculiar low physical and mental characteristics' (1873: 64–6). Lombroso (1891) took a similarly uncharitable view, believing in a sort of swings and roundabout model: that people of genius paid a heavy price for their increase in intellectual stature in the form of physical and mental degeneration, in the same way that physical giants have relative muscular and mental weaknesses (Lombroso 1891: vi).

Nisbet thought that the link was well established: better than that, he thought it was through our understanding of insanity that we could view the workings of genius (1900: 56). He believed that the two conditions had much in common: 'the man of genius overflows with ideas, countless memories are stirred in his brain and he discovers combinations and affinities in facts, tones and colours that lie beyond the scope of the ordinary mind. In all these accomplishments the madman is his equal' (1900: 56). He thought genius frequently merged into insanity, and insanity into genius, but both had a common train, that of functional disorders, with each disorder occupying different parts of the brain (1900: 56). Genius and insanity were simply different expressions of a common evil created by an instability or want of equilibrium in different parts of the nervous system (1900: 57). That the evidence for this was at best patchy did not stop Nisbet and others from asserting such a connection, presumably founded on a physiological base.

Lombroso likewise believed genius to be a special morbid condition, where signs of degeneration were found in men of genius as in the insane, but more frequently in the former (1891: vi). So convinced was he that even when it was pointed out that there had been men of genius 'presenting a complete equilibrium of the intellectual faculties', he insisted that if one were to look more closely defects would be found. In his chapter 'Sane Men of Genius', he concentrates on these 'rare exceptions' (1891: 353) yet still finds quirks of nature and odd forms of behaviour among them. Michelangelo, for example, 'did not tremble for the sorrows of his country', when he clearly should have (1891: 354) and Darwin was a 'neuropath' who was 'unable to bear heat or cold' and 'half an hour of conversation beyond his habitual time was sufficient to cause insomnia' (1891: 356), while Erasmus had a 'passionate temper' (1891: 357) – and so on, and so on.

Linking insanity with genius in this way is hardly convincing. That some men of genius were mad is not in doubt, but to insist that all were is to distort the evidence. And whereas sometimes genius was bound up with insanity, in others it was not. John Connelly and Charles Lamb were the sceptics. John Connelly thought that 'there was much popular error concerning the connection of talent with madness' (quoted in Porter 1991: 495). He saw the mad as failures, as 'following every loose and deceptious analogy, mistaking the order of phenomena'. Charles Lamb thought that although there might be a link with insanity, a necessary alliance as he called it, the most impressive of geniuses were to be found in the sanest of writers – Shakespeare, for example. The greatest had, he thought, an admirable balance of faculties, whereas madness was a disproportionate straining or excess (Lamb 1987: 212). The grounds of the mistake, said Lamb, is that the raptures of higher poetry produce a condition of exaltation that lead us to impute a state of dreaminess and fever to the poet. But the true poet is not possessed by his subject, he has dominion over it (1987: 212–13).

In this Charles Lamb could speak with personal authority, for he spent a period in Hoxton asylum and Mary, his sister, was a frequent detainee there too. A friend described them on one of their journeys to the asylum:

> Whenever the approach of one of her fits of insanity was announced … Charles, her brother would take her under his arm to Hoxton Asylum. It was very affecting to encounter the younger brother and his sister walking together, weeping together, on this painful errand; Mary herself although very sad was conscious of the necessity for temporary separation from her only friend. They used to carry a straightjacket with them. (Burton 2002: 200–1)

In a similar vein Dr Johnson maintained that genius resulted from a mind of large general powers being turned in a particular direction, and Goethe held that the genius summed up the best qualities of the family or the race to which he belonged (quoted in Nisbet 1900: vii). So too did Lombroso, who thought genius differs from insanity in one essential respect: through self-control. 'The genius which cannot regulate itself is not very distinguished from insanity' (Lombroso 1891: 119).

Connelly and Lamb saw a difference in form and content between the mad and the genius, for while both may have a certain heightened awareness, they differed in important respects. According to Charles Lamb, the mad have phantoms that are lawless, and their visions are nightmares. They do not create, for creativity implies shaping and consistency. The genius may be content to be mad, but never lets go of the reins of reason. Where the genius seems most to recede from humanity he will be found the truist to it (Lamb 1987: 213). And whereas the mad are inconsistent and uncontrolled, the genius is the opposite; genius is control. In this it is not be confused with madness.

There were, of course, certain social implications to consider, especially the impact the genius might have on the less stable, more disturbed members of society. Whether deranged or not the genius could create madness in others. W.A.F. Browne, a Victorian expert, noted how poets and writers have done much towards the elevation of the human race, but with the unprepared, ill-balanced and sanguine minds their works exercised a pernicious dominion and sometimes caused madness (quoted in Scull 1991: 38–9). Similarly it was recommended that Blake's works, with all their beauty, should not be put in the hands of anyone neurotically inclined (Porter 1991: 509). Insanity was 'the dark side, indeed the product of the growth of civilisation and an expanding threat to the social order and domestic peace' (1991: xxii). Dorothea Lynde, a Victorian epidemiologist (quoted in Porter 1987: 8), thought that madness more often occurred as a result of the pressure of civilisation, with progress creating problems 'where the intellect is most excited and health lowest'. The poor were the most vulnerable. Large urban populations placed pressure on these groups, and the pressure became too much for them. For here was the dilemma: on the one hand the Victorians wanted to continue the march of progress, and extol genius; yet, madness was the price to be paid. There were, said Dorothea Lynde, a greater proportion of insane in cities than in large towns, and proportionately more insane in villages than scattered settlements (Porter 1987: 9). However, according to G.M. Burrows (in Porter 1987: 10), even among those less civilised than the urban poor 'the passions of barbarians are always strong and sometimes furious'.

Most of the major poets were not mad either. Harold Nicolson (1947) studied 32 great British poets (he didn't say which) and believed only two to be mad: Cowper and Swift. The former was a manic-depressive, the latter became senile, but only then at the age of 74. Nicolson said that it was a fallacy that poets were mad; it was a view brought about by the poets themselves who fostered that sort of romantic image. 'All writers and especially poets feel it dull to be thought completely normal. They thus divulge and even display their eccentricities' (1947: 711). Most were certainly odd, but Nicolson thought their eccentricities cultivated; in the modern idiom, they put their own spin on their lives. And to quote Macaulay, 'perhaps no person can be a poet, or can even enjoy poetry without a certain unsoundness of mind' (in Nicolson, 1947: 710).

To the question, what is the link between genius and madness?, the answer then is that if there is one, it is rather weak. While some men of genius were mad, many others were clearly not. Of those that were mad many were not creative during their madness: Robert Schumann went mad in later life, but that followed a lengthy period of creativity; Tchaikovsky was probably always a manic-depressive; but no other great composers showed any special proclivity to madness. The painter Dadd spent lengthy periods in an asylum and did some of his best work there, but it is impossible to know whether he was mad or temporarily in remission when he was painting. Some creative artists were certainly odd, and many were difficult to live with, but most were not mad. Being a great artist does not guarantee madness, but then it does not guarantee being a likeable or even acceptable human being either. Bernard Levin wrote of Richard Wagner (*The Times*, 10 October 1978) that he was unique in the breadth of the gap between his measure as an artist and as a man 'in which in the latter capacity he was about as detestable as it is possible for a man to be'.

For the second question, on the background of the genius, there are ample accounts of the lives of geniuses, but mostly of the potted history type. Nisbet (1900) and Lombroso (1891) were the main purveyors of this approach, although others took a lengthier in-depth study (Ellis 1904). Nisbet (1900) gives descriptions of the lifestyles of those he calls genius, interwoven with descriptions of their insanity. By modern standards this is unsatisfactory on two counts: there is no control group, and no clear idea of what was genius or madness. Many of those he included would be considered no more than talented men of letters (Southey, Lamb, Walter Savage Landor), while those he called mad we might simply describe as odd, such as Beethoven or Wagner. Additionally, there was no attempt to show how genius and madness was interwoven. In contrast, Felix Post used modern social scientific methods in his systematic study of 453 'exceptionally creative men' (Post 2004). Nonetheless, nearly all who have studied genius have used the same method: that is, making a selection of important figures, such as Newton, Einstein, Beethoven, Mozart, and examining their lives, background and achievements. Francis Galton was one of the first to do so. In his book *Hereditary Genius* (1869) he studied a selection of eminent people, regarding eminence as showing itself through rank (politicians, judges); but, in a way that we would nowadays regard as sociologically naive, concluded *inter alia* that eminent people had eminent relatives – his own cousin was Charles Darwin! Eminence came through intelligence, and intelligence he said, was inherited.

The problem with most of these studies is they never get past the basic definitional problems of 'genius' and 'madness', while the backgrounds of those selected, including their madness, seems to have been carefully crafted to prove the point: Shakespeare apparently experienced 'extreme nervous agitation' just before his death, the evidence being that documents signed by him showed an unsteadiness of hand; Robert Burns was said to have an 'irritable and nervous bodily condition' and 'extreme sensibility'. Nisbet (1900) is able to find constitutional weaknesses in all his men of genius, derived, he thinks, from a well-marked strain of neuropathic disorders, insanity being one of the family of 'nerve-diseases' (1900: 109). All have a marked family weakness – they have family members who are 'ne'er-do-wells' (Bramwell, the brother of the Brontës, for instance) or eccentrics (this being a sign of neuropathic disorder) or show genetic disorders. They rarely married, rarely had children, and often were of active habits – although not, it seems, Wordsworth, who was 'slow and inactive' (1900: 256). What runs in the blood of these families is nerve disorder, said Nisbet, of which genius is the occasional outcome. Genius is an accident of the cerebral and nervous organisation (1900: 325). Stripped of its pretentions this is not an uncommon view; genius is often seen as a quirk of nature thrown up occasionally by who knows what – some genetic upheaval, perhaps. However, Nisbet's message about family weaknesses is not wholly convincing – those he describes can be found in most families if one looks hard enough.

In spite of Nisbet's claims there seems to be no common feature in the background of the genius, although it clearly helped to be middle class and financially independent. Yet Dvorak came from working-class roots, although he was lucky enough to be helped by generous benefactors. How many 'mute inglorious Miltons' we have missed is difficult to say – probably not many. Some geniuses were child prodigies (Mozart), others not (Einstein); some died young (Mozart, Keats, Shelley) while others lived longer than the average for their time (Newton, Handel, Verdi). Harold Nicolson (1947) in his study of 32 famous poets found that 19 lived beyond the age of 60, and seven to between 50 and 60. He suspected that a control group of clergymen, lawyers and merchants living at the same time would show similar death rates. There was no difference in health; men of genius were no less healthy than any others, although Shelley, 'having little gift of self criticism', persistently regarded himself as very ill (Nicolson 1947: 711).

Genius can arise as a solitary figure, or can be part of a centre of excellence such as that in Athens at the time of Pericles. Bertrand Russell describes their achievements as perhaps the most astonishing in all history; out of a population of about 230,000 philosophy, art, literature and science advanced as never before (Russell 1946). Europe in the nineteenth century produced many great composers, as did the city states of north Italy in the fifteenth and sixteenth centuries. Was this a chance constellation of genes – or, for the more sociologically inclined, a special set of socio-economic circumstances that encouraged creativity? Who can say?

In those few insane geniuses it is not clear whether insanity produced the ideas, or the madness was incidental and an outcrop of an abnormal mind. William Blake, described as a 'transcendent genius', was said to be capable of 'sublime beauty of conception and exquisite execution but at times incoherent and subject to hallucinations where much of his writing is pure rhapsody. He brooded on certain ideas and churned them up in a froth of fancy. He took orders from Ezekiel' (Crighton-Browne quoted in Porter 1991: 508–9). And if he was mad, then it was not clear which parts of his madness produced sublimity and which the incoherence. Nisbet describes how Blake was able to draw the subjects of his hallucinations as if there was a living sitter before him (1900: 79). His madness may not have advanced his creative skills but they certainly did not diminish them.

For the third question, linking creativity to madness, those who saw a link with genius speak of it as a mental malady. Of course, one does not have to be a genius to be creative – many journeyman poets, philosophers or scientists have been creative without reaching the higher levels. Creativity in varying forms exists throughout every stratum of society. All stages of creativity follow a pattern, beginning with an interest in the subject – although the term 'interest' understates the case, since often this is more like being overwhelmed by one's subject. This is followed by the appearance of the idea, and finally – one of the hardest parts – the execution (Pickering 1974: 269). What seems to set the genius apart is the level of concentration, and the corresponding way these ideas are turned into practice.

First, an interest in the subject. There has to be an indispensable psychological precondition necessary for creativity; Nietzsche called it intoxication, a 'heightened excitability of the entire machine' which produced the spark (quoted in Porter 1991: 498). The genius seems to have this in abundance, a sort of intoxication of the soul, and it arises in the person irrespective of his or her origins. It is a sort of aesthetic activity. W.A.F. Browne called it the 'monomania of imagination', defined as the mania of accomplishments. It is displayed in attempts to do everything perfectly; the mathematician, the poet, the painter striving for excellence, constantly involved in struggles to attain it. Everything must be at the level of the superlative (Scull 1991: 38–9).

The driving force, that urge to create, is another important component in creativity. It produces a thrill of achievement, related to the beauty of form of what has been newly created. This is true whether for the scientist, the mathematician or the poet (Pickering 1974: 274). Galton went further and insisted that genius was about zeal, a capacity for hard work and a passion for the subject. This was picked up and reported by later researchers (Pickering 1974) who emphasised the importance of passion, adding that personality was as important as intelligence. Or as one researcher said (Cox in 1926, quoted in Pickering 1974: 268), 'high, but not the highest intelligence combined with the greatest degree of persistence will achieve greater eminence than the highest degree of intelligence with somewhat less persistence'. Havelock Ellis (1904) spoke of the passion of one's soul, which is to be distinguished from ambition, the latter being too selfish. Ambition is about getting on in the world, but passion is, in Einstein's terms 'cosmic religiousness' or a deep longing for understanding (quoted in Pickering 1974: 308). Felix Post was clear; all 453 subjects in his study were able through their outstanding industry, meticulousness and perseverance to produce works and get them accepted as cultural advances. Their fame was due to their ambitions, drive and ability, with some help, of course, from supportive social circles (Post 2004: 316).

Then there is the appearance of the idea. This is perhaps the least understood and most difficult aspect to fathom. Yet there can be no ideas without imagination, and Nicolson accepts that a powerful imagination is a necessary prerequisite for creativity. But powerful imaginations play tricks, requiring additional sensibilities; some of these make the creative person receptive to new ideas, some lead to madness; some lead to new levels of sublimity of feeling, others to a loss of the grasp on life. Do not be fooled, says Nicolson; receiving great ideas is no different from receiving ordinary ideas. Both come from a spontaneous activity of the cells and fibres of the brain wherein new combinations and impressions are constantly being formed. It is about what happens after the ideas arrive that determine the future, whether of the idea or the person.

Many suggest that the idea simply arrives, usually after periods of intense thought, and often away from the desk or workplace, perhaps during walks, reverie or dreams. Nicolson describes a whole range of situations in which geniuses worked: Mozart preferred to be surrounded by the hum of conversation in which, incredibly, he would participate while composing; Schubert wrote one of his loveliest songs when listening to a band in a beer garden; Dr Johnson wrote best in a post-chaise, Thackeray in the Athenaeum, Victor Hugo on a bus, Milton only between October and March, Byron and Dostoevsky only at night, and so on. Nicolson concluded that if there was such a thing as artistic temperament then assuredly it assumes diverse forms (1947: 712). Occasionally serendipity plays a part, as with Pasteur and the discovery of penicillin, but it was an Oxford group of biologists who developed the drug, for almost always creativity follows the prepared mind. Pickering thought creativity also followed periods of illness, but of his selected geniuses illness had no role in Elizabeth Barrett's poetry. Yet in others it did: illness provided the idea and the execution for Joan of Arc, Mary Baker Eddy, Sigmund Freud and Marcel Proust, but with Charles Darwin and Florence Nightingale it simply protected them from the drudgery of daily life (1974: 282–3). When Bertrand Russell was asked how he 'thought', he said he just did, and Mozart described how musical ideas simply came to him. Either one has it or one doesn't; only a very few have it, most of us do not.

How much does madness play a part in the creative process? Havelock Ellis (1904) says that as so few geniuses were mad – he thinks about 5 per cent – 'we must put out of court any theory of genius being a form of insanity'. But of those few that were mad, and creative during their madness, how did their madness inspire them? To a small number it was assisted by opium, as with de Quincey, or Coleridge, but more likely their madness remained apart from or independent of their creativity. But sometimes not. Was Van Gogh mad when he painted those self-portraits, or was he, as Porter asks, simply painting misery? (Porter 2002: 182). And how much of modern art is the work of mad people – or perhaps of con artists?

Many have claimed madness to be indispensable to their creativity, but one needs to retain some scepticism about such claims. Not that the claims were necessarily false, or that the artists feigned madness, rather that they were being disingenuous, or simply talking about something different. Virginia Woolf said that she sought madness as an adjunct to creativity: 'madness was terrific' and 'not to be sniffed at' (quoted in Porter 2002: 83). So too with Blake, Dryden or Cowper, but I wonder how severe their condition was. They saw insanity not as a moral dread but a path to creative enlightenment. Small wonder they longed for it. Cowper said to William Blake: 'O that I were insane always. I will never rest till I am so'. Others expressed similar sentiments – it was lucky to be mad.

But was this really madness? I doubt it. To me it more closely resembles 'exquisite melancholy' rather than any full-blown madness. Charles Lamb was also sceptical; his experiences of madness were such that he knew madness produced pain, and the condition as a burden. He wondered why those who craved madness did not see it that way. I agree; their madness does not ring true, or at least it does not fit easily with those whose wail of protest was against their condition, and against those who detained them. Or with the painter Dadd, or the poet John Clare in Northampton Asylum. Janet Frame in her 1961 book *Faces in the Water* (quoted in Porter 1991: 494–5) described her fellow patients as provoking hostility and impatience: 'Their speech did not appeal as immediately poetic. They wept and moaned they quarrelled and complained.' No Ophelias here.

Finally, the hard part, that of execution. Having received the original imaginative idea, it must be fully developed and executed – the latter, some suggest, is more difficult than the former. A number of us have original ideas, but few translate them into practice. Others before Darwin had considered natural selection; he transformed, developed and executed it into a theory (Pickering 1974: 274). Like other successful creative people, geniuses included, he was able to translate those ideas into a useful format. To do so requires tremendous skills, of patience, commitment, perseverance, and an overriding belief in the importance of their idea, or of their art. Some, like Mozart, appeared to do it effortlessly, others such as Beethoven with more effort. But all needed those skills that translate the idea into a coherent whole, aided of course by a little bit of luck, and a patron perhaps, or something or someone to help on the way. But the levels of concentration and commitment are the key. This is genius in action.

The general conclusion then is that if some geniuses were mad, others were not. And if some were creative while being mad, others were not. There was no hard-and-fast rule; at best madness seems to be a necessary rather than sufficient condition of genius and then only for a small number. Perhaps it is the commitment to their art or science that makes the genius appear to be mad – that type of single-mindedness is unusual. Or might it be the genesis of creativity? Is that the ultimate conundrum? How do great ideas appear in one person and not the next? Is it simply that the prepared mind is able to receive them, or something else? Most believe it is that 'something else', yet what that is remains a mystery. Whatever the answer, the genius still excites our curiosity, and the creative spirit our own imagination. Whether the genius is also mad simply adds to that.

I think Harold Nicolson should have the last word. He describes a pyramid of creativity where at the bottom are the journeymen (my words not his) who do the best they can. They are gifted with a certain capacity for observation, but are happy and unperturbed with their lot. Above them, in a higher scale, and in much smaller numbers, are the novelists, who from their memories and associations construct an imaginary world that becomes more than one half of their reality. For them imagination is a constant frame of mind, and when inspiration comes it is as a welcome dissolution of an accumulated perplexity. But, says Nicolson, raised above all others, and very small in number, are those living in a rarefied ether of their own, the mighty poets, who are a race apart. For them imagination is no happy mood, but a superb and agonised bewilderment. The gods visit them, and not amicably but in a flash of flame and fire. Not for them the tiny pleasures, the small disappointments, the trivial success and failure of lesser breeds. They know that they have caught a glimpse of inspiration, which however short is beyond the reach of all others.

Remember, says Harold Nicolson, that those at that highest level are not quite so mad as they believe themselves to be, or as they tell others, or as they seem (Nicolson 1947: 713–14).

What does all this mean in terms of our understanding of madness? First, I think, that genius should not be equated with madness. Genius is about control and the mad are out of control. Second, and here lies the clue about what distinguishes the mad. It is their irrationality, their inability to be able to act coherently; or, put differently, they are dominated by their systematic false beliefs. Most of us have ideas, and as with the mad, some are original and others not, one difference being that the genius is able to develop them in a systematic way. Lamb and Connelly saw the difference. Lamb said that the true poet is not possessed by his subject, he has dominion over it (1987: 212–13). Connelly believed the mad to be failures, as 'following every loose and deceptive analogy, mistaking the order of phenomena' (quoted in Porter 1991: 495). That phrase 'mistaking the order of phenomena' is the key; or as John Locke said, the mad put together ideas wrongly. It is the emphasis on control and on ideas, especially the order in which those ideas are presented. This seems to be the distinguishing feature of the mad.

References

Burton, S. (2002) *A Double Life: A Biography of Charles and Mary Lamb.* London: Penguin Viking.

Ellis, H. (1904) *A Study in British Genius.* London: Hurst and Blacket.

Galton, F. (1869) *Hereditary Genius.* London: Macmillan.

Lamb, C. (1987) 'Sanity of True Genius', in *Elia and the last essays of Elia.* Oxford: Clarendon Press (World Classics), 212–14.

Locke, J. (1690) *An Essay Concerning Human Understanding* (ed. J. Yolton). London: Everyman Library, 1961.

Lombroso, C. (1891) *The Man of Genius.* London: Walter Scott.

Maudsley, H. (1873) *Body and Mind.* London: Macmillan.

Nicolson, H. (1947) 'The health of authors', *The Lancet* (Nov): 709–14.

Nisbet, J.F. (1900) *The Insanity of Genius.* London: Grant Richards.

Pickering, G. (1974) *Creative Malady.* London: George Allen and Unwin.

Porter, R. (1985) '"The Hunger of Imagination": Samuel Johnson's Melancholy', in W.F. Bynum, R. Porter and M. Shepherd (eds) *The Anatomy of Madness*, Vol. 1. London: Tavistock, 63–88.

Porter, R. (1987) *A Social History of Madness.* London: Weidenfeld and Nicolson.

Porter, R. (1991) *The Faber Book of Madness.* London: Faber and Faber.

Porter, R. (2002) *Madness: A Brief History.* Oxford: Oxford University Press.

Post, F. (2004) 'Comment Based upon a Study of Biographies of 453 Exceptionally Creative Men', in A.H. Crisp (ed.) *Every Family in the Land*, revised edn. London: Royal Society of Medicine, 313–16.

Russell, B. (1946) *History of Western Philosophy.* London: George Allen and Unwin.

Screech, M.A. (1985) 'Good Madness in Christendom', in W.F. Bynum, R. Porter and M. Shepherd (eds) *The Anatomy of Madness*, Vol. 1. London: Tavistock, 25–40.

Scull, A. (ed.) (1991) *The Asylum as Utopia.* London: Routledge.

Part 3

Restraining the mad: justifications for compulsory detention

Detaining the mad

It was that titan of nineteenth-century psychiatry John Connelly who posed the relevant question. He wanted 'to determine whether or not the departure from sound mind be of a nature to justify the confinement of the individual'. He concluded that such enquiries were likely to show that 'complete restraint is very rarely required' (quoted in Scull 1985: 129). For 'complete restraint' read 'compulsory admission'.

Some have insisted on their own sanity while seeing their captors as mad. Roy Porter quotes the Restoration poet Nathaniel Lee; when compulsorily committed to mental hospital he reputedly said: 'They called me mad and I called them mad, and damn them they outvoted me' (Porter 2002: 88). And this from a detained patient: 'A favourite thesis among us, was that psychiatry smells of baloney and that all psychiatrists are nuts. They often seemed so' (Porter 1991: 15). Or, 'to speak truth the world is a great Bedlam where those that are more mad lock up those that are less' (1991: 3). Another patient, certified in 1947, noticed that he was confined with artists, musicians, teachers and doctors. It was only when he encountered psychiatrists that he saw his first lunatic. He described what he saw as the hopelessness of present-day psychiatry: 'Alas! Physician, heal thyself! But no, he cannot, nor can any other do so' (quoted in Porter 1991: 16). So, one either gets better or one doesn't; it is all a matter of luck. And for a modern twist on who is mad and who should be detained take the views of one feminist: '"Crazy" is when a woman doesn't want to live with her husband any more. "Sane" is when she decides to wear a skirt and apply for a job at Bell Telephone' (1991: 20). And within the world of the mad contradictions abound; on the one hand they claim and have been ascribed special powers of perception and rationality, on the other they are perceived as idiots and imbeciles. Or they see themselves as all-powerful, invariably through their ascribed status (usually as a king, queen, or senior politician) but in practice are powerless through the legislation that has confined them.

Roy Porter reminds us that the writings of the severely mentally disturbed leave one thing very clear; the business of being forcibly detached from their regular surroundings and removed to an asylum has invariably proved traumatic (Porter 1991: 198). Many patients believe it responsible for a shocking setback in their condition, involving disorientation, demoralisation and depression. The experience of institutionalisation, even for voluntary patients, has often been found forbidding and humiliating; how much more so when detention is formal? More recently it was found that sectioned patients were likely to be more dissatisfied with their care than the non-sectioned (Churchill *et al.* 2000: 4). There have been notable exceptions; William Cowper was pleased to be taken into an asylum by his clergyman brother, seeking relief from 'the pains of hell' and 'the sounds of torments' which he experienced alongside 'the very sorrows of death' (2000: 204). But most have found commitment painful, and the period in detention no better.

There have always been questions about the justification for detention, including how best to secure the patient's rights, and defining the duties of those detaining. Perhaps those who agonised most were the Victorians. Their instincts towards liberty supported leaving alone the mad and eccentrics, but their therapeutic and paternalistic ethics urged them to help (Porter 1991: 101). One case exemplified the problem, that of so-called 'Mad Lucas', a notorious rich Hitchin hermit: namely whether or not a man who acted and lived as he did ought to be interfered with. It was clear that this could not be done merely on the grounds of the neglect of his property, or his mode of life, 'seeing that our law … allows unthrifts and wasters to do as they like' (Whitmore (1983) quoted by Porter 1991: 101). But assuming that proof of his insanity was conclusive, would it have been desirable to place him under care? 'He was not dangerous to others, nor was he dangerous to himself, except in a very general sense, but might he not have benefited and been really more comfortable if under medical treatment and control?' (1991: 101). The answer for the Victorians was forever equivocal. Had Mad

Lucas been a contemporary of ours most likely we would seek an order for detention, believing that he would benefit from treatment and be made more comfortable. And of course that would be true, but perhaps of doubtful value if he was imprisoned against his will. Comfort, tidiness, treatment, control – all words that spring to mind and are used regularly – become justifications for interventions and control, but all walk round the problem.

The Victorians tried to resolve their dilemma through legalism: legislation aimed at providing the courts with powers to decide on admissions, while restricting the asylum managers and those conducting treatment. Each facet of the patient's life and treatment was controlled according to a detailed set of rights and duties imposed on patients and staff alike, all based on the assumption that no one ought to be confined without legal safeguards. Their deep suspicions of those claiming expertise to diagnose and treat the insane supported their beliefs.

The Victorian world-view continued throughout the first half of the twentieth century. Questions about the quality and the veracity of treatments, reliability of diagnosis and the fear that mental illness could be confused with anti-social behaviour, were regular features of the psychiatric literature. As late as the 1960s the *British Medical Journal* agonised about the difference between 'social misdemeanour and mental illness' after a young man, apparently incorrigible and resistant to the crime and punishment formula of the courts, was handed over to a psychiatrist for a leucotomy. In the subsequent correspondence one doctor thought it was indeed fortunate that leucotomy was not practised 100 years earlier lest Dostoevsky might well have been a candidate, and the world a poorer place as a result – without *The Brothers Karamazov*, for instance (quoted in Greenland 1970).

That they worried about such matters was comforting, but legalism was never without its critics. The 1890 Lunacy Act, the embodiment of legalism, was criticised at the time, but in the next century was seen by many commentators as an anachronism (see particularly Jones 1960). Nowadays the law has become the vehicle by which treatment and therapy are advanced, not the means by which the zealot, or the treatment provider can be controlled. Detention has become the prerogative of the medical profession, and as Jill Peay rightly points out, mental health law is now largely applied by non-lawyers (Bean 1980; Peay 2003: 160). Members of that profession, not the courts, are given the primary responsibility and the powers to decide who should or should not be admitted, and on the treatments to be provided. The courts retain limited powers, but there are fewer checks and balances than before.

The Expert Committee in their Review of the Mental Health Act 1983 rarely considered justifications for compulsion, rather it concentrated on the most efficient way of proceeding (Expert Committee 1999: para. 13). Its precepts were almost carbon copies of the Percy Commission (1957). Where the Percy Commission stated: 'People with mental illness should as far as possible be treated in the same way as people with other illnesses or mental conditions', the Expert Committee extended that recommendation by asserting that authority to impose compulsory assessment lies, and should lie, in the hands of mental health professionals (1999: para. 13). Again, where the 1957 Percy Commission said, 'There will always be some people with mental disorder who are either unable or unwilling to seek care or treatment. They may not realise, or not accept, that such care and treatment will be in their best interests if it helps prevent their condition from getting worse or makes it less likely that they will harm themselves or take their own lives' (Percy Commission 1957: para. 2.2), the Expert Committee echoed that view: 'where a patient lacks the capacity to consent to care and treatment for mental disorder then society should have the power to provide that care and treatment even in the absence of the person's consent' (1999: para. 4.1).

Underpinning the assumptions of these committees – the Percy Commission and the Expert (Richardson) Committee – was a willingness to accept that mental conditions can be diagnosed and treated by competent professionals. In addition, patients requiring compulsion can be distinguished by the nature and severity of their condition from those who do not. Moreover no credence is given to the competent refuser – the person who is ill but seeks his own salvation by different means. Nor is credit given to the unequal power distribution between the competent professional and the mentally disordered patient.

Times have changed since legalism held sway, and the knowledge, prestige and powers of medicine have accompanied those changes, often to the benefit of the patient but not always so. We have done away with the traditional Victorian or pre-Victorian madhouses, replacing them by multi-purpose modern buildings where the insane are treated according to modern methods of medical care. That involves new forms of treatments, replacing older ones that were painful and degrading – although some would say that modern treatments are no more effective (Clare 1983). Accordingly, patients now benefit from standards of care beyond the dreams of our Victorian forebears, whether they be of comfort from surroundings, or from modern chemical medications – a markedly different experience from earlier robust forms of treatment (see Minto 1983).

Yet the Victorians maintained a clear distinction between detention and freedom; by implication this meant being treated or not treated. The patient was either detained or not, treated or not. That straightforward division has gone, and with it a belief that such distinctions are irrelevant. Nowadays boundaries are blurred. Compulsory detention takes place in hospitals, hostels and the community. Treatments are more varied. Some treatments, which may be damaging, will be given only with the patient's agreement; while others, which are benign, can be imposed. Patients being treated in the community or living in a halfway house who receive long-term intra-muscular psycho-active medication might not regard their predicament as restrictive, or feel that they are detained, at least formally, as they would be were they in hospital, although in fact they are. They may not be subject to a formal hospital order, nor need to be, but neither are they free in the true sense of that term. The formal demands of legalism, with the court order, the imposition and listing of formal rights, would be seen as inappropriate for modern methods of care, and a clumsy mechanism to deal with these patients.

Modern mental health legislation is characterised by looking towards the rights and privileges of the professionals, not backwards towards the imposition of duties. The Expert Committee put the position thus: 'the law is likely to have only a limited impact unless it is congruent with the values of those who use it', it must 'reflect the ethics of health care to encourage rather than to deter good practice,' so that 'the more in tune any new legislation is with the aspirations of those who have to use it the more it will be followed in practice' (1999: para. 1.4). Not much here for the aspirations of the patients.

Hopefully this does not overstate the case; for others it rather understates it, particularly those among the anti-psychiatry group common in the 1960s and beyond. If it is a reasonably accurate account then perhaps the time is right to assert a different view, less fashionable nowadays, one that nonetheless sees the act of commitment how it always was. This view is set against those who assert the primacy of treatment, or the professional demands of groups such as nurses, social workers and the like, or the new and varied methods devised to control patients in the community, such as community treatment orders. It challenges those who argue for the type of mental health legislation currently in vogue, and who seek justification for the use of or increase in executive powers. At its extreme it disputes with those who see legislation as providing further opportunities to treat the mentally disordered, using that legislation to advance a particular form of therapeutic culture. It stresses that involuntary commitment requires justification. This is over and above saying that justification is solely on the grounds that the patient needs treatment, whether the patient is in a hospital or in the community, or wherever treatment is given without the patient's consent.

The essence of this position is that whenever a patient is detained against his will, and has no choice about the length of his stay, or about his treatment, whether he is in the community or otherwise, that requires justification in the same way as other forms of state detention. It is based on a sociological view that detention is an expression of the power of the state. Its use might be necessary, but whether that is so or not, detention always raises questions about the rights of those being detained, and about the duties of those doing the detaining. It is legalism in a modern form.

Starting from the assumption that all forms of detention pose threats to liberty – negative liberty in this context – the method here is to hold up some basic features of the modern legal system, especially those from criminal law, and see how mental health legislation compares. It is similar to looking at a mirror; I want to see how the image of one compares with that of the other. Using a socio-legal framework I examine the way current mental health legislation defines compulsory detention, and show how it works in practice. Inevitably, I rely on the 1983 Mental Health Act, which applies to England and Wales, but I want to include other legislation, especially the Mental Health Bill 2006. I do not intend to get involved in a detailed legal debate, and even in reference to the 1983 Act and the 2006 Bill I will be selective (House of Lords 2006). For example, the Act includes Guardianship, but this is rarely used nowadays. I am more concerned with those aspects that determine the major forms of compulsory detention. Also, affecting the 1983 Act and the 2006 Bill is the Human Rights Act 1998, which brought into force in October 2000 the rights set out in the European Convention on Human Rights (Bindman *et al.* 2003). Again, I shall refer to these as appropriate.

The task would have been easier had there been more empirical evidence on which to draw, to show the effect of detention, detrimental or otherwise; there is nowhere near enough. A small number of papers look at the impact of the legislation (see especially Department of Health 2000b) aided by one or two more ambitious tasks on the way the law works (Peay 2003). There are numerous patient accounts, but these are often self-justifying, claiming conspiracies against them by families, friends and the medical profession, sometimes containing a belief in their own sanity compared with that of their jailers. Offsetting the more truculent patient's accounts are the oft-quoted expressions of gratitude, the so-called 'thank you theory of psychiatry' given when patients return to normal life. On both sides complaints and gratitude are doubtless sincerely given, that is not in issue, but they are poor substitutes for good-quality research. For always the important questions remain. Was detention necessary? Did it have positive effects? Were there any damaging side effects? If so, what were they and how long did they last? What of those patients of a similar condition who were not compelled? Would any have been better off under an order? How did their treatments differ, and did detention affect the length of time taken to recover? Given the state of research most of these questions go unanswered. In practice, of course, the lack of empirical research cuts both ways; it can be as comforting to the complainant as to the detainer, for both sides can marshal supporters if there is no data to confound them. But that will not do. Psychiatry claims to be data-led, yet here is a major aspect of its work that too often relies on unsupported, anecdotal evidence; with one or two notable exceptions little has been done to evaluate it.

But where to begin? Perhaps the first port of call is to refer to the Declaration of Hawaii, approved by the General Assembly of the World Psychiatric Association in July 1983, a body incidentally without executive powers outside its membership. Its membership is large, even if it does not necessarily represent international opinion. The declaration was thus:

> No procedure shall be performed nor treatment given against or independent of a patient's own will unless because of mental illness the patient cannot form a judgment as to what is in his or her best interests, and without which treatment serious impairment is likely to occur to the patient or others.

Few I think would quarrel with the general terms and sentiments of the declaration. It sets out justifications for detention on the basis of impaired judgement due to illness, and what the effect of that illness might be if no treatment is given. The problems lie in the detail, as much in what is not said as what is: what constitutes a serious impairment, what constitutes best interests, for how long should detention continue, what treatments may be given and who decides whether to proceed with treatment? Above all, what constitutes a procedure? Nonetheless the declaration fits into an earlier justification for detention offered by Anthony Clare, presented in his objection to Szasz; that is, detention is justified when the psychiatrist judges the patient's ability to choose freely is gravely compromised by his mental state (Clare 1978: 1198). Again, there is no dispute about this as a general principle; the problem is again in the detail.

With this in mind I suggest the next step is to deal with a set of basic epidemiological questions, namely how many are detained, who they are, and under which sections of the legislation, and proceed from there.

De jure and de facto detentions

It is neither easy nor straightforward to determine the numbers of patients formally detained in England and Wales – especially if we include those on community orders. There is first and foremost a definitional problem; what constitutes detention? From this apparently simple question matters turn out to be quite complex. To deal with the more straightforward aspects first, that is, the legal provisions: there are formal direct legal controls, as under Sections 2 and 3 of the 1983 Act. Section 2 allows for detention for assessment, and/or treatment for a maximum of 28 days, while the renewable powers of Section 3 effectively allows for indefinite detention for treatment. These are largely retained under the new Mental Health Bill. The Mental Health Act Commission (or MHAC from now on), in their tenth Biennial Report (MHAC 2003), states that these powers have separate criteria, and therefore separate safeguards, but adds that it is a matter of professional judgement as to which Section is appropriate (para. 8.29).

MHAC official data shows that 20,136 patients were subject to Section 2 orders in the year 2001–2002, and 17,940 under Section 3 (MHAC 20003: para 8.31 and Figure 7). To these must be added those patients detained under Section 4, which allows for emergency admissions based on a single medical recommendation. There were about 2,000 of these – this compares with about 3,500 in 1984 and about 1,500 in 1992–93 (2003: para 8.41). These figures add up to about 40,000 for that year. I say 'about' because as I show later no one really knows the correct number.

Translated into numbers of patients, as opposed to the number of orders, the official point prevalence figure for 31 March 2002 shows a total of 13,459 patients subject to Sections 2, 3 and 4 compulsory orders (2003: para. 8.26). MHAC rather alarmingly states that not only is there a general increase in the use of the Act, but the proportion of compulsory patients to informal patients remains large. Kmietowicz (2004) also reports an increase of over 40 per cent in compulsory orders in the last decade.

Who are these patients? Audini and Lelliott (2002) examined 31,702 detentions over a comparable period and concluded that the highest rates of detention were of the 25–34 age group, with 47 per cent aged 20–39, the mode being 25–29 for men and 30–34 for women. In the 25–39 age group men accounted for 59 per cent of admissions, but the difference in gender reverses after the age of 40; in the over 80s group 72 per cent were women. Detentions were over six times more likely for black people than for white (450 against 68 per 100,000; for Asians the figure was 112 per 100,000). The explanation offered was that there was a higher prevalence rate of schizophrenia in black populations, coupled with a mistrust of services, poor compliance with medication leading to delays in seeking treatment, plus a greater history of violence and greater contact with the police. This was largely confirmed by Churchill *et al.* (2000). In addition, McPherson and Jones (2003) found that older people were more likely to be detained because of self-neglect and physical illness and a diagnosis of organic mental disorder, whereas young people pose a greater risk to others and a risk of suicide. Webber and Huxley (2004) argued that there were four risk factors in admission: a risk to self and others, bipolar affective disorder, non-white ethnicity, and low social support, the last being an important variable, as high admission rates are associated with deprived inner-city areas. To these could be added the dramatic increase of illicit drug use among the seriously mentally disordered; another is the promotion of risk management strategies, which may have the unintended effect of producing more defensive practice (MHAC 2003: para. 8.27). Whatever the reasons, the number of orders made, whether for assessment, treatment, emergency or in the community, is considerable and it seems there is little hope of a reduction in the near future.

What also seems to be happening is a changing pattern of psychiatric care, not incidentally confined to the UK (Priebe *et al.* 2005). The number of psychiatric beds has been falling, and with the number of admissions rising, that means a shorter period in hospital. Set this against the period before community care and the changes are stark. Then the mental hospitals were full of elderly long-stay patients who took up most of the psychiatric services. The social composition was quite different, as was the length of stay. (Incidentally these elderly patients have long since gone, but where to? Almost certainly to hostels, bed-and-breakfast accommodation, single bedsit apartments, usually in inner-city high crime-rate areas. What quality of life they have is anybody's guess, nor is it clear about the quality of psychiatric services they receive.)

Added to the more direct formal orders are those patients detained under Section 136 where the police have powers to detain patients in the community in order to be psychiatrically examined. This is not a power normally included within standard definitions of compulsory powers *per se* as it lapses after 72 hours unless other sections are invoked, such as Sections 2 and 3. Nonetheless, it involves a period of detention. MHAC reports over 3,000 are detained annually under Section 136. I want also to include those detained under Section 5(2): the informal patients who can be detained for up to 72 hours if the doctor in charge of treatment reports that an application under Sections 2 or 3 ought to be made. Throughout 2001–02 there were about 10,000 of these (Salib and Iparragirre 1998). Then there is Section 5(4), which provides for nurses of a prescribed class to invoke a holding power in respect of a patient, for up to six hours. In 2001–02 there were about 2,000 patients so detained. I am not including here Guardianship Orders, Section 135 orders (patients detained due to neglect) or orders for offender patients.

The information MHAC collects comes from hospitals or detaining authorities. There is no dispute about an increase in numbers, although one should be careful about official figures; this is confirmed by the work of Audini and Lelliott (2002), who say that no data sets are accurate, and if our own research is anything to go by hospital data are seriously deficient and often flawed (Bindman 2000). In a study on the use of compulsory powers in mental hospitals in the London area (Nemitz and Bean 1995) we had to change the research design as there were no valid data from which to act as base line for the study. Massive discrepancies existed between the data published by the Department of Health and that retained by the hospitals themselves. There were similar inaccuracies within the hospital system, and numerous discrepancies between the hospitals in the way data was collected and recorded. For example, some patients were officially listed as being discharged and re-admitted when they moved from one ward to another, others listed as separate patients when their legal status changed from, say, Section 2 to Section 3. Some hospitals overstated the numbers of compulsory admissions, and others the reverse. It was difficult to see how the data was of much value, whether for planning or research. ('Rubbish in, rubbish out' was how one official described it.) Our proposed solution was that all compulsory admissions should be notified to MHAC (as happens in Scotland) where the Commission could collect, evaluate and analyse the data. This suggestion has not been taken up.

Take the data on Section 136. MHAC reports that detentions under this section do not include those detained in police stations – yet these are substantial, as police stations are the most commonly used premises for this section (Bean 2000). MHAC goes on: 'We consider it to be a serious lack of mental health statistics that there are no total figures available for the use of these powers' (MHAC 2003: para. 8.51). This scant regard for data indicates a deeper malaise. It is not that the numbers of orders may be greater or lesser than supposed, or that planning and research are restricted, rather that poor data creates the impression that detention is unimportant. Faulty data encourages a casual approach; it conveys a lack of urgency, a sort of 'if that's the way they do things then why worry' sort of attitude. And indeed, why should one worry if that is the way things are done. And if there is a conspiracy theory worth stating it would be that the hospitals encourage such a casual approach as it allows them to hide behind the inaccuracies. I don't always believe this, but often things get mightily close.

That apart the numbers listed above are the *de jure* detentions. It is probable that the *de facto* detentions are much greater, for instance those admitted as 'voluntary' patients who are to all intents and purposes detained. These voluntary patients are regarded by MHAC as 'representing one of the clear advances in mental health legislation in the twentieth century and a legacy which society should seek to preserve' (2003: para. 8.1). But how many voluntary patients are there? In *R. v Bournewood Community and Mental Health NHS Trust, ex p. L. (1998)* the House of Lords held that so-called voluntary patients fall into two categories: those that have the capacity to consent to the admission and do consent – to be called the 'voluntary patients' – and those who though lacking capacity do not object – called 'informal patients'. This distinction, at last finally acknowledged, shows the complexity of the so-called voluntary group (see Hodgson 1997; Jones 2003: 1149). But it still leaves other matters unclear.

How many of the 'voluntary' group – those who have the capacity to consent and do consent – are really voluntary, and how many coerced? Coercion can take place at different levels. There is coercion by the legislation. Whenever there are compulsory powers patients' decisions will be tainted, by either implied or overt threats. The mere presence of compulsory powers so distorts matters as to make them *de facto* detainees. In my own research (Bean 1980) an oft-heard comment by the psychiatrist was, 'You can go in voluntarily or compulsorily; it's up to you'. Most accepted the voluntary option. (Occasionally a psychiatrist would recommend compulsory detention even though the patient wished for voluntary admission. The fear was the patient might change his mind.) More recently Thornicroft (2000) and Churchill *et al.* (2000) came to similar conclusions. In Thornicroft's study of 85 admissions, two-thirds of whom were voluntary, almost half believed that they would be detained if they attempted to leave.

Then there is coercion as a result of social or physical conditions. Many so-called 'voluntary' patients may have the capacity to give consent but are elderly and enfeebled. They have nowhere else to go, and even if that were not the case they lack the willingness to state and assert their freedoms. In my research of some 20 years earlier I wrote:

> Consider the elderly. They lacked financial independence and were already recipients of a wide range of services ... Their physical health was often poor ... (A)bout 80% of those ... over the age of 65 were receiving back-up services, and about 95% were currently being treated by the GP for physical conditions. The dependence of the elderly on the technical skills of medicine made them a compliant group. Lacking resources, they could not afford to offend those who might relieve their physical ailments. (Bean 1980: 121)

This is a different form of coercion but equally powerful.

Finally there is coercion by friends and family. In *Jane Eyre* Mrs Rochester was coerced and *de facto* detained, but the sympathy was for Jane. Understandably families call in the professionals when they can no longer cope, and of course they too can be coercive – albeit lacking formal powers. Patients know this and often acknowledge that they have reached the end of the line. They are likely to agree to admission at this point, even if reluctantly. Of course, being compliant is different from being coerced, but being compliant simply adds weight to the assertion that 'voluntary' is a difficult concept to handle. Thornicroft (2000) found the distinction between legal compulsion and voluntary treatment unclear, with many patients feeling coerced. He then added somewhat darkly, 'If compulsory treatment is extended to the community it may be that even patients who are not in fact subject to compulsion will feel increased coercion in their relationship with services' (2000: 16).

And what of the 'informal' patients, that is, those lacking capacity? Again in my own research, I described the situation of the 'informal' patient:

> To be old and enfeebled, particularly when this was associated with some degree of intellectual impairment, meant their opinion was rarely considered … For the severely demented patients who no longer appeared to recognise their husbands or children, any agreement was illusory. To put it crudely, they seemed to regard one place like any other. They resembled severely handicapped children who could be deposited in a hospital and remained there because they lacked awareness of their surroundings. (Bean 1980: 120–1)

Formal acknowledgement of their plight came in 2004 through the judgement of the European Court of Human Rights (ECHR) in the case of *HL v UK* – the so-called Bournewood Judgement. This involved an autistic man who was kept at Bournewood hospital against the wishes of his carers. The court held that admission to and retention in a hospital of HL under the Common Law of Necessity was in breach of Article 5(1) deprivation of liberty and 5(4) right to have lawfulness of detention reviewed by a court. The Bournewood decision affirmed that informal patients have the right to leave hospital whenever they like. For a patient not detained there must be a complete removal of restraint. There must be no half measures; there must be freedom to leave whenever the patient wants to, there must be no locked wards, and no enforced treatment, especially those treatments that render the patient unconscious. The upshot of this is that the ECHR judgement has been included in the 2005 Mental Capacity Act and the new Mental Health Bill: in the former there are procedures to authorise the deprivation of liberty of a resident who lacks capacity to consent; the latter states that people with ongoing needs should be cared for in ways that promote their independence, well-being and choice. Deprivation of liberty should only be authorised if identified by independent assessment as a necessary and proportionate course of action to protect the person from harm (House of Lords 2006).

What does this mean for the 'informal' patient? A right to leave? Yes, certainly. But if so, to go where? Law is one thing, practicalities are another. Patients now have the right to consent to treatment, or decide not to receive treatment, especially if the treatment is not to their liking, yet they remain dependent on those suggesting it. How realistic is this? We can but hope that relatives and doctors will consider the patient's best interests, but this may not always be so. If not, then who else takes responsibility? The answer is nobody. Richard Jones makes the point (2003: para. 1–1150) that until the recent ECHR judgement there was no legally established mechanism for reviewing either the reasons for an informal patient's admission to hospital or the justification for continued hospitalisation. Once an informal patient had been admitted no person or body was under any legal obligation to inform him of his legal status, including his freedom to leave whenever he wishes. Jones hopes that the MHAC will one day be responsible for reviewing the care and treatment of such patients, but that may be a while yet. In the meantime patients have to rely on the goodwill of others. However, after *HL v UK*, under the Mental Capacity Act 2005 new procedural safeguards developed for the protection of those falling within the 'Bournewood gap' have appeared in the *Draft Illustrative Code of Practice* (Department of Health 2007). I refer to these below.

There are a number of patients detained on community supervision orders (CSO) or community treatment orders (CTO), and the figures here are even more difficult to determine. I will not discuss CTOs in detail as I suggest that they offer a special case which would need separate consideration. Detention in the community is different from that in a hospital. However, CTOs were introduced because there was evidence that patients who failed to take their medication deteriorated, and supervision encouraged compliance. Community treatments are central to current government strategies, as ministers have argued for years that some patients require community treatment; this in spite of the complexities and anomalies of this type of order.[1] The niceties of the legislation need not concern us, except to say that there are, generally speaking, two types of order: those attached to a patient on discharge from a hospital who has earlier been admitted compulsorily, to be introduced through the 2006 Mental Health Bill; and those for patients without immediate prior hospitalisation who are already in the community. For convenience they are both referred to as community treatment (see Bean 2001 for a discussion on these orders; also Part 4 of this volume; and Hansard 2007).

I do not want to debate the effectiveness of community treatment, or about the number of orders required to prevent homicides (see Baroness Murphy's comments in Hansard 2007). For our purposes two matters stand out: that community treatment involves *inter alia* the requirement that the patient receives medication while in the community, and that refusal to do so will lead to sanctions, and ultimately compulsory hospitalisation. Other conditions may include that the patient be drug tested, or must notify any change of address – but the central requirement involves the forcible administration of medication outside a hospital.

One gets the impression that those favouring community treatment see the community as a sort of mild or poor-quality mental hospital, or an earlier stage in a continuum of compulsory care. The Expert Committee said that it was content to recommend the introduction of an authority to administer compulsory medication in a hospital outpatient setting, a sort of pre-hospital world, but added that its main concern was about shortages of services to apply the treatment. Yet control over patients in the community, outpatient setting or not, differs from control over patients in a hospital. There may appear to be similar therapeutic opportunities but the settings are worlds apart. Compulsory medication in hospital is in front of a limited audience, most of whom are therapeutically inclined; in the community or outpatient setting it is in the public arena before a larger and potentially unsympathetic audience. The community *per se* does not and cannot offer a milder form of therapy; it is geared up to different demands making it more unforgiving towards its deviants. And what community treatment does to the doctor–patient relationship one dare but ask.

This may all be bad enough, but what of using hospital as a sanction when community treatments fail? How can that message be reconciled with the view that the mental hospital is like any other hospital, and mental illness like any other illness? Are we to see the hospital as a place of punishment – is this the final acknowledgement that hospital is a prison, just as the anti-psychiatrists always said it was? There is an equally pertinent question about whether we need these orders in the first place. Existing mental health legislation provides adequate powers to deal with people who require compulsory detention, including those whose condition deteriorates, as a result of a failure to take medication or otherwise. Community controls have simply added a whole new set of unnecessary procedures, as well as duplicating those already there. And we know how control procedures have the ability to expand and enlarge themselves. This has not stopped the government pressing ahead with supervised community treatment orders under the new Mental Health Bill for patients following a period in hospital – creating in mental health a sort of old-fashioned detention centre after-care.

Finally, a brief comment on the mentally disordered in prison; though not formally detained under the Mental Health Act – unless in high-security hospitals – they are detained nonetheless. They do not have the protection of MHAC although they are of course protected as offenders under criminal justice legislation. In some ways they are a vulnerable group, yet in others they have greater protection than under mental health legislation.

A root of the difficulty lies in the definition of 'hospital' within the 1983 Act. A prison is not a hospital and therefore cannot have patients detained under Sections 2 or 3 of the Mental Health Act. Nor can it assess or treat patients without their consent. Any suggestions that the prison should be a 'hospital', or that hospitals should take more mentally disordered prisoners, oversimplify a complex problem. Many prisons lack both the facilities to provide necessary treatment and appropriately qualified psychiatric expertise. The long-term solution must be to provide adequate psychiatric facilities within the criminal justice system generally, and prisons in particular, but this could only ever be for the larger prisons; it would be unrealistic for a prison with only 200 inmates to have a fully fledged psychiatric service.

MHAC is deeply concerned about what it calls the lack of monitoring, overview, or general protection provided in relation to mental health care in prisons (MHAC 2003: para. 14.18) Yet some proposed solutions would, if introduced, make the situation worse; the consultative document for the draft Mental Health Bill recommended making the prison a hospital: 'there should be similar flexibility for patients to receive treatment in prison' (Bowen 2000; Department of Health 1999: para. 3.35). To do so without raising the level of prison psychiatric services to that of mental hospitals would be disastrous for the psychiatric prisoner. Kinton (2002) suggests removing mentally disordered prisoners 'to a designated treatment environment for the duration of that treatment' (2002: 307). That simply would not be possible. It would require qualified psychiatrists and nursing staff on a 24-hour basis, in effect creating a separate centre, or a prison within a prison. It would have all the defects of compulsion with few of its safeguards.[2]

Clearly the fears of MHAC are well founded. As things stand a large number of mentally disordered prisoners are detained with too many opportunities for exploitation by the ruthless and for mentally disordered prisoners to express their violent tendencies. However hard one might try, a prison remains a prison. It must be said that many prisoners prefer the certainties of prison – especially the certainty of the release date – to the uncertainties of the hospital world. Some will have been in hospital already and may have disliked the treatment given; in prison they are left alone. That may not be a justification for leaving the mentally disordered in prison but it is a point worth making.[3]

The high-security hospitals such as Rampton, Broadmoor and Ashworth in England and Wales and Carstairs for Scotland and Northern Ireland are a quite different type of facility. The point I want to make here is that some patients, after a period of treatment, may no longer need that level of security, but where do they go? Getting out is mightily difficult, for no one wants to take them. Their plight raises important questions about keeping patients in conditions of security over and above what they need. I have said elsewhere that legislation is long overdue to improve this situation but nothing changes. This is not a new problem; it has been going on for decades.

A note on liberty

I now want to examine some of the procedures for detaining patients. Traditionally, justifications for compulsory detention have been based on two major platforms: mental disorder, and dangerousness, which means danger to self and to others. I want to retain that format. I do not argue that there is no justification for compulsion – quite the reverse: my view is that compulsion is necessary and desirable for some patients, but the question is, for which ones? I argue that within that tripartite framework the current system needs revising, and I will make reference to the new Mental Health Bill currently before Parliament. But before that the debate needs to be placed in a socio-legal framework, which in this case means a discussion about liberty.

There are numerous ways by which to examine compulsion and seek justifications. Here I adopt the model of a process evaluation: essentially questioning whether the processes are appropriate and valid. That is, do they hang together, are the rules appropriate, and do they do what they were intended? Moreover, are those operating the Act doing so within the rules, are they suitably trained and qualified, are they able to determine which patients require compulsion, and which do not? And so on. We begin by asking, how does compulsory detention stand up against the demands of liberty?

Liberty is a ubiquitous and prescriptive concept, usually expressed to create approval in the minds of others. To say a person is free is to say very little unless and until we specify what he is free from (Benn and Peters 1959: 197). For these purposes to be free means a person should not be impeded by restraint or limitation imposed by mental health legislation except through justifiable means.

I use the term 'liberty' following one of the classical traditions of English political thought, which interprets liberty negatively. Others define it positively; they see the proper aim of law as an opportunity to remove hindrance, such as to provide employment for the unemployed, education for the uneducated, and health for those who are ill. Positive liberty becomes a means of righting social wrongs by extending choices; so health is freedom from disease, contentment is freedom from aggravation, and so on. The positive libertarian might point to an anomaly where an individual confined to his bed can legitimately scoff at a legal system that grants him freedom of movement, or a poor man scoff at one that (were he able to afford it) allows him to buy a Rolls Royce. The negative libertarian would show, rightly, that in spite of any inability to realise their ambitions both the man confined to his bed and the poor man without a Rolls Royce would be additionally worse off if they were not allowed to express their opinions, or their opinions were criminally proscribed (Feinberg and Gross 1975: 114).

Negative liberty is more proscribed – freedom from as opposed to freedom to – whereas positive liberty can mean as much as one wants it to mean. It can be relevant to all measures aimed at extending social justice. As such the term becomes weakened. If the proper end of law is to do good, that does not say very much, and if the proper end of law is to make people free from hindrance then there is no conceivable object of social organisation and action that cannot be called freedom (Feinberg and Gross 1975: 212). Positive liberty would see mental health law as directed towards promoting mental health; in contrast, negative liberty, defined as absence of restraint, sees that law as potentially impeding the patient by threatening to restrain him. To the negative libertarian those restraints, where they exist, must be subject to certain conditions that place limits on the occupational groups given power to enforce the rules.

Adopting a negative view of liberty means that the central question must be, by what purpose can the state rightly restrain the mentally disordered, or interfere with the liberty of these citizens? Or, put slightly differently, for what purpose can the state justifiably detain a mentally disordered person who does not wish to be detained? In democracies the legal system is the primary means by which restraints are imposed. So as a general rule certain kinds of conduct are directly prohibited by criminal statutes, others by regulatory devices that employ criminal law less directly. Compulsory detention of mental patients operates under one of these less direct legal statutes. Invariably behaviour or conduct that is prohibited under those statutes usually conforms to the 'harm principle', that is, conduct likely to harm others. Harm to oneself is, generally speaking, less often prohibited; where it is, it comes mainly through the so-called 'morals offences', such as drug abuse or prostitution, where there is no traditional victim, or all parties are willing to the proceedings.

Most philosophers and lawyers adopting a negative libertarian position agree that restrictions of liberty require justification (see Berlin 1948). Feinberg's view is typical. Feinberg says that because the exercise of liberty is morally valuable, the burden shifts to the State to justify the use of the law to constrain or control it (*The Times*, Obituary, 23 April 2004). It is not sufficient to rely on the beneficence of others in order to be treated fairly; individuals have rights that entitle them to demand such treatment. 'A world without rights is one in which our status as persons is diminished and our relations to one another precarious' (*The Times*, 23 April 2004). Underlying this view the onus or justification rests on the would-be restrainer, not upon the person restrained. The state must justify detaining the patient; the patient does not have to justify or make out a case for not being restrained. The presumption is always in favour of liberty, and of that form that views restraint as evil. Leaving people to themselves is always better than controlling them. Critics would, of course, adopt a different view. Roth and Kroll (1968: 91) view as dangerous the value system that reveres freedom of choice above all other considerations. They suggest that it acts to the detriment of the mentally disordered, where the slogan is 'better to let a few ... mentally ill die than risk our liberties'. This view is not unusual. Trenchant critics of negative liberty say that this can lead to a poor level of service where patients get no help from anywhere, either from the state or from any other source.

That apart, the case for liberty is further enhanced as being necessary for the development of self-expression and realisation. Various political theorists have argued that the absence of coercion is a necessary though not a sufficient condition for individual self-realisation, and the full flowering of intellectual virtues (Feinberg and Gross 1975: 113). J.S. Mill said that all restrictions on the expression of opinion are illegitimate; all sanctions violate the individual's autonomy as a rational human being and thereby weaken his intellectual muscles; so, in a subtle way, harming him and to some degree the intellectual life of society (1975: 113). Feinberg and Gross underline the point: 'the case for an unhindered open debate of public issues necessary to the pursuit of truth was never made more impressively than by Mill' (1975: 116). Indeed that is so.

But what of the mentally disordered themselves? They are not involved in an unhindered debate; more often they are ignored. They may present a series of incoherent ramblings, where the ramblings themselves form the basis on which their detention is determined. And did not Mill say that the demands of liberty only apply to those in full possession of their faculties? That may be so, but we are talking of the period prior to their detention, before they have been so diagnosed, and about the way in which they and the rest of us can be protected against unjustified detention. It is about those procedures that initially take away liberty, not about those after it has been taken.

Moreover, if the mad are seen as presenting 'incoherent ramblings' herein lays one of the dangers. They may not always be ramblings; they might be statements of truth. The use of mental health legislation to silence critics, whether in totalitarian societies or not, has been sufficiently documented to alert us to the dangers of dismissing the 'ramblings' of the so-called deluded. Mental patients may also be coherent, and be capable of making decisions; they may speak unpalatable truths. The dangers arise when that point is forgotten, and this is no more so than when psychiatry becomes the tool of the state operating within a political ideology. The safeguard is to move away from a practice embedded in ideological foundations, which emphasise political, impressionistic and experiential qualities, for these pose the greatest threat to liberty. Conversely the more psychiatry is based on evidence, clear and unequivocal, the greater the likelihood that liberty will be sustained.

Yet in spite of its obvious value, liberty can be overstated. Liberty should be seen as relative not absolute (Roth and Kroll 1986: 104). It may be precious but it is by no means the only social value worth fighting for. Nor should it be the value that overrides all others. Feinberg and Gross (1975) argue that liberty is but one value among many; it can conflict with other values, and in some circumstances may not be worth its price when measured against others (1975: 114). They give the example of a society, that may enjoy political liberty but yet permits large-scale social injustice; they suggest that where liberty and social justice may conflict, the presumption should be made towards the latter. Whether so or not, we return to the original assertion – that while liberty is relative, not absolute, the negative libertarian tradition in western societies is of value and to be preserved.

Nineteenth-century legalism provided rules and regulations for every contingency, yet failed to convince. Might a more up-to-date version, accepting the basic premise of earlier legalism but without many of the earlier details, be relevant? I hope so. It retains the central features of negative liberty – that detention ought not to be arbitrary, and that those undertaking the detaining do so on the basis that the onus is on them to justify it. It retains too the value of procedural rules, aimed at reducing capricious decisions, rules that were developed in common law with the clear aim to protect against arbitrary arrest and punishments. And as a secondary matter it asserts that the greater the level of clarity for these rules the better, for without clarity there is always the possibility of equivocation, which protects those making the decisions. Clarity, as Jill Peay says, does not always ensure consistent outcomes (2003: 164), but it helps. All this means that its central premise is that freedom of choice is to be revered, if only because a greater measure of freedom leads to personal development, and that flourishes in conditions that require restrictions on those who would restrain us. Freedom is as appropriate for the mad as for others; the mad need the security that formal rules provide in the same way that the rest of us do, and similarly require protection from idiosyncratic behaviour.

The first point to note, then, is that set against these standards the law relating to mental health falls short. Under mental health law there are few procedural rules offering protection to the compulsory patient. As is shown later, there is no opportunity to offer a plea, no right to be legally represented, no right of appeal prior to detention (there is a right to go before a tribunal after detention but that is not the same). Nor is there an opportunity for a patient to sue his captors for wrongful detention, even if he could show that he was not mad, did not require treatment or was even the wrong patient. Without such rules the fear is that the door is open to arbitrary decisions. There is an equal fear that without procedural rules the onus is no longer on those doing the detaining; as they no longer have to negotiate according to such rules, any emphasis that there might have been on them to justify detention is weakened.

Such failings would be set aside by those emphasising treatment. Offering a plea, being legally represented and so on would, they say, simply get in the way; the aim is not to promote rights but secure treatment. It is also about reducing suffering. They might accept that offenders receiving punishment need to be protected, but assert that the needs of the mentally disordered are different. Of course in some respects they are: offenders receive punishment; mental patients receive treatment. And prisons differ from hospitals, or they should do. But do they? Well, yes and no: yes, in the sense that the aim in the hospital is more therapeutic; no, in the sense that it is a place of detention that involves a loss of certain basic rights. So once there is a suggestion that mental health legislation involves compulsion, which further involves forcible restraint, then the argument falls, and the negative libertarian stakes his claim once more. And with that claim the debate returns to questions about rights and liberty.

Mental health law and formal law

An equally strenuous approach using the 'looking glass' of negative liberty is to examine the legislation to see how it compares with what I call formal law – that which approximates to criminal procedures. The first point is that to call it a 'Mental Health Act' is to mislead. It is hardly, if at all, about mental health; it is more about regulating the compulsory powers provided for detained patients admitted and discharged from hospitals. It also includes consent to treatments – itself a new feature of mental health legislation in England and Wales, albeit limited in scope – alongside provisions for offender patients involved in criminal proceedings, including detention by the police. It deals with the introduction of a Mental Health Act Commission; and with a number of other matters such as patient after-care. The Mental Health Bill 2006 continues the line taken earlier, and follows the tradition established since 1959. It is not radical.

Current mental health legislation fits into the category I have referred to in another context as 'therapeutic law' (Bean 1975). Therapeutic law does not fit the tradition of negative liberty. It differs from the more standard form of law in that the aim is to protect the person who is unable to protect himself: it is based on the concept of *parens patriae*. In criminal law the state is the accuser; in therapeutic law the state aims to look after those members of vulnerable groups unable to look after themselves. Therapeutic law is very much a twentieth-century concept, having been invoked in various Royal Commissions. Its origins, however, lie deep in the past, for example in the legislation on Chancery lunatics whose mental conditions led them to squander their fortunes.

In therapeutic law, of which mental health legislation is a good example, key terms are not defined, which leave the basic components to be formulated in ways that permit professional discretion. For example, Section 1(1) the 1983 Act defines the generic term 'mental disorder' and three of the four specific categories: mental disorder, severe mental impairment, mental impairment and psychopathic disorder. Richard Jones says all the definitions are remarkably similar in their scope – and, he could have added, almost impossible to understand. (I defy anybody to know what the definition of 'severe mental impairment' means.) 'Mental disorder' is defined as meaning mental illness, 'arrested or incomplete development of mind', but mental illness itself is not defined. This is surprising given that mentally ill patients form the bulk of admissions. There have been opportunities to arrive at more succinct definitions of these categories; there was the famous definition of mental illness by the DHSS that was abandoned 'partly because of the difficulties of producing a definition which would stand the test of time, and partly because there had not been much evidence that the lack of definition of mental illness leads to any particular problems' (quoted in Jones 2003: para. 1–023). To whom was it not a problem? Presumably to those enforcing the rules. The Expert Committee fared no better. It said it favoured 'a broad primary diagnostic criterion', but added that it would provide safeguards through more rigorous entry criterion (Expert Committee 1999: para. 4.3). What all this means is that the balance remains tipped favourably towards those making the decisions. Mental illness is what a doctor says it is, and if others disagree, then so be it. And in practice others may well disagree; the level of convergence of opinions in psychiatric diagnoses is not that high.

Under the 2006 Mental Health Bill things have in fact got worse. The Bill replaces the four types of mental disorder with a single definition: 'any disorder or disability of the mind', (clause 1(2)), first introduced in the Green Paper (Department of Health 2000a: chapter 4 section 2). The effect is to widen the application of the provisions in question to include forms of personality disorder that do not fall within the current definition of psychopathic disorder because they do not result in seriously irresponsible conduct. Also included might be certain types of psychological dysfunction arising from brain injury or damage in adulthood. However, a definition not dissimilar to psychopathic disorder is smuggled in under a definition of a variant of 'learning difficulty': 'A person with learning difficulties shall not be considered by reason of that disability to be suffering from mental disorder … unless that disability is associated with abnormally aggressive or seriously irresponsible conduct' (House of Lords 2006: clause 2(2)). That puts things almost back to square one.

Returning to the matter of procedural rules, a feature of all therapeutic law is that there are few such rules, so much so that where those making the decisions get the procedures wrong they can later be corrected. Jones reports (2003) that although primary responsibility for checking the completed statutory forms rests with the applicant, hospital managers and local social service authorities should each designate an officer to scrutinise the documents as soon as they are completed, taking necessary action if they have been completed improperly (Jones 2003: para. 1–141). In other words, it doesn't matter too much if they get it wrong, others will put it right. Now, I am not criticising this procedure or saying that such provisions ought not to be included. After all, if the aim is to encourage members of the social work, medical and psychiatric professions to operate the compulsory admissions procedures then it would be wrong to expect them to act at the level of the Crown Prosecution Service, and condemn them for legal failings. What I am saying is that procedural rules, which *inter alia* protect the defendant in criminal courts, are lacking in therapeutic law, and without them all sorts of abuses may occur.

Many would say, of course, that comparisons with formal law are inappropriate. Mental health law is not concerned with justice. It matters not to the psychiatrist what happens to other patients in similar situations. Equality before medicine is not the same as equality before the law. The psychiatrist bases his decisions on the health of the patient; this will differ according to the particular prognosis, so that each sick person becomes uniquely important. Comparisons are out of place in a way. Another obvious difference is that there is not the same requirement to enforce mental health law as there is in criminal law (see Eastman and Peay 1999). That is, medical personnel do not have to recommend that the patient be compulsorily detained even though by all accounts he fits the criteria. Admission becomes a matter of discretion based on professional judgements. Eastman and Peay (1999: 11) point out that in practice compulsory powers are not used on everyone who fulfils the conditions, but on a selected sample of patients; the Act is in fact used much less frequently than could be legally justified. Some patients who could be compulsorily admitted, are admitted voluntarily, others not at all, or they are diverted to other systems including criminal justice. Eastman and Peay conclude that mental health law is used as a method of last resort, not of first choice (1999: 11).

Mental health law is almost a different species, or perhaps a sub-species, of law, and it fits uneasily into that formal law tradition.

It more closely resembles the law on probation, or childcare, where rules are exercised by administrators using a relatively wide range of discretionary powers. Standard definitions of law (e.g. as a command of the Sovereign backed by sanctions as defined by Austin) are clearly not relevant here. If that is so, ought we to judge therapeutic law by different standards, that is, being less concerned with issues such as deprivations of liberty and more with the patient's welfare? Such is the view of those who suggest that mental health law cannot incorporate the concepts and thinking of another science or academic discipline (Eastman and Peay 1999: 21). On that basis jurisprudence, or, sociology, cannot provide a satisfactory critique. A different species it may be, but it still packs a heavy punch, in extreme cases providing for virtually unlimited detention. That cannot easily be put aside. Therapeutic law or not, detention is still detention.

What we have then is a law, the Mental Health Act, that is unlike most other laws in that it includes major differences in its structure, and its approach, and in the way it permits decisions to be made. Its aim is to promote welfare. Professionals operate it without the opportunity for the patient to challenge or debate their decisions. It stands in contrast to the legalism of the 1890 Lunacy Act where decisions to detain were made by the courts. These decisions followed the legal tradition expounded by formal law and approved by the Justices Clerks Society, who stated: 'there is not a single exception in times of peace ... to the well established principle of our common law that a man may not be put under restraint save by due process of law as signified by the order of a judicial officer', that is, a court (quoted in Bean 1980: 16).

The Expert Committee tried to nudge things towards a more formal version, without losing the modern touch – the inputs from the professionals. It proposed an Independent Decision Maker (IDM) to confirm admission to compulsion. The IDM would be used to amend defects (Expert Committee 1999: paras 5.43–5.49), would make decisions openly, and act as an independent body, placing the formal responsibility for compulsion outside the reach of the clinical team. The Expert Committee thought that the IDM would improve the consistency of decision-making. The IDM would be a lawyer whose presence would reassure the patient, the family and the carers, in fact all who doubted the present system, for it would 'appear to be essential that such decisions are taken openly and accountably by an independent body' (1999: para. 5.47 i). All well and good, but why not go the whole way and return to the courts? The Committee recognised defects in the existing system when it talked of the need to allay fears about the use of compulsion in the community, acknowledging that the imposition of control is a common feature of community treatments, but went no further along this path. And in any case the government would not agree if it did.

Clearly mental health law, or any form of therapeutic law, offers professionals a choice as to whether to use the legislation or not; if they choose not to, so be it. If they do choose to use it they avoid the threat of legal redress if they get their decision wrong. Presumably the IDM would operate somewhere midway between the existing system and the courts; the IDM would be likely to attract slightly more legal opprobrium if he got it wrong but not at the level of the courts. But the IDM would only be called upon after admission, and that remains the crucial difference.

Is it indeed the crucial difference? Well, yes. In formal law legal protection is provided before and after detention; in therapeutic law there is little or nothing before, and it has to be said not much after. No one denies that the state has a duty to protect the vulnerable, and for these purposes the mentally disordered are vulnerable, although no one denies that these matters are complex, with definitional and diagnostic problems everywhere one turns. I do not wish to evoke a Szaszian argument that dismisses all forms of compulsion as unwarranted, as it avoids the difficult question about whether compulsion is an effective remedy that alleviates suffering, which is an empirical question yet to be answered. But Szasz is correct in one respect; questions about liberty will not go away, and the manner in which supporters of current mental health legislation have been able to opt out of the debate is not easily understood. Did we need to travel that far on the treatment path? Why not provide an opportunity to be legally represented? What is wrong with a right of appeal before committal? And what is wrong with making those who detain being more responsible for their actions where they fail to act appropriately? The mad ought not to lose their rights because they are mad. Certain basic rights found under the negative liberty banner should be available to all, including the mad.

Typical legal justifications and their limitations

At the time of writing the 1983 Mental Health Act remains in operation, but certain changes will be brought about if the Mental Health Bill 2006 becomes law.[4] There is no doubt that new legislation is needed for in one respect the 1983 Act was out of date before it began – the old-style mental hospitals had been largely replaced by a care in the community philosophy. Also, in 1983 the concept of 'mental capacity' was rarely invoked; nowadays it is becoming a key determinant. Yet the new Bill retains much of the old, providing more of a tidying-up exercise than anything else.

Civil commitment statutes in most jurisdictions include three conditions for involuntary commitment: the mental disorder itself, the need to protect others, and the need to protect oneself. Some such as Thomas Szasz argue that these conditions have never provided adequate justification, nor can they ever, for he remains convinced that mental illness is a myth and hospitalisation a modern form of state-controlled warfare. His critics (Roth and Kroll 1986: 90–1) say that such views ignore the reality of mental disorder, the agonising and the hardship, both in the patient and in the family, of what is a painful condition. In my view Roth and Kroll are right. Of the three conditions, the first and most important is the mental disorder, although mental disorder alone is not sufficient to justify compulsory detention. Most psychiatrists would, however, view a serious mental disorder as, by definition, sufficient to require protection for the patient, for others, or for both.

As we do not detain patients who suffer from other illnesses, why do we do so for mental disorder? The answer can be found buried deep within the Percy Commission (1957), which set out the principles that the Commission believed were capable of justifying compulsion (see particularly Hoggett 1984: chapter 2 for an incisive legal summary of the problem). There were four: first, there had to be a mental disorder that required treatment; second, care could not be provided without compulsion; third, there was a refusal to accept treatment that suggested that this was due to the disorder itself; and finally, the patient would benefit from treatment, either by the regulation of his own behaviour, or by the protection of others (Percy Commission 1957: 56). Brenda Hoggett says that the Commission did not suggest that these principles should be expressed by statute, but recommended a scheme that distinguished various types of mental disorder – mental illness, psychopathy – by restricting long-term treatment for two categories, the mentally ill and the severely subnormal, and by adding additional restrictions that were to be satisfied before commitment was made. These are *inter alia* that the patient's disorder must be 'of a nature and degree which warrants detention in a hospital' and 'the patient ought to be detained in the interests of his own health or safety'. As said above, the 1983 Act retained these criteria but the new Bill rids us of these divisions.

Following and paraphrasing Brenda Hoggett (1984: 65), what this amounts to is that there must be evidence of a mental disorder; the best place for treatment is in a hospital either for the patient's own safety or the protection of others; and compulsion is the only way of getting the patient there. Leaving aside for the moment the question of safety, there remain legislative gaps that need filling. Take, for example, the two principles that compulsion is justified on the basis that the patient has a 'mental disorder which required treatment' and that 'care would not be provided without compulsion'. These surely cannot of themselves justify compulsion. A patient may suffer from appendicitis and can be accurately diagnosed as such, but no one would suggest that he should be compulsorily detained were he not to accept treatment. There are, of course, some physical conditions that of themselves justify compulsion, mostly involving illnesses or diseases that lead to severe epidemics, such as typhoid, and therefore are a danger to all members of society. But these are different.

How about 'a refusal to accept treatment due to the disorder itself'? It seems more acceptable that compulsion may be necessary when the mental disorder takes away the capacity to make appropriate decisions, and as such this makes a clear distinction between physical and mental illness. I have no problem with this, for as I said in Part 1, what distinguishes the floridly mad from the rest of us is their system of false beliefs, delusions and wild extravagant behaviour, all of which renders them incapable of understanding their predicament. Accordingly, if madness is about making irrational decisions, in my view this is the beginning of a satisfactory justification for compulsion. Or rather, so far so good. We need to be clear about the mental capacities. What is meant by an inability to make rational choices, and which choices are to be regarded as irrational? Which beliefs are created by the mental condition, and which are not? I may believe quite wrongly that the earth is flat, or that someone close to me no longer loves me when in fact they do, but these may have nothing to do with my manic-depressive condition. In contrast my beliefs that I am invincible, can swim the English Channel, and am destined to be a Lottery winner on which basis I buy six houses, may well be relevant.

Current legislation does not deal with this, nor is it included in the new Bill. Legislation, at least since 1959, has assumed that once the patient is diagnosed as suffering from one of the forms of mental disorder, and compulsion is required, then nothing more needs to be said. Questions of capacity become irrelevant. Brenda Hoggett was well aware of this and wanted to exclude eccentricity, caprice, forgetfulness, and the inability to make choices which others regard as wise or good (1984: 68). The Expert Committee took matters further and recommended the introduction of a capacity test to regulate treatment, so that patients with sufficient capacity would not have their wishes overruled except when there were real and serious risks to others. The pity of it is, the government did not accept this recommendation.

A considerable body of opinion would prefer that mental health legislation drew a clearer distinction between the capable and the incapable when determining the limits of compulsion (see MHAC 2003: paras 4.2–4.10). Recent research has supported that view:

> Until quite recently, it was common for clinicians to presume that serious mental illness, mental retardation or cognitive impairment *per se* rendered a patient incompetent to consent to treatment. This presumption frequently was recognised in the legal system as well. Courts often accepted a clinician's diagnosis of mental illness as all that was required to settle the matter. The most fundamental, important, and uncontroversial maxim we can offer about the modern concept of legal incompetence is that this presumption is obsolete. (Grisso and Appelbaum 1998: 118)

Grisso and Appelbaum found that most patients hospitalised with mental illness performed certain tasks as well as a comparison group with no history of mental disorder. Initially, there were thought to be long-term implications of this research, with considerable impact on legal and psychiatric thinking, perhaps greater than from any recent research initiative. For if patients retained the mental capacity to decide their treatment it is difficult to accept that they should be treated compulsorily – a position supported by Georg Hoyer who said that commitment was only justifiable when the patient's mental capacity was reduced as a consequence of mental disorder (1999: 3). That, of course, would place immediate impediments on clinical freedoms.

To some extent Georg Hoyer's claims have been met. The 2005 Mental Capacity Act (MCA) fits with the new Mental Health Bill in that those concerned will need to consider whether the patient needs to be detained under mental capacity legislation or the proposed Mental Health Act (MHA). The *Draft Illustrative Code of Practice* (Department of Health 2007: 20) states that compulsion under the Mental Health Act should be required only when there are reasons to think that relying on the Mental Capacity Act is either not possible or inadequate for some reason. The Code adds: 'This is a judgement for the professionals concerned. There is no obligation to ask the Court of Protection for a ruling that the MCA should not be relied upon before using the MHA' (para. 2.10d). The Code then lists a number of reasons why detention should be considered under the MHA rather than use the MCA, and these include the need for a degree of restraint (para. 2.10f). The Code seems to suggest that the two pieces of legislation will dovetail into each other.

Yet this promise of change may turn out to be illusory; this pessimism is shared by the MHAC who doubt 'whether the concept of mental capacity can, in fact, provide the panacea of natural justice which its supporters seem to suggest' (MHAC 2003: paras 4.1–4.10). The Expert Committee following the Law Commission, were more confident, but as elsewhere there are problems of subjectivity and definition: where does one define the point at which the patient's incapacity is detrimental to his ability to make decisions? Placing undue reliance on professionals is also worrying. Nonetheless, the potential for undermining the current system is there, even if it is some time before legal precedents help to define practice and an acceptable workable definition finds its way into legislation. Were this to happen it would provide a powerful ethical base on which to determine patient's autonomy. It requires an assessment of cognitive capacities and as such would be a move towards eliminating subjective assessments of madness, and also be applied to conditions that mimic psychiatric disorders (as in substance abuse), allaying Brenda Hoggett's fears about eccentricities, caprice, forgetfulness, and such like (Hoggett 1984: 68). It would deal the final blow to those wanting to include personality disorder and psychopathy within the rubric of the legislation.

What of the other two conditions, that is, the need to prevent harm to others or to self? The 1983 legislation does not use the term 'dangerous' it says that admission is 'necessary for the safety of the patient or for the protection of other persons that he should receive such treatment and it cannot be provided unless he is detained under this Section' (Section 3(c)). Brenda Hoggett says being 'dangerous' implies a level of risk where the patient would be expected to attack and harm someone, whereas the law simply requires that it be necessary to 'protect other persons' (Hoggett 1984: 63). The distinction is important, although for convenience 'dangerous' is a useful shorthand description.

The 1983 Act does not prescribe levels of 'safety' or 'protection' or give adequate definitions of the terms. Most likely protection covers physical and emotional harm, but could extend to actual or threatened damage to a person's property (Jones 2003: 1–041). There is no requirement that persons should be protected from 'serious harm' – the 'precise level of risk is not (surely cannot be) spelt out.' (2003: 1–041). Reducing these to more convenient terms, such as 'danger to self' and 'danger to others' or to 'self-regarding' and 'other-regarding' acts, then a useful starting point is to reaffirm the negative liberty argument and begin with John Stuart Mill's so-called harm principle. He thought that interference would be legitimate to prevent other-regarding acts, but not the self-regarding. This harm principle provides a presumption in favour of liberty. It can be overridden where the individual's conduct is likely to affect others, but if so, the harm must be relatively serious. Harm includes personal harm, and that caused by theft of property, air pollution, even damage to public institutions, but does not include personal slights or trivial insults. It must be more than conduct that is merely offensive, or based on mere dislike (Feinberg and Gross 1975: 114–15).

Living with a mentally disordered person is often unpredictable, disruptive, disturbing and almost always disputatious. The type of harm experienced cannot always be quantified but it is likely to be significant. If threatening or intimidating it undermines individual safety; even if not it remains a considerable burden that family members must bear. Nonetheless, the harm principle provides a procedural maxim that indicates where the justification lies (Benn and Peters 1959: 222). In that sense it is purely formal but it promotes a presumption in favour of freedom that can be put aside only by matters more persuasive. So, to follow Feinberg and Gross' rule of thumb, the cautious theorist will begin with Mill's principles and then apply them to the various problem areas under review, in this case the detention for mental patients. That is to say, before the presumption can be overruled conduct must be identified that is harmful; this excludes conduct that is merely offensive or not to our liking, alongside immoralities and actions that harm no one but the perpetrator (Feinberg and Gross 1975: 115). It then becomes possible to produce 'solutions that are both plausible and consistent' (115). Of course, the behaviour of mental patients can change, speedily and fleetingly, from self-regarding to other-regarding acts, making plausible and consistent solutions difficult to come by. Even so, that seems the way forward. There is no dispute that actions that involve harm to others require restraint, or that actions that involve mere dislike do not. In between, however, is a range of actions, from the more severe where safety is imperilled, to the less severe when there is a possibility, albeit remote, that the situation could become tense and unpleasant. Procedurally, personal safety outweighs liberty only at the point where safety is imperilled.

How does mental health legislation meet this maxim? The answer is, rather poorly. It does not specify the levels of harm required, or how harms might differ in mental health legislation from those prohibited by the criminal law. It suggests that mental health legislation produces a new surrogate criminal code, it being far from clear why harms to others that do not meet the level required by the criminal law should be regulated. Assaults, yes, but behaviour regarded as distasteful, no. Threats, yes, but rudeness, no. If the aim is to protect families from the disruption, heartache and gross disappointment created by looking after a mentally disordered family member, then this should be made clear. I am not minimising the suffering created. I am saying that if this is so it should be spelt out, and in such a way as to specify the level of suffering to be tolerated. A common failing of current legislation is that it permits too much. 'Danger to others' is acceptable, but if, and only if, those dangers are at a certain level.

Interference in self-regarding acts is an altogether different matter, (Benn and Peters 1959: 220). Mill was clear; interference for the person's own good, either physical or moral, was not a sufficient warrant. The distinction between self-regarding and other-regarding has always been difficult to maintain, for example, drug abuse may be self-regarding, but other-regarding when the drug user takes up valuable public health resources and creates unhappiness and disruption. So too with mental patients. They inhabit that grey area midway between self-regarding and other-regarding acts in what they do, and what they are. They can be self-regarding and other-regarding at the same time: self-regarding in that they need help, and other-regarding in that others need to be free of them.

There remains that tricky question about serious, possibly fatal, self-regarding acts. However much one may laud the principle that we have no right to interfere with self-regarding acts, what if they involve allowing the person to harm himself fatally? What does one do? Nothing? I doubt it. Few I suspect would be able to stand back and watch someone kill himself, by cutting his wrists, or jumping over a parapet, even if he is presumed sane. Nor is it moral to leave unattended a person in a depressive stupor who has not eaten for days, or a paranoid schizophrenic who sees demons in all he does.

The natural reaction, and this applies to the sane and insane, and in my view the correct one, is to act: that is, do more than remonstrate, and intervene, if only on the reasonable belief that tomorrow or some time later the person may change his mind. I suggest therefore that 'self-regarding' acts should be seen in similar terms to 'other- regarding' acts: intervention is justified where patient's safety is imperilled, but only then. And as with other-regarding acts, patient safety is best seen on a continuum; at the top of the scale intervention is justified and at the bottom is not. In between are grey areas where behaviours that justify intervention need to be identified.

In summary, then, not only are the terms poorly defined in mental health legislation, but too much is left to the professional to make decisions that are essentially moral, political and social and therefore beyond that level of expertise. It is not specified what levels of harm we should be protecting ourselves from, or the type of self-harm we must prevent. In my judgement this is unacceptable.

The impact of compulsion

What we know of the impact of compulsion is limited to a few studies and a number of personal accounts. In the latter claims are often made that the mad are no different from the rest of us. The notion that the whole world is mad is not a new idea. Thomas Tyson (quoted in Porter 1991: 1) put it thus: 'To speak truth the world is one great Bedlam where those that are more mad lock up those that are less; the first presumptuously knowingly committing evils against God, their neighbours, and themselves, but the last not knowing what they do are as it were next door to innocency.'

If commitment was a series of evils, against God, neighbours and self, and undertaken by the innocent, who may be more mad than those they lock up, was it always thus? Charles Lamb would not have thought so (Burton 2003: 200–1) but the modern view is less sentimental. It does not see those as 'innocent' nor as acting as an evil against God. The stage or ship of fools is more secular nowadays. Rarely are criticisms made of the mental health services for wrongful detention. The sin is not to lock up but to let out. There has been little or no media comment in the last decade that has reported on the wrongful detention of patients, but numerous on the failure to detain.

From the patient's point of view compulsion would be regarded as posing the more severe alternative – 'severe' defined in whatever way one might wish, in the sense of the patient's condition, prognosis, need for treatment or dangerousness. Compulsion carries with it a suspicion of being uncooperative, recalcitrant and wayward, and is made worse should there be a hint of drug abuse. Compulsion also produces stigma, which is related to the type of hospital concerned. It is bad enough for non-offender patients detained in traditional hospitals; much worse if they are detained in a high-security hospital, such as Rampton, Broadmoor and Ashworth. Formerly for the 'criminally insane' these institutions provide the highest level of security and the greatest levels of supervision. One wonders how many ever recover from the stigma attached to having been in Rampton or the like? How do such patients, if they disclose their background, ever manage to get and hold down a job, or live a normal life thereafter? How do family and friends assist with reintegration?

The Code of Practice (Department of Health and Welsh Office 1993: para. 2.6) requires professionals to consider the impact that compulsory detention might have on the patient's life after discharge but what of the impact while in hospital? And what is the effect of compulsion on the doctor–patient relationship? Surely the relationship must be damaged, as the doctor is suddenly transformed into a quasi judicial, executive figure with extraordinary police powers. Churchill *et al.* (2000) found evidence that some clinicians avoided using the Mental Health Act fearing damage to future clinical relationships. Other critics see compulsory powers as having a detrimental effect on psychiatry being a 'knife that cuts both ways' (Adserballe 1985: 37). According to Darcy (1985: 100), 'psychiatry will not develop until legal interventions are excluded or relegated to a secondary role. A critical evaluation of legal interventions in psychiatry must question whether the existence of legislation is in the interests of either psychiatry or its clients.' All, however, are agreed, in spite of little empirical evidence to support them, that when compulsory treatment involves serious disturbance in personal relationships it will have a negative influence on the patient's powers of recovery (Brun 1985: 73). The solution: encourage psychiatry to develop its own practices that protect the patient rather than rely on legislation such as the Mental Health Act.

Other evidence comes mainly from the user groups, who may be unrepresentative of the population, but nonetheless point out how the psychiatrist–patient relationship differs from other doctor–patient relationships. Psychiatrists have powers of detention and for that reason are not seen as being on the patient's side. Sometimes that complaint is bound up with the service received while in the hospital (see particularly Jensen and Pedersen 1985), such as on the length of time spent in hospital before seeing the psychiatrist (8 to 19 days in some cases) or the failure to provide information on the patient's rights, or the poor quality of courses offered (rehabilitation training courses produce the strongest criticism) (Jensen and Pedersen 1985: 52). Anne Rogers *et al.* (1993) confirm that mental patients do not hold their psychiatrists in high regard: 'they barely reach a majority vote of confidence' (1993: 48) – but psychiatrists get a poor press anyway.

Nor does it seem that mental patients are convinced by the psychiatric rhetoric that 'mental illness is an illness like any other'. In a manner that offers support to 'labelling' theory they report that few patients were prepared to identify their problem as an 'illness'. They did not internalise a bio-medical view, rather they saw their condition in social psychological terms. In my own research some 25 years earlier patients referred to being in hospital 'to have a rest', a term also used by some patients in Jill Peay's study some 30 years later (Peay 2003: 35). In their research Rogers *et al.* go on to say:

This suggests a widespread rejection of medical labels as an acceptable way of construing distress. The potential benefits of medicalisation, such as the removal of individual liberty for the presentation of unacceptable behaviour seem to have failed to convince users that problems formulated in bio-medical terms are helpful or comforting. Instead they are generally viewed as unhelpful and stigmatising. (1993: 175)

In the research by Rogers *et al.* psychiatrists were criticised by their patients as being 'cold, aloof and uncaring' (1993: 39–54). The authors explained this in terms of the historic links with social control, whether as superintendents of lunatic asylums, or as those who warehoused patients into the old-style mental hospitals. They believe the powers granted to psychiatrists under mental health legislation promotes their remoteness, aided by a psychiatric view of mental disorder where the patient's communications are of interest to doctors only as revealing symptoms. 'This historical picture helps us to understand why some doctors behave in a cursory, coercive and impersonal way at times and why patients object to such conduct' (1993: 53).

How many compulsory admissions are necessary? In my own research on emergency psychiatry I thought that almost all those committed were appropriate admissions; that is, their committal fitted in with the accepted normative systems under which psychiatrists operated and according to the legal criteria (Bean 1980). But to ask how many were false positives is a more difficult question. A patient may fulfil the legal criteria for admission, but clinically may not require it, or may turn out not to be dangerous to self or others. How many are those? We do not know, and we have no data on which to make any supposition. So, questions about how effective the legislation is, how necessary it is, how best to amend it to meet the required standards, or how much mental disorder we can tolerate, have to be put aside. This means that large numbers of patients will continue to be detained, through a process that is not data-led, but according to a set of clinical variables based on a series of assertions about the nature of mental disorder. Small wonder that Rogers *et al.* concluded that the traditional territory in which mental health professionals operate was viewed with suspicion (1993: 176). Only a more rigorous approach to data collection will remove suspicion and doubt.

Who does the detaining?

We now turn to questions about who does the detaining – who are the personnel involved? What does the law provide? Who undertakes the tasks? Does the legislation make sense – that is, does it work to advantage? Moreover, do the regulations under which those detaining operate provide adequate measures of protection for the patient against arbitrary decisions? If not, then clearly amendments are required. Answers to questions about the personnel involved and the detention procedures are generally not dependent on the answers to issues raised about the justifications for detention. Although, of course, some are. We may say that detention under existing mental health legislation is unacceptable, in which case there is no point in further discussion on the personnel involved in the procedures. Or we may find the justification acceptable in principle, yet find the procedures and personnel unacceptable.

Questions about who should undertake the task, that is, who should detain and provide treatment, are answered in different ways by different countries. Some countries and certain states in the USA have granted powers to the police to decide who is to be detained. The patient is seen by a member of the medical profession, not always a psychiatrist, and only *after* admission. Other countries use local politicians, the mayor, for example, while still others use the courts, or specially trained welfare officers. We use the courts sparingly; for instance when granting the police a warrant to enter the premises of a person deemed to be insane (Section 135 of the 1983 Mental Health Act), preferring to leave the bulk of compulsory admissions to the medical profession supported by an application from a social worker.

We operate an odd system in England and Wales. In order to be compulsorily detained an application needs to be made either by the nearest relative of the patient, or by an Approved Social Worker (Mental Health Act 1983, Section 11(1)). That application for admission, whether for treatment or assessment, must be addressed to the managers of the hospital to which admission is sought. The Act sets out the rights of the nearest relative, and who that should be, in order of precedence – wife before brother before cousin, for example – and when they should be consulted; all this is amended in the new Bill. The applicant, in this case the social worker, has a duty to transport the patient to the hospital and check that the documentation is correct; this regulation is found in the Mental Health (Hospital Guardianship and Consent to Treatment) Regulations 1983 (Reg. 4(2) and 5(2) (see Jones 2003: 79), although hospital managers and local social service authorities are expected to assist.

The application must be supported by medical recommendations, two in the case of Sections 2 and 3, and one for the Emergency Order under Section 4. Section 12 of the 1983 Act specifies the requirements that apply to medical recommendations. Where two are required, Section 12(2) states that one shall be approved by the Secretary of State as having 'special experience in the diagnosis and treatment of mental disorder'; the other to be approved preferably by someone who has previous acquaintance with the patient, often the GP. Where one doctor is required that doctor should if practicable be one of those above; if that is not possible any doctor will do.

I want to deal first with the Approved Social Worker (ASW) and/or nearest relative who makes the application. It is odd that there should be an 'application' – most other countries seem to do without it and as in the USA this duty is undertaken by the police. There are three features to the application that can only be explained historically (and even within those historical developments anomalies remain). First there is the role of the ASW as a 'mere transporter' of the patient to the hospital (Hargreaves 2000). Second, there is the expectation that the ASW will contribute to the assessment by providing information on the social situation of the patient, and of the facilities available.

Third, the ASW is expected to act as a corrective to an over-zealous psychiatrist. All three can be traced back to the duties of the old-style Mental Welfare Officer of the 1890 Lunacy Act. He transported the patient to the hospital, an important job given that patients could and still are interviewed in their homes, or in the community; he was expected to provide additional 'social' information, presumably to add to the medical knowledge from the psychiatrists; and he was to stop psychiatrists 'railroading' patients into hospital who would not otherwise be detained. The modern twist to the ASW's current position is the emphasis on the latter, the corrective role, where the ASW can refuse to make the application if in his view an alternative decision could be made. Of course, were he to refuse there is nothing to stop the nearest relative from making the application, or the psychiatrist or ASW bringing in another ASW, in which case an ASW would still be required to transport the patient to hospital.

Yet it remains unclear why there should be an application at all. The three main tasks of the ASW do not need the legal trappings of legislation. Conveying the patient to the hospital could be done by the ambulance service or the CPN. Providing a social input presumably means providing a social dimension to the patient's condition; if so, will it help those making the medical recommendations? In her research, Jill Peay thought that it did in so far as they translated information through a 'social model' (Peay 2003: 66). My view is probably not, for at the point at which a medical recommendation is made the psychiatrist is predominantly concerned with determining the severity of the patient's psychiatric condition. Social aspects are rarely considered, and if they are, which are relevant, and which known exclusively by the ASW? The psychiatrist might find it interesting to know where the patient lives, with which relative, and where the patient is employed. But he can find this out for himself; and this assumes that this type of data would affect his decision, which may not be the case. Social matters assume more importance when considering discharge, but the ASW is not involved in the care or treatment of the patient. The ASW's input finishes at the point at which the patient is conveyed to the hospital.

As to the third aspect of the ASW's role, to act as a brake on an overenthusiastic psychiatrist railroading patients into hospital, this is an oft-stated and major claim by ASWs. Again, Jill Peay's research offered some evidence to support this, as did that of Eastman *et al.* (2000) and Eastman and Peay (2000), but these studies used a vignette methodology, where practitioners were asked to consider hypothetical cases. How valid these answers are is difficult to say, as the pressure of emergency psychiatry may well produce different responses and actions. I am personally sceptical about the value of the ASW's role and find it difficult to see how the ASW can have a major part to play. As I have said before, the ASW is hardly in a position to withstand a recommendation by a psychiatrist; there is a clear imbalance of knowledge, an equally clear imbalance of access to resources, and a similar imbalance in legal recognition. Take the following typical scenario, which is in fact a case history.

> A psychiatrist made the medical recommendation on a patient he diagnoses as psychotic and considers detention under Section 2. The ASW disagreed. After a short discussion the psychiatrist said he has undertaken all the necessary procedures and will leave the matter there – adding darkly that should the patient commit suicide the Coroner will be informed accordingly.

What is the ASW to do? He knows less about psychiatry than the psychiatrist; the psychiatrist has presumably been offered access to hospital resources in times when resources are scarce (railroading is not the problem nowadays – finding facilities to get patients into treatment is considered more the problem) and the ASW is faced with the threat of explaining a suicide to the Coroner. The solution: make the application – and this is in fact what the ASW did.

I am not suggesting that all cases are open to such immediate resolution, but that the ASW's powers to affect psychiatric decisions are limited. Richardson and Thorold (1999) are correct when they say that the Act tries to impose a brake on psychiatry by demanding involvement of a non-medical opinion, but in practice the brake proves ineffective. 'Social work it seems is unable to provide sufficient challenge to the professional hegemony of psychiatry; the communication is unequal' (1999: 114). Yet if the ASW cannot act as a corrective to the psychiatrist, might the opposite be true? Does the psychiatrist act as a corrective to the ASW? Perhaps yes, although this is rarely mentioned. In emergency psychiatry the ASW invariably sees the patient first and then calls the psychiatrist to make the medical recommendation. In my own research the psychiatrist admitted only about 33 per cent of all requests to assess patients, which means in effect that in many cases the psychiatrist refused to admit where the ASW thought otherwise, or at least considered the possibility of admission (Bean 1980).

If this, the third of the planks of the ASW platform, is removed, what are we left with? Precious little, it seems. The Mental Health

Act Commission still believes in the value of 'decisions ... taken by a multi-disciplinary group of professionals' (MHAC 2003: para. 8.76), but seems to be accepting the inevitable that the ASW's influence is on the wane. Hargreaves (2000: 146) sees the role of the ASW as an amalgam of legal, professional, administrative and practical functions accumulated over two centuries. He thinks that they 'do not sit comfortably on the shoulders of a modern social worker in a present day mental health service'.

Such views do not fit the new legislation, as the Mental Health Bill follows the recommendation of the Richardson Committee to retain the application. Instead of the ASW we now have the Approved Mental Health Professional (AMHP), defined as someone approved to act in that role by a local services authority. The AHMP will be trained to 'take on the role to bring a social care perspective to act independently and assess whether all the conditions for compulsion are met, or whether the patient's needs can be met without compulsion' (Department of Health 2007: para. 1A.12). Even allowing for that training and assuming it was of value, that role could still be provided without a statutory input; and it leaves the question unanswered as to what evidence there is to suggest that such an input qualitatively improves the compulsory admission procedure, defined in whatever way one wishes.

The ASW's counterpart, the 'nearest relative', is in an even more invidious position. Largely ignored by social workers in the 1970s and beyond (Bean 1980) the 1983 Act under section 26 set out a list of the 'nearest relatives', in order of priority, able to make the application.[5] Few commentators favour the retention of the nearest relative; the Expert Committee recommended that the nearest relative's powers should be removed (1999: para. 5.7), while Rapaport (2003) said the nearest relative was 'better known for vices than virtues'. One illustration of this was of a patient who said her husband had used his powers to enhance claims for custody of the children (2003: 60). There were other cases, and Rapaport concluded that 'if the relationship was poor, [or] the nearest relative had abused the patient or vice versa, or the relative did not know the patient well enough the safeguard was worse than useless' (2003: 60). The Mental Health Act Commission cited a similar example of a patient who alleged that she had been sexually abused by her adoptive father who happened to be her nearest relative under the Act. She did not want him to act for her but she had no right to have him replaced by someone else (MHAC 2003: para. 3.30).

The current legal powers of the nearest relative owe as much to legislative inertia as anything else. Originally introduced two centuries ago on the basis of sanguinity, the role was included within the 1983 Act in much the same form as before. Clearly, relatives have a part to play; some consultation is required with an appropriate carer, who may incidentally provide more useful background information than an ASW; but there is a difference between consultation and having statutory rights. If the suggestion to remove the application and all that goes with it had been accepted, the nearest relative role would have been dispensed with too. Even if the ASW had been retained I can see no need for the nearest relative. As things stand the Mental Health Bill retains the nearest relative, but gives the patient the right to apply to displace their nearest relative, through the county court, where there are reasonable grounds for doing so. In addition the provisions will be amended to include civil partners among the list of relatives.

Taking away legal powers does not mean taking away influence. A Swedish study showed that in general psychiatrists were influenced by opinions expressed by relatives in making decisions about compulsory admissions. The authors suggested three possible reasons: first, that when the family insists on hospitalisation this might indicate the severity of the crisis; second, the psychiatrist might consider the relative as an ally who is also trying to protect the patient; and finally that psychiatrists find it easier to hospitalise someone when they act according to the wishes of a significant third person (Jacobson *et al.* 1996: 394–5). Accepting that relatives have influence is not the same as giving them legal powers.

The same sort of questions can be asked of the medical personnel who make the medical recommendations: does the law make sense, and if not in what ways should it be amended? Before a patient is detained under Sections 2 or 3 there must be two medical recommendations. Why two? It seems for a number of reasons: the first doctor to provide additional information on the patient – the doctor should ideally have previous acquaintance with the patient – and the second to act as a corrective against the zealot. I have said on a number of occasions that the practicalities do not measure up to the ideals. The days are long past when the patient could expect his GP to be part of the procedure; nowadays it is more likely to be someone assisting with the emergency services, a locum perhaps. The psychiatrist runs the service; he has access to the resources of the hospital. The GP – I am assuming the second doctor is a GP or of equivalent status – cannot get someone admitted if the psychiatrist opposes it, and the psychiatrists knows more about mental disorder than anyone else. Moreover, if the GP asks the psychiatrist for assistance he is hardly likely to disagree with the psychiatric assessment. I have suggested elsewhere that it might be time to take a more honest approach and remove the illusion. Why not accept the reality that the psychiatrist is the dominant figure and give him sole responsibility? (Bean 2001: 48). Eastman *et al.* (2000) seem to agree. The results of their research (a questionnaire sent to 2,052 respondents with a 43 per cent response rate for non-Section 12 GPs to 85 per cent for Approved GPs) showed that GPs displayed significantly lower levels of knowledge than other groups and the authors 'question whether GPs should lose the power of formal recommendation' (2000: 23).

That leaves the psychiatrist in sole charge, or someone classified as a Section 12 doctor (a doctor with special experience in the diagnosis of treatment of mental disorder). Would that be such a bad thing? Well, no, but it depends on other safeguards. Under the present system there is no right of appeal, at least not before the patient is admitted. A tribunal is available after admission but that rather weakens the idea of an appeal, which should allow the appellant access to a higher judicial authority as soon as possible after the initial hearing. Most likely the patient will have been treated before meeting the tribunal, which is presumably what he is appealing against, so that rather defeats the objective. The Expert Committee tried to rejig the argument by offering the Independent Decision Maker, who would confirm admission. The Committee suggested that the independent person would be available by the seventh day after admission, with powers to request further information from the care team and on exceptional cases to call for an expedited tribunal (1999: para. 5.82).

One wonders why the Expert Committee did not go the whole hog and suggest a return to the courts. The lawyer as the Independent Decision Maker comes as close as anyone to returning the procedure to its earlier rightful position, that is, before a properly constituted legal authority, with its own built-in legal safeguards, including a right of appeal. Criticisms of the courts pre-1959 were *inter alia* that they rubber-stamped the powers of the medical profession, and criminalised an essential medical matter. Things have moved on since then; there is no reason why the same problems should exist; properly constituted mental health courts already exist in the USA and have a track record of dealing with mental patients. There is much to learn from them. The Independent Decision Maker could also be accused of the same 'rubber-stamping' exercise as the earlier magistrate. As for criminalising a medical matter, the decision to detain compulsorily was never other than a quasi-legal exercise. We have closed our eyes to this. It is time the judiciary should bear a greater risk.

But what of Section 4 – the emergency order where only one doctor is required? This provides, in the case of an urgent necessity, for the compulsory admission to a hospital for assessment for up to 72 hours. An application is required from an ASW or nearest relative, plus one medical recommendation, from any medical practitioner. Patients detained under this Section are not subject to the consent to treatment provisions and therefore, in this respect, are in the same position as an informal patient. Needless to say the opportunities for abuse are legion; Section 4 becomes a shorter, easier and less complicated method than Sections 2 or 3. It has been the subject of a number of enquiries and MHAC has taken a more than passing interest; perhaps as a result its use has declined, both proportionately and in aggregate terms. The legislation states that it is to be used only in 'a case of urgent necessity' but MHAC doubted if all Section 4 admissions met the criteria. Although treatment cannot be given without consent, from my experience it invariably is. Section 4 encapsulates many of the criticisms of mental health legislation including the potential abuse of power.

Having said earlier that I regard the presence of two doctors as unnecessary in addition to the psychiatrist, it may appear contradictory to criticise the single doctor under Section 4. But there is an important difference. Section 4 permits *any* doctor to make the order, not a psychiatrist, or a so-called Section 12 doctor. And without a psychiatrist all sorts of problems can arise. Psychiatrists may be less than eager to do a home visit and may rely on others to make the decisions for them – this is not as fanciful as it seems. In a study on Section 136 for the Leicestershire Police the greater distance a police station was from the central hospital the less likely the psychiatrist would visit, and the more likely a Section 4 order would be made by a police surgeon. And what is an 'emergency'? Rarely do situations arise that cannot wait for a psychiatrist. And once in a hospital all the trappings of a compulsory order arise including the likelihood of treatment.

Section 5 of the 1983 Act provides two sets of holding powers for patients already in hospital; Section 5(2) provides powers for an informal patient in hospital to be detained for up to 72 hours if the doctor in charge of his treatment reports that an application under Sections 2 or 3 ought to be made. I will not enlarge on this here, having mentioned earlier about patients feeling coerced as long as such a section remains (but see also Hall *et al.* 1995; Jacob and Freer 2005). I will, however, say a bit about Section 5(4), which provides for nurses of a prescribed class to invoke a 'holding power' in respect of a patient for a period of not more than six hours.[6] During this period the appropriate medical practitioner in charge should examine the patient with a view to making a report under Subsection 2. A nurse invoking this provision is entitled to use the minimum force necessary to prevent the patient from leaving hospital (Jones 2003: 1–075 and 1–082). Section 5(2) is often used as an easy way of detaining patients compulsorily, and as a trial period for compulsory detention (Bean and Mounser 1993: 82–6). The Expert Committee recommended that consideration be given to competing interests from other professional groups, other than the medical profession. 'Thought should be given to extending the role to include other mental health professionals who are not psychiatrist' (1999: para. 1.3) – a view endorsed in the 2006 Mental Health Bill, and probably referring to psychologists, community psychiatric nurses (CPNs); CPNs are employed by the Trusts and trained in mental health matters. The Mental Health Bill (Clause 18) talks of 'Approved Mental Health Professionals', approved by the local social services authority details of which will emerge later, presumably in line with the Richardson proposals. It is not clear who these mental health professionals are. Have empirically sound and tested reasons been produced to prove that they should be so involved? Has their training and experience equipped them for such tasks and what additional knowledge do they have to justify these claims? I suspect that the decision to include other professionals is political; professional groups have made demands that they should have equal rights to detain patients, and those demands have been accepted. If so, then to accept those claims panders to a spurious form of democratisation or egalitarianism. Whatever the justifications, this would have horrified our Victorian predecessors. In my view this is a mistake and I suggest that the time has come to do more than rethink Section 5(4); better to dispense with this provision altogether.

I have to confess that I have never seen the need for Section 5(4). I have never been able to accept that a nurse, however well qualified and experienced, should be allowed to take away a patient's liberty, with all the attendant matters associated with that. The official reason was that these powers were needed to prevent a patient leaving hospital before a psychiatrist could reach the scene. It is difficult to accept that; emergencies rarely happen in that way, and if they do then surely a physician could be found. In fact the Draft Code of Practice admitted that 'Most patients who express a wish to leave hospital can be persuaded to wait until a doctor or approved clinician arrives to discuss it further' (Department of Health 2007: para. 9.2). And of those that cannot? Well, if they are that disturbed one would expect a doctor would be close by. As I have argued throughout Section 5(4) does not represent the direction I wish to travel (Ashmore 1998).

Finally, to turn to Section 136, which involves the police. There is much hostility towards police involvement and the use of the police station as a place of safety. The police are regarded as an inappropriate group to deal with the mentally disordered and police stations as unsuitable likewise. In an ideal world this must be correct; the problem is that there is no one else to deal with the mentally disordered in a public place, who are often intimidating and frequently violent (see Bean 2001 for a more detailed discussion on Section 136). The police are reluctant enforcers yet were Section 136 to be repealed, the police would rely on public order powers to detain the mentally disordered. In my view, this section needs amending – the length of time the order lasts could be reduced, and a clarification needs to be made of the duties of the mental health services in relation to the responsibility of those undertaking the interviews. But whether we like it or not, the police will remain key figures in the compulsory admission procedure. The growth of community care is responsible for determining that, more patients in the community means more police involvement.

This brief overview of the roles and legal requirements of those enforcing the legislation shows that the current system relies on a mixture of nineteenth-century legalism (the Approved Social Worker, two doctors, the police) and twentieth-century professionalism (the use of GPs and nurses). While there have been numerous nods towards the protection and promotion of liberty by various committees, they have not always been translated into hard proposals. Nor does the government seem interested in moving in that direction. That is the failing.

Paternalism v. autonomy

Implied throughout has been a nascent conflict between paternalism and autonomy. Paternalism in the form used here is close to *parens patriae*, literally the state as father of the people, where it is the duty of the state to look after those unable to look after themselves. An early manifestation of *parens patriae* in English law was in the fourteenth century, in the recognition by Edward II of the Sovereign's responsibility towards the property, and later the person, of the insane (Kittrie 1971: 9). A modern example albeit in a slightly different context can be found under the National Assistance Act 1948 whereby elderly people may be removed from their homes when they cannot care for themselves. Under *parens patriae* certification has been regarded as a privilege that brings benefits. As the state has a duty of care, so its agents have a duty to see that care is offered in the circumstances appropriate to the person's needs. In its purist form there is no interest in the aetiology of the condition; its effects are the important determinants.

In one sense, of course, aetiology is important, for the case for *parens patriae* is better made if the patient's condition is seen to be the result of a lack of responsibility to make other than harmful decisions. There are numerous historical precedents for this: Kittrie describes how the insane of the seventeenth and eighteenth centuries lacked responsibility, and how in the history of unreason the insane were gradually segregated from the criminals (1971: 61). Ultimately where it can be shown that there is a defect of reason occurring as a result of mental disorder, the person can be exonerated from any criminal act. In less dramatic, more routine, occurrences it is enough to assert that the person has lost some power of reasoning and is not fully responsible for his actions: the court may then accept this as mitigation.

Few people nowadays would be unconditional supporters of *parens patriae.* Critics see it as providing an excuse for imposing an increasing number of social controls – the modern term is 'net-widening' – and for imposing greater measures of preventative detention under the guise of providing help. 'As long as therapeutic science and skills remain underdeveloped, confinement in the name of *parens patriae* was almost certainly more of a preventative detention measure for the benefit of society than an individually orientated programme' (Kittrie 1971: 61). While few would cite it nowadays as a justification for compulsory detention, it is occasionally smuggled in to justify intervention in patient care; it may be more associated with paternalism, but its strength is to awaken us to the needs of the less fortunate. Its weakness is to permit intrusion into people's lives – based on the judgements of those claiming to know best; in mental health this often means giving treatment against the patient's wishes.

At the other end of the spectrum, those supporting autonomy would presumably cite the Szaszian type argument that mental illness is a myth, and accordingly there is no justification for compulsory detention. What most call an illness Szasz calls a problem of living, and he is vigorous in his critique of psychiatry and mental health law as a means to incorporate into the criminal justice system behaviour that is disliked.

It is interesting to examine not only the merits of these arguments but also their practical application. What sort of world would it be for the mentally disordered were paternalism to be practised in an unrestrained form; or indeed were autonomy to be similarly practised? In the first, levels of insecurity would be raised, with the knowledge that anyone deemed mentally disordered (or in need of help) could be detained and treated at the whim of those claiming to assist. In the second, patients would have to fend for themselves – in the same way that offenders are left to their own devices, with the resulting accusations when they continue committing offences. Neither world seems particularly attractive. In the one there is an absence of controls, in the other controls are shifted from mental health legislation to the criminal law. One exudes compassion, but promotes coercion, the other offers disdain, but promotes control. In practice both may promote lower levels of care.

In the debate of 'paternalism v. autonomy' we can begin with two suppositions: that it is better to prevent the need for compulsory detention through the provision of better psychiatric care; and that the practical realities surrounding methods of detaining patients may turn out to be more important than any legal precepts. In one sense the Expert Committee were correct; we must take the professionals along with us if the legislation is to operate appropriately, for within the current climate there is little hope for change politically let alone from the psychiatrists. Modern governments are concerned primarily to promote public safety and are not keen to enter this sort of debate.

What is the evidence for paternalism? As a general rule the greater the levels of intervention in people's lives the more trouble is created. We are not good at doing things to or for people, as the history of public intervention shows. And acting in people's best interests, whether they agree or not, has been even less fruitful. Nor has psychiatry been able to demonstrate that it has been overly successful in terms of treatment outcomes (Clare 1983). But few would deny that compulsion is needed for some patients, and they may be unwilling to accept it. What then matters is how paternalism is practised.

The major justification for paternalism, as for mental health legislation generally is to reduce suffering. But in order to achieve that paternalism must be restrained; and subject, I suggest, to certain restrictions – to clarify the level of harm, for instance. The age-old adage applies: whether paternalism assists the solution or contributes to the problem. Mental health legislation can easily do the latter; it is much more difficult to make it do the former. In saying this I recognise that the current climate does not favour a public concern for patients' rights; protection of the rest of us is more in vogue. Unfashionable though this view may be, I think it worth stating: unrivalled paternalism is dangerous, not just to the patients but to the rest of us as well. Security in the knowledge that we are protected by appropriate procedural rules is important.

Summary and conclusion

Mental health legislation uses detention to solve what is essentially a socio-legal-medical problem. It provides detention through an alternative legal system with minimal restrictions of formal procedural rules, and without the usual set of rights granted to offenders within criminal justice. It solves many of the problems in dealing with the mentally disordered using professional (medical) personnel. To this scene the courts are thought inappropriate; historically they were criticised because they criminalised mental disorder and ended up ratifying the professional's demands. They did not appear to act as an independent tribunal. Current legislation grants professionals wider and more extensive powers, almost to the point where they can fashion individual remedies according to a disease model of illness, with few inhibitions or limitations based on those powers. Nor is there a groundswell of opinion that wants to curtail them – public sentiment more often goes the other way. In effect, compulsory detention is treated separately from other forms of detention, although in practice a patient can spend lengthy periods in confinement and can be given powerful treatments unless consent to treatment regulations apply. The criminal justice system aims to ensure that decisions approximate to a desired system of justice; although no one has arrived at a successful formula to ensure that it will, or produce an even-handed exercise of discretion. All agree, however, that this is a desired attribute (Casey 2004). No such aims appear in mental health legislation.

Involuntary commitment derives ultimately from moral and social considerations, not medical ones. A patient may be detained in order to receive treatment but the detention itself is the vehicle by which treatment is provided. Moreover, considerations that determine commitment – danger to self or others – are also moral and social. What constitutes a 'risk' is socially and morally driven; 'risks' today are not the same as risks yesterday, and will be different from risks tomorrow. 'Risks' and 'dangers' are socially specific, not just in the sense that they change over time, but by reference to their populations. The general population is rarely at risk from a particular patient; the risk is more likely to be to a specific person or social group, often close family members. Changing the social situation changes the nature of risk.

Within this social and moral nexus lie a number of extreme views about compulsory detention. The extreme libertarian position states that no one should be coerced unless convicted of a crime, and the extreme paternalistic position states that coercion is appropriate for everyone whose behaviour deviates from that which is in his or her best interests (Buchanan 2002: 36). In between there is a medley of proposals, some more interesting than others. The extremes are not very attractive. An extreme libertarian position leaves unattended those who do not harm others since they have committed no criminal offence, even though they may harm themselves. As suicide or attempted suicide is not a crime there is, on this basis, no justification for intervening. But madness is more than harming others or committing offences; it is more than being involved in criminality, and more than (as is suggested by the labelling theorists) a conspiracy by those who enforce the label. That takes away the dignity of madness and sets aside their suffering. No one denies that identifying, defining and diagnosing madness is usually difficult, sometimes impossible, and often highly subjective; but most of us know madness when we see it, and the mad are rarely so out of touch that they fail to recognise their own condition. Depression is more than sadness or exquisite melancholy, and mania has little or nothing to do with extremes of happiness or enthusiasm, while the inner world of the schizophrenic also has little to commend it. The mad deserve more than to be told that they have the right to be left alone as long as they do not harm others, in which case they become offenders – or that their condition is nothing more than a conspiracy by groups of self-seeking professionals.

At the other, paternalistic extreme things are no better. Here the mad are detained in their best interests. The literature is replete with examples of the damage wrought by overenthusiastic interventionists and the way paternalism diminishes self-respect. The saying: 'He helps others. You can tell the others by the haunted looks on their faces' remains the watchword. Had Mad Lucas, the notorious rich hermit, been compulsorily detained, he would have been given more comfort in his new surroundings, but he would not necessarily have been more comfortable. Those who detained him may have experienced the warm glow of a job well done but Mad Lucas may not have shared that feeling. Most of us would prefer not to be patronised, and to be allowed to make a mess of our lives as well we might.

The extremes take away dignity: libertarians because they do not accord the mad sufficient respect, and the paternalists because they give too much. But where, within the midway position, is the appropriate response? Too much libertarianism may turn out to be as destructive as too much paternalism. There is no one mid-position, but a series of positions, some erring in one direction, some another. The libertarians see no justification for any paternalism, but this cannot be correct. The law is full of examples where the state recognises and acknowledges its duties to protect the vulnerable, not just in the so-called morals offences but for special groups such as juveniles and substance abusers; also in certain special situations that may appear trivial but are not so: building regulations, for example, where we as citizens are protected from those with expertise who could take advantage of us. The concept of *parens patriae* embraces a wide range of activities; there is no reason why it should not apply here. And the mad are as vulnerable as any, if not more than most.

But what sorts of madness should qualify for state intervention? Certainly the mentally ill when their conditions are sufficiently severe. As far as the psychopath or the personality disordered are concerned, as I have said throughout, in my view they do not qualify. They are not mad or vulnerable; they exploit others, and may end up isolated and alone as a result, but that is their lot. Neither should the substance misusers be included, nor the neurotic, the worried well, the unhappy or those who cope less well than they ought. If compulsory detention is to mean anything it must be only for the mad or severely mentally disordered (Dixon *et al.* 2000).

Insisting on a certain level of severity is to state the obvious, and to many psychiatrists working with limited resources almost fatuous. Why should they consider cases other than the severe? Yet stating guidelines helps underscore the basic precepts; they give added measures to its mission statement that helps promote agreement. People need to know where they stand, including the limits of intervention. For our own sense of security it should be clear to whom the rules apply. Obfuscation promotes insecurity and distrust; clarity rarely does.

The least the mentally disordered should expect is to receive the same protection as offenders. They could spend similar lengths of time in detention, may even live alongside offenders in a high-security hospital, and receive equally unpleasant treatments, with damaging implications. Their identity will be damaged, and they have to face up to some unpleasant legal consequences; some occupations will be closed to them, and visa restrictions apply in some countries. There is a price to pay for compulsory detention, socially and legally.

The negative libertarian position provides the best protection of our freedoms. It places the onus on those doing the detaining, requiring them to meet the demands of procedural rules. Obviously the prosecution has rights too but these are ably provided for. Held up against a mirror of liberty the current legislation fails in almost every respect. There is little or no opportunity to defend oneself against accusations, and the procedural rules are minimal. The cards are heavily stacked against the patient often with only the integrity of the professionals to protect against unwarranted detention. That cannot be right. (Nor is it right, as is sometimes suggested, that procedural rules are unnecessary as the patient is mad anyway. That presumes the outcome before we start.) Patients deserve something better.

The question of liberty and its demands are played down by those who see the object of the exercise as increasing and promoting psychological well-being. Introducing better legal safeguards and increasing and promoting patients' rights may seem worthy, but does little to reduce suffering. Indeed, the argument would be that as the need to reduce suffering is dominant, legal provisions interrupt the smooth exercise of medical procedures, and in fact sometimes hinder it. We need to speed up procedures, at the same time as adding to the psychiatrist's knowledge of the patient. So, instead of getting rid of the ASW or nearest relative, why not replace them with a nominated or designated support person along the lines of the Appropriate Adult?

Clearly, the overarching goals of psychiatry should be to reduce suffering, and any impediment to those goals must be resisted. One can see that an emphasis on liberty may have the effect of extending the period before treatment and therefore, realistically, extend the patient's illness. The aim of a Mental Health Act is, or should be, to provide help and treatment to people who suffer, and the need for legal safeguards is, or should be, correspondingly downplayed. That much is accepted. On that basis the fewer restrictions the better, and the speedier the patient is taken into treatment. One can see too that questions about liberty might appear to some to be the wrong questions. Emphasising a reduction in suffering approaches the situation from a different direction, based on a different premise.

Even so, few would argue, presumably, that unbridled powers should exist to coerce patients into treatment, even if the aims were laudable and suffering dramatically decreased. Procedural rules of some sort inevitably rear their head, liberty in some form waits in the wings. But there is within this discussion a clash of values – liberty on the one hand versus powers to reduce suffering on the other. Or, justice versus outcome. There is no easy middle ground. Having said earlier that liberty can never be absolute, the same should be said of other values. It would be wrong to accede to all claims to reduce suffering – some may be bogus, others misplaced; and in the process more suffering may be added than is reduced. There must be a mix of values; my complaint is that the present system has not moved sufficiently in the direction of liberty. It is too concerned with outcome, and that defect needs to be addressed.

Invariably objections are that we should trust our professionals. But if the presumption is that professionals are rarely likely to abuse their powers then this is plainly wrong. 'Railroading' into mental hospitals is not a problem nowadays, but Jacobson et al. (1996) in their survey of Swedish psychiatrists found that 33 per cent of psychiatrists reported abusive practices. In Sweden there emerged new forms of abuse, described by the authors as being 'very closely related to what was considered abuse of psychiatry in the former Soviet Union' (1996: 395). Abuse was often reported in the psychiatric care of asylum- seekers, especially those facing deportation. Some psychiatrists believed that psychiatric diagnoses were used to prevent deportation, others that refugees were declared healthy despite having obvious mental disorders (1996: 395). Corruption, it seems, is never far from any activity, professional or otherwise.

Emergency psychiatry is a world away from the sheltered environs of the courtroom, where facilities are available should things go wrong, and staff on hand to deal with the unexpected. The courtroom is a tranquil and ordered place compared with the situations in which most psychiatrists work. What time or place for legal niceties when faced with the floridly mad in the early hours? That point is well made; but incidentally the time and place are no worse than many situations in which the police find themselves. Yet whatever the situation, diagnoses still have to be made, treatments considered, and decisions made about how best to proceed; the psychiatrist makes decisions according to a psychiatric and legal orthodoxy. The debate is about how to strengthen that orthodoxy: in practical terms, to decide which legal rights to insert, and at which point in the proceedings. What also matters is the political will to introduce change: if that exists facilities and opportunities will follow.

The first gap to fill is to provide a right of appeal. I do not mean the current system where after a period of time, and always following treatment, the patient is considered by a mental health tribunal. I mean prior to admission and prior to treatment, and appeal to an outside body, perhaps a court. As I have said elsewhere, it could work something like this (Bean 2001: 44–6). For an appeal against an order, the hearing could be either in court or in hospital, the patient would decide, and would be held immediately after the order is made. The evidence would be presented and a decision made. For an appeal to be meaningful it must take place before treatment is given, unless a delay would present a serious risk to the patient or to others. The patient should be entitled to an appeal hearing within 12 hours of the compulsory order being made, although expect to remain in detention for those 12 hours.

A likely criticism would be of the 12-hour detention period. But many floridly mad are kept in police cells under Section 136 for longer than this, and without treatment, and there are many others detained for offences who are never given treatment. I don't support this practice, and if this is a major objection to an appeal system it is strange that no one has objected to such practices before. What of a plea, legal representation or the right to sue for wrongful detention? It would make little sense to suggest a plea, as pleading not guilty to a charge of insanity is hardly suitable or realistic. The patient could be represented, or could call on the services of a support person familiar with proceedings. Could a patient sue for wrongful detention, whether through error in diagnosis or in the preparation of documents? Again, surely yes. It is too important not to. Rogers *et al.* (1993) and Humphreys (2000) report that some psychiatrists knew little of the legal details of the legislation. That is not good enough.

Liberty must be seen to be firmly embedded in mental health law. It should be more than a general concept, brought out from time to time, often in token form, whenever questions are asked about the way patients are dealt with. Introducing these safeguards pulls mental health law away from therapeutic law. An obvious objection was made by the Percy Committee decades earlier against the then legalism; that insanity becomes criminalised, and psychiatric decisions turned into criminal decisions with patients turned into offenders – or something mightily close to it. Yet committal carries a stigma:

it may be a decision made by medical personnel but it is more than a medical decision. Madness is about conduct, about ourselves, and about all of us, not just a part, as in appendicitis. Current legislation may not try to criminalise us directly, but we criminalise ourselves. We may not be wholly responsible for our insane behaviour, but madness is seen as a failure to live up to expectations – after all, we are often told to pull ourselves together – and compulsory detention as a sure sign of our wilfulness. We are blamed for a defect of reason. That attitude is not likely to change; the notion of blame is too deep within our public consciousness, and if we allot blame then we need protection. It cuts both ways.

There is more to liberty than providing legal representation. Too little attention is currently given to defining basic concepts, or the boundaries of the behaviour under review. Madness is what psychiatrists define it as, and without an adequate definition there is never the possibility of mounting a successful challenge. Concepts like 'mental illness' can be defined, they can meet operational requirements, and they need to be defined if progress is to be made. This is a problem not just for admission; the same criticisms can be levied at the legislation on discharge procedure – about which I have said little as I think it requires its own special attention. Richardson and Thorold are equally scathing about discharge legislation; it is full of uncertainties that promote a culture of caution and a consequential diminution of the Mental Health Review Tribunal's strength as a protector of the patient's right to liberty (1999: 117). Patients, it seems, face similar hurdles when they go out as when they come in.

There remains the question about whether improvements to procedures will bring about an overall improvement to the patient's condition. How will better patient safeguards and increased patients' rights promote psychological well-being and aid recovery? If we knew know more about the impact coercion has on patient outcome it would help, as it would to know the impact of legal rules on those doing the detaining. Without that research we continue to stumble around, but it seems that the more tedious and bureaucratic the procedures, the less will be the use of coercive interventions. So any attempt to streamline them may not always be in the patient's best interests, even if they lack a substantial contribution to a realistic and rational assessment of the facts. Of course, I am not saying that such complex procedures should be introduced in order to put off applications, just that it seems the fewer the hoops there are to go through, the more encouragement there is to go through existing hoops. But, the more those hoops are legalistic the more difficult it is to overturn them; so decisions made by the courts are likely to be more permanent than decisions made by clinicians. This would seem to suggest that the optimum set of legal rules would be few but precise, and coming from high-status organisations.

Finally, the personnel concerned. It may seem perverse to criticise the few safeguards that are there – the ASW (including the nearest relative) and the second doctor. The former offers a counterpoint to medical psychiatric opinion, and by refusing to sign the application can prevent admission. The second doctor, preferably a GP, acts as a corrective to any over-zealous psychiatrist. For the emergency order (Section 4) only one doctor is needed but the order lasts for only 72 hours. The criticisms are not that these safeguards are too weak, but that their structural position prevents them from doing what is required. The psychiatrist, usually a consultant, knows more about psychiatry than the ASW or the second doctor, has access to the resources, and will be responsible for treatment. Where there is an associated medical condition, as there often is, or a psychiatric history, the psychiatrist is not going to divulge this to an ASW. The psychiatrist runs the compulsory admission procedures, and no social worker or GP can compete with that expertise or challenge this access to resources. Better to acknowledge this at the outset and avoid repeating the tokenism inherent in the legislation. That means giving the psychiatrist full responsibility, with of course the attendant safeguards listed above. There is no need for Section 5(4) and it should be repealed.

I have tried to show that compulsory detention poses complex social and legal problems, which in our eagerness to secure treatment and cause the minimal inconvenience to the professionals have been glossed over, or not given the attention they deserve. My instincts are towards liberty. In addition the debate could have been enlivened and enriched with high-quality research upon which to draw, showing the effects, for good or ill, of compulsion. Research will not solve ethical and moral considerations, but it helps answer some basic empirical questions. There has been too little, reflecting perhaps the importance governments have given to compulsory detention. Yet compulsory detention involves a sizeable group of people who deserve better.

Notes

1 On 1 January 1994 Supervision Registers were introduced into Britain, and a year later the Supervised Discharge Order was introduced under

the Mental Health (Patients in the Community) Act 1995. These two orders were part of a more complex system of community controls that include Guardianship (section 7 of the 1983 Act), extended leave (section 17) and the Probation Order with a Condition of Treatment (Powers of Criminal Courts Act 1973) See Bean (2001) for a discussion on these.

2 Turning the prison into a hospital has long been seen as the solution. Kinton (2002) says, 'if appropriate treatment units were available within prisons it would make sense to allow compulsory treatment there'. Well, yes, but clearly not for all prisons; those with under about 400 prisoners would be too small. And what of the other complications? What level of security would be needed? Some prisoners might finish up under more secure conditions than they would otherwise in order to receive treatment. Where would the staff come from? We are not recruiting enough psychiatrists to run a health service, let alone to find large numbers of additional staff prepared to work full time in a prison. If only it were that simple.

3 England and Wales are not alone in this. The *New York Times* (22 October 2004) reported that with roughly one in six inmates suffering from mental illness the American prison system has evolved into something of a mental institution by default. It says mentally ill inmates receive little or no help while they are locked up, and on release they are usually dumped on the streets with neither treatment nor medication. For psychotic inmates psychiatric care is particularly poor. A local study had found that nearly a quarter of the inmates in disciplinary lockdown, i.e. confined to small cells for 23 hours a day, were mentally ill. Their symptoms worsened in isolation and many tried to commit suicide. The same newspaper commented: 'Forty years ago, America's seriously mentally ill were housed in psychiatric hospitals that kept them too long and often without good cause. As those hospitals closed, a promise to provide care in communities went unfulfilled. At the same time, America's prison capacity grew; it has quadrupled since 1980. People with untreated mental illness are often poor and homeless. Many commit petty crimes, creating arrest records that often lead to harsh sentences. Today some 250,000 Americans with mental illness live in prisons, the nation's primary supplier of mental-health services' (31 October 2004).

4 I do not go into too much detail about the time taken to produce the Draft Mental Health Bill 2006 and the long line of earlier government proposals, as this can be found in any legal commentary (see particularly Bowen 2000: 99–120). However, as Moss and Prins point out (2006) the current proposals to amend the law have had an astonishingly long gestation reflecting perhaps the degree of opposition to the many proposals. Over 20 organisations reflecting a wide range of professional interests have formed The Mental Health Alliance, representing powerful interests. They have expressed concerns over a number of earlier proposals including the use of compulsory detention for those who *might* commit dangerous

acts, and to broaden the definition of mental disorder – the latter to no avail. Moss and Prins say, 'perhaps the most worrying is the exclusion of the "escape" clauses in the 1983 Act in respect of sexual and addictive behaviours'. These have, however, been included. They believe: 'Of great significance in the current proposals is the introduction of a new label "Dangerous Severe Personality Disorder" (DSPD). This is a political not a clinical term' (Moss and Prins 2006: 190–1). The government has now (2007) withdrawn the controversial Second Draft Mental Health Bill and amended only a small number of features of the 1983 Act.

5 Section 11 sets out the rights and duties of nearest relatives, especially their right to be consulted. The legal requirements are complicated but without getting too detailed, briefly, Section 11(1) states an application for admission to treatment may be made by either the nearest relative or approved social worker. Subsection 3 requires the ASW to inform the nearest relative and Subsection 4 requires consultation with the nearest relative if the nearest relative objects. Under Section 23(2)(a) the nearest relative has powers to order the patient's discharge from hospital.

6 The Mental Health (Nurses) Order 1998 (S.I.1998 No. 2625) prescribes the class of nurse for the purpose of Section 5(4) of this Section as 'a nurse registered in any part of the register maintained under Section 7 of the Nurses, Midwives and Health Visitors Act 1997 which is mentioned in paragraph 2'. These will usually be first and second level nurses (see Jones 2003: para. 1–085).

References

Adserballe, H. (1985) 'When is Compulsory Admission Justifiable?', in K. Jensen and B. Pederson (eds) *Commitment and Civil Rights of the Mentally Ill*, Copenhagen: Sind, 36–47.

Ashmore, R. (1998) 'The nurse's holding power: Patterns of use in mental health', *British Journal of Nursing*, 7(21) (26 Nov–9 Dec): 1323–8.

Audini, B. and Lelliott, P. (2000) 'Are there groups of the population sectioned more often than others? An analysis of Mental Health Act assessment data', in Department of Health, *Shaping the Mental Health Act: Key Passages from the Department of Health Research Programme* (Mimeo). Department of Health, 9–12.

Audini, B. and Lelliott, P. (2002) 'Age, gender and ethnicity of those detained under Part II of the Mental Health Act 1983', *British Journal of Psychiatry*, 180: 222–6.

Bean, P.T. (1975) 'The Mental Health Act 1959: Some issues concerning rule enforcement', *British Journal of Law and Society*, 2(2): 228–38.

Bean, P.T. (1980) *Compulsory Admissions to Mental Hospitals*. Chichester: John Wiley.

Bean P.T. (2000) *Section 136: An Evaluation of Procedures*, Report to Leicestershire Constabulary (Mimeo).

Bean, P.T. (2001) *Mental Disorder and Community Safety*. London: Palgrave.

Bean, P.T. and Mounser, P. (1993) *Discharged from Mental Hospitals*. Basingstoke: Macmillan.

Benn, S. and Peters, R. (1959) *Social Principles and the Democratic State*. London: George Allen and Unwin.

Berlin, I. (1948) *Four Essays on Liberty*. Oxford: Oxford University Press.

Bindman, J. (2000) 'What is the variation in the use of the Mental Health Act at local level? A study in eight Trusts', in Department of Health, *Shaping the Mental Health Act: Key Passages from the Department of Health Research Programme* (Mimeo). Department of Health, 17–21.

Bindman, J., Maingay, S. and Szmukler, G. (2003) 'The Human Rights Act and mental health legislation', *British Journal of Psychiatry*, 182: 91–4.

Brun, B. (1985) 'Patient/Therapist Relationship During Compulsory Admission and Treatment', in K. Jensen and B. Pederson (eds) *Commitment and Civil Rights of the Mentally Ill*. Copenhagen: Sind, 66–81.

Bowen, P. (2000) 'Reform of the Mental Health Act 1983: Convention implications of the Green Paper', *Journal of Mental Health Law* (No. 4): 99–120.

Buchanan, A. (2002) 'Psychiatric detention and treatment: A suggested criterion', *Journal of Mental Health Law* (Feb): 35–41.

Burton, S. (2002) *A Double Life: A Biography of Charles and Mary Lamb*. London: Penguin Viking.

Casey, T. (2004) 'When good intentions are not enough: Problem-solving courts and the impending crisis of legitimacy', *Southern Methodist University Law Review* (Fall).

Churchill, R., Wall, S., Hotopf, M., Buchanan, A. and Wessely, S. (2000) 'Centrally collected information: What can the data tell us?', in Department of Health, *Shaping the Mental Health Act: Key Passages from the Department of Health Research Programme* (Mimeo). Department of Health, 2–8.

Clare, A. (1978) 'In defence of compulsory psychiatric intervention', *The Lancet*, No. 8075, Vol. 1: 1197–8.

Clare, A. (1983) 'Treatment and Cure in Mental Illness', in P.T. Bean (ed.) *Mental Illness: Changes and Trends*. Chichester: John Wiley, 137–62.

Darcy, P.T. (1985) 'The Myths of Mental Health Legislation?', in K. Jensen and B. Pederson (eds) *Commitment and Civil Rights of the Mentally Ill*. Copenhagen: Sind, 95–101.

Department of Constitutional Affairs (2007) Mental Capacity Bill 2005, Summary (28 January).

Department of Health (1999) *Reform of the Mental Health Act 1983: Proposals for Consultation*, Cmnd 4480 (Green Paper). London: Department of Health.

Department of Health (2000a) *Reforming the Mental Health Act, Part 1*, Cm 5016-I. London: Department of Health.

Department of Health (2000b) *Shaping the Mental Health Act: Key Passages from the Department of Health Research Programme* (Mimeo). London: Department of Health.

Department of Health (2007) *Draft Illustrative Code of Practice* (Mimeo). London: Department of Health.

Department of Health and Welsh Office (1999) *Mental Health Code of Practice*. London and Cardiff: Department of Health and Welsh Office.

Dixon, M., Oyebode, F. and Brannigan, C. (2000) 'Formal justifications for compulsory psychiatric detention', *Medicine Science and the Law*, 40(4): 319–26.

Eastman, N. and Peay, J. (1999) 'Law Without Enforcement: Theory and Practice', in N. Eastman and J. Peay (eds) *Law Without Enforcement*. Oxford: Hart, 1–38.

Eastman, N., Peay, J. and Roberts, C. (2000) 'A study of the attitudes, legal knowledge, decision processes and decision outcomes of professionals with responsibilities under the Mental Health Act 1983', in Department of Health, *Shaping the Mental Health Act: Key Passages from the Department of Health Research Programme* (Mimeo). Department of Health, 22–5.

Expert Committee (1999) *Report of the Expert Committee: Review of the Mental Health Act 1983* (Richardson Committee). London: Department of Health.

Feinberg, J. and Gross, H. (eds) (1975) *Liberty in Philosophy of Law, Part 2*. California: Dickenson.

Greenland, C. (1970) *Mental Illness and Civil Liberty*, Occasional Papers on Social Administration No. 38. Bell.

Grisso, T. and Appelbaum, P. (1998) *Assessing Competence to Consent to Treatment*. Oxford: Oxford University Press.

Hall, A.D., Puri, B.K., Stewart, T. and Graham, P.S. (1995) *Doctors' Holding Power in Practice: Section 5(2) of the Mental Health Act 1983*. London: Department of Health.

Hansard (2007) 'House of Lords Debate on the Mental Health Bill', *Hansard*, 17 January: col. 696.

Hargreaves, R. (2000) '"A mere Transporter" – the legal role of the Approved Social Worker', *Journal of Mental Health Law* (Dec): 135–46.

Hodgson, J. (1997) 'Detention, necessity, common law, and the European Convention: Some further aspects of the Bournewood case', *Journal of Mental Health Law*: 23–32.

Hoggett, B. (1984) *Mental Health Law*. London: Sweet and Maxwell.

House of Lords (2006) United Kingdom Parliament (Lords) Mental Health Bill (Explanatory Notes) and Text for 17 January 2007.

Hoyer, G. (1999) *On the Justification for Civil Commitment* (Mimeo).

Humphreys, M.S. (1999) 'Psychiatrists' knowledge of Mental Health legislation', *Journal of Mental Health Law* (Oct): 150–3.

Jacob, C. and Freer, T. (2005) Cross sectional survey of the use of Section 5(2) Mental Health Act 1983, within a psychiatric hospital', *Medicine Science and the Law*, 45(2): 129–34.

Jacobson, K.G., Lynoe, N., Kohn, R. and Levan, I. (1996) 'Practices and attitudes among Swedish psychiatrists regarding the ethics of compulsory treatment', *Acta Psychiatrica Scandinavica*, 93: 389–96.

Jensen, K. and Pedersen, B. (eds) (1985) *Commitment and Civil Rights of the Mentally Ill.* Copenhagen: Sind.

Jones, K. (1960) *Mental Health and Social Policy 1854–1959.* London: Routledge and Kegan Paul.

Jones, R. (2003) *Mental Health Act Manual,* 8th edn. London: Sweet and Maxwell.

Kinton, M. (2002) 'Should we allow compulsory mental health treatment in prisons?', *Journal of Mental Health Law* (Dec): 304–7.

Kittrie, N.N. (1971) *The Right to be Different.* Baltimore: Johns Hopkins University Press.

Kmietowicz, Z. (2004) 'Admissions to hospital under the Mental Health Act rise by 40% over 10 years', *British Medical Journal* (10 April): 854.

McPherson, A. and Jones, R.G. (2003) 'The use of Sections 2 and 3 of the Mental Health Act (1983) with older people: A prospective study', *Ageing Mental Health,* 7(2): 153–7.

MHAC (Mental Health Act Commission) (2003) *Placed Amongst Strangers: Tenth Biennial Report of the Mental Health Act Commission 2001–2003.* London: The Stationery Office.

Mill, J.S. (1859) *On Liberty.* Indianapolis: Liberal Arts Press (1956).

Minto, A. (1980) 'Changing Clinical Practice', in P.T. Bean (ed.) *Mental Illness: Changes and Trends.* Chichester: John Wiley, 163–78.

Moss, K. and Prins, H. (2006) 'Severe (Psychopathic) Personality Disorder: A review', *Medicine Science and the Law,* 46(3): 190–207.

Nemitz, T. and Bean, P.T. (1995) 'Discrepancies and inaccuracies in statistics for detained patients', *Psychiatric Bulletin,* 19: 28–32.

Peay, J. (2003) *Decisions and Dilemmas.* Oxford: Hart.

Percy Commission (1957) *Royal Commission on the Law relating to Mental Illness and Mental Deficiency,* Cmnd 169 (Percy Commission). London: HMSO.

Porter R. (1987) *Mind Forged Manacles.* London: Athlone Press.

Porter, R. (1991) *The Faber Book of Madness.* London: Faber and Faber.

Porter, R. (2002) *Madness: A Brief History.* Oxford: Oxford University Press.

Priebe, S., Badesconyi, A., Fioritti, A., Hansson, L., Kilian, R., Torres-Gonzales, F., Turner, T. and Wiersma, D. (2005) 'Reinstitutionalisation in mental health care: Comparison of data on service provision from six European countries', *British Medical Journal,* 330: 123–6.

Rapaport, A. (2003) 'The ghost of the nearest relative under the Mental Health Act 1983: Past, present and future', *Journal of Mental Health Law* (July): 51–65.

Richardson, G. and Thorold, O. (1999) 'Law as a Rights Protector: Assessing the Mental Health Act 1983', in N. Eastman and J. Peay (eds) *Law Without Enforcement.* Oxford: Hart, 109–32.

Rogers, A., Pilgrim, D. and Lacey, R. (1993) *Experiencing Psychiatry: Users' Views of Services.* London: Macmillan.

Roth, J. and Kroll, J. (1986) *The Reality of Mental Illness.* Cambridge: Cambridge University Press.

Salib, E. and Iparragirre, B. (1998) 'Detention of inpatients under Section 5(2) of the Mental Health Act 1983', *Medicine Science and the Law*, 38(1): 10–16.

Scull, A. (1985) 'A Victorian Alienist: John Connolly FRCP, DCL (1794–1866)', in W.F. Bynum, R. Porter and M. Shepherd (eds) (1985) *The Anatomy of Madness*, Vol. 1. London: Tavistock, 103–50.

Thornicroft, G. (2000) 'Supervision and Coercion Studies', in Department of Health, *Shaping the Mental Health Act: Key Passages from the Department of Health Research Programme* (Mimeo). Department of Health, 13–16.

Webber, M. and Huxley, P. (2004) 'Social exclusion and the risk of compulsory admission: A case control study', *Social Psychiatry and Psychiatric Epidemiology*, 39(12): 1000–9.

Part 4

Madness and crime

Some methodological problems in the madness and crime nexus

Research on the links between madness and crime has tended to concentrate on the mentally disordered offender, a term that is neither legal nor psychiatric, nor does it refer to any clinically homogeneous group. Traditionally, it has been applied to any offender on whom a psychiatric diagnosis could be given, or to an offender whose behaviour is sufficiently odd to suggest some form of psychological disturbance (Halleck 1987). Included are the eponymous psychopaths and similarly defined personality disordered, who almost by definition, are offenders.

Nearly all this research has an inbuilt bias. Populations or sampling frames are invariably taken from offender groups, where there is an existing or pre-established link between mental disorder and crime. This type of research usually involves an examination of the background of diagnosed mentally disordered offenders in detention, whether in prisons, police stations, or high-security (special) hospitals, as NHS or private patients (Jones *et al.* 1998). At the more rarefied level research has been done on selected offender populations, on parricide or on stranger killers in high levels of security (Baxter *et al.* 2001). Although these studies give valuable information, they fall short in providing answers about the links, if any, between madness and crime.

An inbuilt problem with these 'arrest rate studies', as Monahan calls them (1992), is that they rarely have a control group for comparative data. They also tend to measure the activities of the criminal justice agencies, more so if the agency is a police station, and the station in a poor neighbourhood. Mostly, these offenders have a criminal record so bias is inevitable; they are seen as police property; and they know this is how the police see them. They are frequently arrested, mostly for petty offences, invariably diagnosed as 'inadequate personalities'. These are often the offenders caught in the research nets. Yet for all its failings this type of research still provides important data on the way the system works – successfully or otherwise. Moreover, the respondents (patients or offenders, call them what you will) will quite likely have been seen by a medically qualified figure and been given a diagnosis. Offenders in prison have access to a medical officer, although perhaps not a psychiatrist and usually this diagnosis will be supported by the opinion of others in the prison medical services, now called health care services. Moreover, follow-up studies are made easier, with some offenders released on licence, or in compulsory after-care, making contact less difficult (Link and Stueve 1996: 138).

Another type of research, 'non-arrest rate studies', or 'patient studies', usually takes the samples from psychiatric hospital in-patients, or outpatients from psychiatric outpatients' departments. Again the bias is obvious and evident. As with offenders, these populations or samples have similar inbuilt limitations in that the studies tend to measure the activities of the psychiatric services. And like arrest rate studies they have similar advantages – although diagnosis may be sound, perhaps better than from the prisons, and improving due to alignment with NHS provisions, follow-up is less reliable.

The most successful way to eliminate bias is to take large-scale populations or samples from non-patient, non-offender groups in the community. There have been no such studies in Britain. In the USA the Epidemiological Catchment Area (ECA) is the best example (Swanson *et al.* 1990). The aim was to determine the extent of untreated mental disorder in the community. This was conducted in five communities with probability samples drawn from each, and respondents interviewed using an instrument that yielded a psychiatric diagnosis. Over 13,000 respondents were interviewed. Data from such a study provides a mine of information, but the costs are huge; mostly we have to be content with smaller versions. Incidentally, a major finding of ECA was that serious mental illness by itself was rare; other findings were more directly concerned with criminality, especially violence, and will be referred to later.

Samples taken from offender or patient populations are, of course, easier and cheaper. This is not so much a complaint, more a recognition of the problems involved. But while most concentrate on resident populations, and the selectivity is understandable, they are likely to exclude the majority of the mentally disordered and criminals (Gunn 1977). Accordingly, what we know, or think we know, is heavily slanted towards producing answers contained in the question. So, if the samples come from offender groups there is bound to be a connection with crime, and if taken from patient groups there will be a similar connection with mental disorder. What is difficult to determine is the extent or magnitude of that bias – one researcher suggests that studies of mentally ill persons sampled from populations of previously hospitalised and arrested individuals overestimate the prevalence of violence by a factor greater than three, that is 26 per cent as opposed to 7 per cent (Swanson 1996: 132).

Obtaining good-quality data is always difficult in criminology but in this sub-specialism the problems are magnified. Not only is the cost huge, prohibitive for most research foundations, the methodology is fragile. Dealing with the floridly mad simply adds to existing problems. A great deal of mental disorder is transitory and denied, yet the sequence of events may be critical to the research. Did criminality precede the disorder, accompany it, or postdate it? Was the person actively mad when he committed the offence (it is usually a 'he' but not always)? Was there a history of violence preceding the criminality and mental disorder? Cooperation and a clear memory are a prerequisite for good data; the mentally disordered are not always the ideal respondents to interview.

Then there is the terminology and the application of that terminology to add to the researcher's woes. All self-report criminology studies rely on respondents assessing their own behaviour as criminal, and categorising it as an offence. So too with mental disorder; respondents have to self-diagnose and report on episodes considered as periods of madness, or mental disorder. The results then have to be translated into a psychiatric diagnosis, with all its attendant problems. If that is not bad enough there are problems about the unreliability of psychiatric diagnoses, which is well known. Chadwick, writing in the *Independent*, sums it up rather well: 'To the cliché about getting seven different diagnoses from six psychiatrists could be added another to the effect that even if they agreed on the diagnoses you could get seven different treatment plans' (6 October 1992). There is no agreed terminology to fall back on.

Yet establishing links between mental disorder and crime is more than an academic exercise, for there are practical consequences to consider. If mental disorder leads to or causes crime, then treatment for mental disorder will expect to lead to a reduction in crime rates. Conversely, if it does not, then treatment will not affect crime rates. And if crime and mental disorder are not linked then the treatment of one will not affect the outcome of the other. Presumably criminal justice systems, alongside psychiatric services, require answers to these questions, not least because they need to acquire a better understanding of the outcome of various patient groups, alongside an understanding of the nature of any stigmatising process (Link and Stueve 1994: 137).

We know that there are large numbers of mentally disordered offenders within the criminal justice system, but can we go further? Can we do more than suspect or hypothesise that there exists a link between mental disorder and crime? That there is a high correlation is obvious, but we need to know more; which is the independent variable? Perhaps some mentally disordered persons are coincidentally criminal, in which case the link is less strong. If the term 'cause' is to be used, or have any relevance, it can only be in its weakest sense; that is, as similar to an association or statistical correlation, or as a necessary rather than a sufficient condition. It means going no further than stating that one condition (mental disorder or crime, it matters not which) is present at the same time as the other (crime, or mental disorder).[1] That is to say, at the time of committing an offence the person was mentally disordered, or, as is often the case, had an earlier mental disorder. Sometimes all one can say is that there are two morbidities that have occurred together – which in statistical terms is presented in the form of a correlation.

The difficulties in establishing causal connections are also due to the complexity of the phenomena. What we need to know is how many crimes were committed as a direct result of the mental disorder, or how did the mental disorders arise as a direct result of the crime – a sufficient condition – and not simply committed during the period when the offender was mentally disordered – a necessary condition. That some mentally disordered *are* criminal should not lead to the conclusion that their crimes are due to or caused by that mental condition. They might have been offenders in any case, or perhaps were so before they were mentally ill. Or they might have been mentally disordered anyway. Some may commit more offences as a result of their mental disorder, but some might commit fewer, and some stop altogether. Similarly some non-criminals might be drawn into offending during their period of mental disorder while others might not; again, how many and for which offences it is difficult to determine. And some criminals might become more mentally disordered during their criminality, and some less. In order to make a direct causal connection we would need to disaggregate those crimes committed irrespective of the mental disorder from those not, or disaggregate those mental disorders irrespective of the criminality. In practice these are almost impossible tasks.

A further complication is that the terms used, and the parameters set by those terms, are poorly defined and rarely able to offer the level of rigour necessary for an enquiry aimed at establishing causal connections. Leaving aside for the moment problems with the word 'crime', for which there is no settled or agreed definition, how do we define 'mental disorder'? Without labouring or repeating the points made elsewhere, this is clearly a term without a settled or agreed definition. A solution might be to adopt David Farrington's concept of the anti-social personality syndrome which includes, for children, lying, truancy, running away from home, school failure, sexual precocity, and bullying; and for adults, substance abuse, reckless driving, spouse abuse, sexual promiscuity, child neglect and employment instability (Farrington 1992: iv). He regards these factors as indicators of mental ill-health and suggests that they should be the concern of the Department of Health, as opposed to the Home Office: they are health matters rather than criminal justice ones. Unfortunately, to do so reopens that age-old question of the borderline between mental disorder, morality and social deviance. It widens rather than confines the debate; it does not always assist it.

Many of these basic methodological problems are common to social science generally – which for my purposes includes psychiatry and criminology. They cannot be easily resolved. Too often we stumble from one conceptual problem to the next, and from one daunting exercise to another. Madness (or mental disorder) and crime are not wholly impenetrable, but the concepts are mightily difficult to handle. Too often we must make do with correlations, and draw such statistical inferences as we may.

An overview of the problem

I do not include 'psychopath' or 'personality disorder', here or elsewhere in this volume. To do so would be to load the dice; it presupposes a link between mental disorder and crime, suggesting more than could be established otherwise. In fact the legal definition of psychopathy makes the point for me: the definition includes 'abnormally aggressive or seriously irresponsible conduct' (Section 1(2) of the 1983 Mental Health Act) – a certainty for crime.[2] This book is about madness and, as I have said elsewhere, I do not see the psychopath as mad. Psychopathy approximates more to a moral judgement, or is little more than a moral judgement masquerading as a diagnosis (Blackburn (1986) quoted in Gunn and Taylor 1993: 387; see also Cope 1993). I think John Gunn is correct when he says that psychopathic disorders are best understood as a defect of learning and socialisation rather than illnesses (Gunn 1977) and for that reason am puzzled that some still see value in viewing psychopathic disorders as mental abnormalities (Prins 1995: 124). The more so as the Butler Report recommended the term be abandoned. No one has successfully escaped the criticism of Barbara Wootton; she talks of its circularity where mental abnormality is inferred from the anti-social behaviour, and the anti-social behaviour inferred from the mental abnormality. Summing things up, Gunn and Taylor state that there are five agreed facts about psychopathic disorder. First, the definition is unreliable; second, almost all disagree about the definition; third, psychopathy is used in the vernacular as a term of derogation; fourth, it has a legal use in England and Wales; and finally many doctors use the term to indicate that the patient is incurable or untreatable (Gunn and Taylor 1993: 386). That, I think, ought to be the end of the matter.

Nor is it the purpose here to examine detailed legal matters, such as insanity defences, the role of forensic psychiatrists at the trial stage, or the legal decisions concerning sentencing. These can be found elsewhere (see particularly Gunn and Taylor 1993: chapter 2; 21–117). Suffice to say that aside from those offenders claiming one of the insanity defences, or who fall within the special provisions of the Hospital Order (where under Section 37 of the 1983 Mental Health Act a magistrate's court has only to be persuaded that the act was committed in order to detain the offender in a mental hospital or equivalent), the general rule is for courts to consider the presence of a mental disorder only as mitigation. This is so even if there is clear evidence that madness has led to the crime. Gunn and Taylor (1993: 42) call this a pragmatic decision, which produces an apparent paradox. The law expects the mentally disordered offender to exercise control over his behaviour, for to do otherwise would open the floodgates to all sorts of legal defences, some sound, some not.

Yet some critics are beginning to challenge that view, although, it must be said, with limited success. As Tom Williamson says (personal communication), a model is being developed that shows how important mental vulnerability is as a concept in criminal justice. The minimisation of this by lawyers who have remained ignorant of psychological processes has, he believes, done untold harm to the image of the criminal justice system, and been an instrumental factor in too many miscarriages of justice. Given the way in which some offenders are clearly mad when they commit the offence, Williamson wonders why such a disorder is given short shrift. He says that there is a need for all practitioners to have the opportunity of training to ensure a greater understanding of mental health issues in as far as they relate to criminal justice. He thinks there appear to be subtle changes in the English criminal justice system, in that it is becoming a little less accusatorial. Where once victims and witnesses were routinely pilloried, and truth was an irrelevance, current changes, he suggests, begin to hold out prospects for a more measured sensitivity to victims and witnesses. Truth and justice should be available to all, and Williamson thinks that these new systems take us a small step closer to achieving that aim. I am less optimistic. There may be a greater sensitivity to human frailty, but I doubt if much else will change in such a deeply entrenched system.

In any case, most lawyers would believe that the more important question is, to what extent ought the mentally disordered be subject to punishment, if any? This is to enter Jill Peay's minefield (Peay 1997: 692). She wants to disentangle the various strands that have produced fierce debates in criminological/psychiatric circles. Should the mentally disordered offender be treated or punished? And if treated, how should that fit into a modern criminal justice system: if treatment is successful, after, say, a short period, whereas the offence was serious, should the offender then be discharged? And if punished, should this be only where the mental disorder is mild, or not regarded as a direct consequence on the index offence, or lead to future offending?

The minefield is extensive and daunting. It includes preventative sentencing, risk assessments and deciding on matters which, if resolved in favour of psychiatry, would greatly extend its influence. For example, should offenders be discharged from prison if their disorder remains untreated, or is only in temporary remission, especially if there is a high risk of future offending? Should more offenders receive treatment as part of their sentence, having the obvious effect of pushing the prison towards being a hospital? Should mentally disordered offenders be sentenced on the basis of their disorder rather than the offence?

Most lawyers baulk at extending psychiatric influence, and with good reason. Steadman and Cocozza, writing in 1974, in an age more sympathetic to patients' rights, say that an expansion of psychiatric services with in criminal justice would be suspect and detrimental. They find support, not surprisingly, from Kittrie, an ardent human rights lawyer, who concluded that such continued expansion without definite checks would be counter-productive (Steadman and Cocozza 1974: 176). Traditionally lawyers have wanted to keep psychiatry at bay, believing it muddies the waters by undermining legal notions of responsibility. Lawyers may acknowledge the current situation as less than perfect, accepting perhaps that it gives less emphasis on the mental disorder than it might, but believe a lurch towards a greater psychiatric embrace poses more problems than it solves. It would mean coming very close to highlighting a sub-group of offenders, and separating those with mental problems from those without. There is, of course, an existing sub-group of offenders within high-security hospitals who are admitted only by executive decision, but the numbers are small and for these purposes can be conveniently ignored. It would also mean involving psychiatrists at both sentencing and discharge, and for all mentally disordered rather than the selected few as at present. The tariff, that rough and ready guide to sentencing beloved of judges, would be undermined; some sentences would be lengthened, others shortened, but not according to the severity of the offence, rather the severity of the psychiatric condition – what the offender *is* rather than what he has done. This would revive earlier fears of the injustices of rehabilitation and the rehabilitative ideal. Better to keep things as they are, one can hear lawyers say.

Better indeed. But how to keep the genie in the bottle? The trend towards stricter criteria for hospital admission – for this read fewer beds – and for more precise indicators of dangerousness gives the psychiatrist more influence. And the more research there is that shows a high prevalence of mental disorder within offender populations, so the demand will be greater for more psychiatric services. Whether claims will grow exponentially remains to be seen; more likely they will chip away at legal values, unless and until lawyers take serious steps to repel them. Perhaps after all Tom Williamson's plea for less legal confrontation and a speedier search for truth might become an avenue for change.

Psychiatric services in the penal system: an overview

There is no doubt that the criminal justice system has more than its share of mentally disordered offenders. This has produced a number of assertions about the links with crime; such as, the mentally disordered are basically criminal; or there is an inverse correlation between the prison and mental hospital population – the latter was ascribed to Penrose (1939) who supposedly said that countries with a high prison population had a correspondingly small mental hospital population. What he in fact said was rather different: that birth rates, homicide rates, death rates, suicide rates and the size of the prison population were all negatively correlated with the size of the mental hospital population, and that this applied throughout most of Europe. Nowadays we would be more careful about using international data and coming to conclusions based on hospital admissions. Nonetheless, Penrose thought that attention to mental health helped to control the incidence of crime, and in this he was following Cyril Burt a decade earlier, who had also seen insanity, including mental deficiency, as predisposing causes of crime.

Things were different in 1939. Even if we take the national data as valid and reliable, there was a stable if low crime rate, and an equally stable, if largish, mental hospital population. Neither Penrose nor Burt could have anticipated the changes over the next 70 years – the massive growth in the prison population, the reduction in the old-style mental hospitals followed by the emphasis on community care, or the dramatic rise in substance abuse, licit and otherwise. Yet their views are still valid, though not quite for the same reasons, and not as much as they thought: that attention to mental health may help prevent the occurrence of serious crimes, especially homicide. They also said that there is incompatibility between the development of mental health services and the need for accommodation in prisons, but again not as much as they thought. Things are more complicated nowadays, for what we know of the links between mental disorder and crime leads to no simple socio-demographic statements of the type offered by Penrose. And no one would dream of taking national and European figures of crime and mental hospital populations at their face value and extrapolate from them what Penrose did.

The Penrose/Burt contention was a variation on an older Freudian model of aggression, directed either outwards leading to crime, or inwards leading to self-destructive neurosis. If outwards it led to a high prison population, if inwards, to a high mental hospital population. That no longer applies, if it ever did. Nowadays, it is not an either/or, it is both. The modern mentally disordered are also criminal, and many modern criminals are also mentally disordered, the more so when they are substance misusers. To see the extent of the problem I want to show how the criminal justice system is expected to absorb large numbers of mentally disordered offenders at different points throughout, with the largest aggregate figures in the police station, and the largest proportion in the prisons.

Where research has centred on psychiatric offenders the dominating question has been about the quality of the criminal justice services, usually with a subsidiary question about effectiveness. With prisons it has led to a general agreement that the range and quality of medical services are inadequate, or worse; and that prisons are unsuitable places for the mentally disordered, especially the floridly mad. While nearly everyone agrees about that, there is no agreement on the way forward. Rather there remain two separate positions, with other views somewhere in between. One extreme is to take the mentally disordered out of the criminal justice system altogether and deal with them as a health problem, in the health system (Department of Health 1992). This has been widely canvassed. The opposite is to retain them within criminal justice but do more about them than hitherto; that is, improve the quality of the psychiatric services (Scott 1970). This has had less support, but in my view is the correct way forward, for the reasons given below.

Those advocating the first position face the inevitable question: where will they go and to which parts of the health system? Traditionally psychiatrists in the health service have not welcomed mentally disordered offenders, they being in Prins' phrase, 'the unloved, the unloving and the unlovable' (Prins 1995). They take up a disproportionate amount of psychiatric time, are disruptive, and if they are drug takers even more so, with an additionally poor prognosis. Psychiatrists say, with some justification, that they have enough to do treating the rewarding patients without bothering with the unrewarding. And offender patients are very unrewarding.

Those advocating the second position face an equally insuperable question: how can psychiatric services be expanded within criminal justice? Too often the mentally disordered get little or no treatment, even in the most severe cases. In an ideal world they should not be held within the criminal justice system, but if they are, then, so the argument goes, criminal justice should develop appropriate treatment services. This too is not without its problems. First, there are theoretical matters to deal with: criminal justice and health systems do not mix easily, the primary aim of criminal justice being retribution and deterrence, that of health, treatment. Criminal justice sets limits on the time offenders must remain within it; health systems have no such requisites – treatment continues until the patient gets better, or no longer requires it. Then there are economic considerations. Criminal justice is not a health service, and the cost involved in staffing criminal justice programmes with treatment personnel is expensive and probably prohibitive; we can barely staff a health service let alone one that includes a criminal justice system. Finally, there is the fear, a valid one in my opinion, that providing better medical services in prisons will encourage courts to send more people there, and for longer periods. So, in summary, the best we can hope for is a series of incremental changes such as reforming the prison health services, or seeking better arrangements to transfer prisoners, especially the more floridly mad, out of criminal justice into treatment facilities – this incidentally is not always welcomed by the prisoners, as criminal justice has the advantage of specifying the date of release – while discouraging courts to increase prison sentences. This I am sure is the way forward; and if only because of pragmatic considerations, I doubt that it will ever be possible to get all the mentally disordered out of criminal justice into a health system, or some equivalent system of care.

Although there has been a considerable amount of research on the mentally disordered within the criminal justice system the overall effect has been an unbalanced or lopsided approach. Too often it has concentrated on offenders in institutions such as special hospitals, now called high-security hospitals, or prisons, with much fewer in police stations, or in the probation service where the throughput is speedy and the numbers large. I suspect one reason might be that high-security hospitals and the like have complex organisations attached, and to most criminologists they provide more interesting venues for research, opening more theoretical possibilities. Moreover the data is easier to obtain and verify. Yet John Gunn warns of its dangers, for embedded within nearly all these studies is the assumption that offenders are there as a result of their disorder. Accordingly, much is made of their psychiatric condition and less attention given to their offence or criminal history. The result: we know more about their psychiatric failings than their criminality (Gunn *et al.* 1991b).

To begin with policing and the police station. For most offenders this is the point of entry into the criminal justice system. Dealing first with the authority to detain the mentally disordered in a public place, under Section 136 of the 1983 Mental Health Act, the police have powers to take a mentally disordered person to a place of safety, invariably a police station, in order to be assessed by an Approved Social Worker (ASW) and a psychiatrist. An obvious question is whether the police or the police stations are appropriate organisations to deal with these patients? Critics say that the police criminalise mental disorder. On the other hand they provide a secure environment, with a reduced presumption that those detained are mentally disordered, at least until they have been assessed. There is, however, a serious problem with the floridly mad, who may be aggressive and dangerous while in the street, but once detained tend to implode. Deaths in custody are high for this group. Yet for all mentally disordered, florid or not, who best to detain them? The police would prefer not to, but who else is there? And once they are detained, how best to secure the appropriate treatment? Many patients under Section 136 have long psychiatric and criminal histories and are no more welcome than other offender patients in the health service. Yet for the present there are no other obvious candidates to deal with them, and nowhere more secure than a police station.

For the offenders, between 10 and 14 per cent of those arrested and taken to a police station for questioning could be given a psychiatric diagnosis. Police stations in inner-city areas will have the highest rate, and a higher rate again if the catchment area includes an active drug market. Robertson *et al.* (reported in Exworthy 1998) found that 1.4 per cent of all police detainees were acutely ill, and although diversion from prosecution was common, those not diverted were more likely to be arrested for violent offences, persistent petty offending, and the execution of police warrants (Exworthy 1998: 407).

If these estimates are correct they show the enormity of the problem. The police will be dealing with thousands of mentally disordered daily; some will not be charged, some will be released on bail, and others detained in custody. What happens to them is anybody's guess; outcomes may depend on whether the police officer in question is sympathetic to psychiatric values – in which case there is a good chance the offender will end up in the psychiatric services rather than in criminal justice. Some offenders seek or continue treatment within the criminal justice system, many do not; some get better by themselves, some do not; but most reappear as part of that endless circular process of arrest, sentence, release and rearrest. Some are released immediately with a formal warning or reprimand (previously called a caution), but where do they go? No one knows – and a warning or reprimand like a conditional discharge or a fine, does not provide treatment.

Many take part in that grand circular tour between police station, care in the community, mental hospital, and back to police station – a circuit identified many years ago by Henry Rollin (1969). The majority then, as now, were involved in public order offences, such as ripping aerials off cars, walking naked in the street, entering Parliament to dispense justice: clearly mad behaviour, says John Gunn! (Gunn 1977: 321). They help form that large army of offenders who are poorly educated, of low social class, often unemployed (some almost unemployable); when a psychiatric condition is added to their otherwise endless list of personal defects they give the impression of having started at the bottom yet are still able to move downwards. To most psychiatrists they are untreatable; their prognosis is poor and often they are given a diagnosis of 'personality disorder'. Some are relatively harmless, some are not. All are persistent troublemakers of some sort, serious offenders or otherwise. What to do with them remains one of the great unanswered questions; they continue to commit offences and the police continue to arrest them. And so it goes on.

Provisions exist under the Police and Criminal Evidence Act 1984 and subsequently in the Codes of Practice (C Annex E3) for an Appropriate Adult to be present whenever the police interview an offender who is 'vulnerable' – which of course includes the mentally disordered. The aim is *inter alia* to protect them from unfair questioning, but not necessarily to obtain psychiatric treatment. If there is evidence that they are floridly mad, however, then an Appropriate Adult might help secure psychiatric attention. The Appropriate Adult scheme is not about diversion but about ensuring that the offender has his rights secured while under interrogation. That these provisions are rarely used, except for juveniles, merely compounds the problem (Bean and Nemitz 1994). But then, how many Appropriate Adults would be required to cope with this stage army? Certainly many more than are currently available, or ever likely to be.

Invariably the police surgeon, or in today's language forensic medical examiner is the first professional to be called to the police station – and the first to arrive. There is nothing in the Police and Criminal Evidence Act 1984 (PACE) or its Codes of Practice that requires the police surgeon to be called to see someone detained under Section 136, or for the police surgeon to advise on the use of the Appropriate Adult, but this is current police practice. For those detained under Section 136 the Act states the need for a patient to be 'examined by a registered medical practitioner and an ASW to make the necessary arrangements for his treatment and care'. Ideally, the registered medical practitioner should be a GP and/or a Section 12 physician. In practice police surgeons select out the more floridly mad, leaving the others in custody making decisions on their competency rather than their mental disorder. 'Fit to be detained and fit to be interviewed' are their standard assessments.[3]

This means that a few offenders, the more obviously mad, will be picked up, while the others move through the system with their disorders almost unnoticed, rarely being offered treatment. They serve their sentence but are likely to be rearrested soon after release. Too often these offenders have already travelled that well-trodden path through the criminal justice system, but the police station is where it all starts, and the numbers show how daunting is the situation (for a more detailed discussion see Bean 2001: chapters 5, 6 and 7). Various attempts have been made to improve matters. Treatment through diversion from police custody was once the catchphrase, but 'diversion to what?' became the obvious retort. There are no powers under current bail provisions to require offenders to receive treatment. This is a particular defect for drug users, where arrest referral schemes rarely see the offender after the initial visit. Exworthy (1995) describes a number of schemes that divert offenders into a treatment programme, as a diversion out of the criminal justice system or into treatment. These schemes are small in number, and take but a handful of patients. The remaining offenders presumably struggle on as best they can.

Once out of the police station and into the courts the mentally disordered offender can be remanded or sentenced. If sentenced, he – again, it is usually a 'he' – may be under the care of a probation officer or dealt with in similar ways through other community service provisions. Again, no one knows how many mentally disordered are on these orders, or receiving treatment whether informally or as a condition of their order. Or they may go to prison, first as a remanded prisoner and sometimes later as a sentenced prisoner.

Within the prison system high rates of mental disorder are found among the male remand population – about 15 times higher than in the sentenced population generally – and the courts, it seems, use their powers of remand to obtain a psychiatric assessment and/or recommend treatment. Or the offender may be sentenced. In which case, and the most reliable figure comes from the research of Gunn *et al.*, about 3 per cent of the male sentenced prison population are floridly mad (Gunn *et al.* 1991a). Based on current prison statistics of over 80,000 prisoners in 2007, that figure is about 2,500 prisoners. Add to this those with alcohol and drug problems, or personality disorder, and the overall figure of severely mentally disordered runs into many thousands. A few will be transferred to high-security hospitals or secure units of one kind or another, but most will remain in prison to be treated by the medical services as best they can. Some will become mentally disordered during or perhaps as a result of their prison sentence, but most will have arrived in prison as a mentally disordered prisoner (see also Bean 2001 for a discussion on this).

The position is no better for female prisoners. Although their numbers are much smaller, throughout the criminal justice system and in prisons, there is general agreement that they too have high rates of mental disorder. Women prisoners tend to receive proportionately more psychiatric disposals than men (Prins 1995: 114). A study by Parsons *et al.* (2001) of all receptions to two female remand prisons over a 15-week period (during 1998) showed high rates of disorder. Their population was of just under 400 women, of whom 221 (68 per cent) had a lifetime prevalence of mental disorder. Current mental disorder, excluding substance abuse, was identified in 227 (59 per cent) of the 382 women interviewed, 42 being psychotic. Prison screening appeared not to be very successful in detecting mental disorder among this offender group.

The role of prison medical services is under increasing scrutiny, leading to the phasing out of the prison medical service as a separate service linking prisons to the National Health Service. This debate has been long and protracted with prison medical staff claiming that their expertise will be lost if their identity is merged, and accusations being made about the low standards of medical specialists within the prison medical services, and a correspondingly poor-quality service. Sadly, the debate has often been conducted at that level. There was little doubt that those favouring greater integration would eventually win, with the expectation that a better-quality service would follow. This may not happen, of course, nor should there be an expectation of better facilities, or more extensive facilities; as before, only minor matters can be dealt with in prisons, whether medical or psychiatric. The smaller prisons will continue to receive GP services.

Health professionals in the prison services are more than neutral observers in the daily clashes between prisoners and staff. They play a part in the power struggles within the prison. Some prisoners may seek to use the psychiatric services to undermine the discipline staff, whether routinely or when seeking parole. Presumably, psychiatric services play key roles in determining the outcome of the allocation of scarce resources within the prison, and involve frequent decisions about the mentally disordered. Bringing in outsiders may shift the balance of power making it harder for prisoners to negotiate or assert dominance; or the opposite may happen, with outsiders being less schooled in subterfuge than their predecessors. Changes in structure and personnel are rarely neutral. Health professionals based in the NHS may turn out to be less loyal to the prison system.

For juveniles there seems to be a worsening situation. Mental health legislation in England and Wales gives no special protection for juveniles, with formal detention in mental hospitals a rarity (Gunn and Taylor 1993: 233). The best data comes from the USA, and it shows a serious deterioration in the mental and physical health of some juvenile offenders, particularly those attending US drug courts. There is an increase in the numbers of drug/alcohol abusing juveniles who also suffer from mental/behavioural disorders, ranging from clinical depression to ADHD (attention deficit hyperactivity disorder) and beyond. Consequently, many juvenile courts in the USA include mental health professionals in the team (Bean and Nemitz 2000). US studies on juveniles who commit serious violence offences, including homicides, also suggest high levels of psychopathology within their families. The position may be less serious in the UK (Pritchard and Bagley 2001), but there is growing awareness that the US pattern may be around the corner, and we need to be prepared. While there is increasing concern in the UK about dual diagnosis in juveniles (or more accurately co-occurring disorders, often referred to as comorbidities), there is currently less concern about their formal mental disorder. We seem ill prepared for what is to come (Maughan 1993).

It is customary, perhaps almost obligatory, for academics to complain about 'the absence of research', and they usually follow this with a broadside against the government (any government will do) about failing to fund the research community. Sadly, such accusations are true, there *has* been a dreadful shortage of research, leaving little by way of hard data to go on. There has been much speculation – especially from clinicians – about what to do with the flow of mentally disordered through the criminal justice system, and some debate among lawyers about new legislation, but that is not a substitute for data. We seem to be faced with huge numbers of mentally disordered offenders, albeit mainly the inadequate rather than the floridly mad, but mentally disordered according to modern diagnosis nonetheless. Most go untreated – whether in police stations or elsewhere – and most reoffend. The problems seem to be beyond the scope of any single body or government to deal with, and the only hope is in a long-term solution directed towards improving the level of treatment services generally. It is against this background, dire in some ways, that we now consider the links with crime.

A model for examining the links between madness (mental disorder) and crime

We need a model to examine the links between mental disorder and crime. Much of the research on mental disorder, especially the mentally disordered offender, has not been concerned with linking it to crime in a direct sense. Rather it has aimed to show the extent of the problem within criminal justice, and the failings of criminal justice to do something about it. Consequently, the models used to examine mental disorder and crime have tended to be dominated by psychiatric or legal studies. The model to be used here, however, is much wider in scope, and taken from research into drugs and crime where it has been used to great effect (Goldstein 1995; see also Bean 2004). It is simple, straightforward and uncomplicated.

The model provides three ways to establish links.

1 That mental disorder leads to crime.
2 That crime leads to mental disorder.
3 That mental disorder and crime have a common aetiology.

The first area of study includes that large body of research, which while not pointing directly to a link with crime often does so by implication. It includes research on the mentally disordered within the criminal justice system; research on hallucinations, delusions and other psychiatric phenomena; and latterly includes research on substance abuse. This section is the largest and perhaps the most unwieldy. Other areas covered include the way mental disorder might reduce crime, the mentally disordered as victims, and mental disorder and economic necessity.

The second area of research is more restrained and confined, yet strangely underdeveloped both by researchers and clinicians. It includes specific types of crimes that have led to mental disorder, although sometimes that disorder is explained as much by the impact of being sentenced as that of the crimes themselves. Included too are aspects of the way substance abuse, itself a crime, has led to the disorder.

Finally, research on mental disorder and crime as comorbidities. This area of research is also not well developed but the potential is huge and the questions to be asked of great interest, particularly in terms of public policy.

The trouble with using this format is that research does not easily fit, so many questions are left hanging, or supported only with occasional pieces of anecdotal evidence. In that sense it is not very satisfactory. However, it shows areas where there is a surfeit of data, as well as pointing to other areas that resemble a data desert. But it means that sometimes the data are often poor, leaving more than the usual questions unanswered.

Mental disorder leads to crime

This is the most popular, the most widely stated and sometimes the least understood link with crime. It is often used to great effect to dominate debates about future policy. Numerous assumptions arise, and running alongside them are tangled webs of ideologies, pressure group demands and vested professional interests. Sometimes research has played into these, and has been used to develop demands for new policies. Occasionally research has been motivated by, and spawned its own pressure group, supported by various clinicians and social workers seeking their own agendas, sometimes seeking a more coercive stance than before, and almost always fundamentally hostile to criminal justice, albeit seemingly prone to psychiatric values. (Criminal justice is seen as punitive and authoritarian, and often therefore the antithesis of liberal sensitive values.) The result has been a fragmented approach, not always leading to a dialogue – more often a series of rehearsed monologues.

Political pressure groups play their part. When John Monahan confidently stated that psychiatrists were poorly qualified to act as predictors of violence the anti-psychiatry lobby nodded sagely. When he said that of every three disordered persons predicted by psychiatrists to be violent only one will be discovered to commit a violent act, his research was hailed as a breakthrough (Monahan 1993b: 641). Later, when he recanted by pointing to subsequent research, showing these results to be inconsistent – that for every study that reported an increase in predictive inaccuracy from psychiatrists another one found otherwise – he received less publicity, fewer comments, and less interest. Perhaps it was ever thus.

Politics aside, the question as it stands is too large, too unwieldy. 'Mental disorder leads to crime' – but which disorders and which crime? What is the possibility of mental disorder leading to a reduction in crime, or leading to financial impoverishment – called 'economic necessity' in drug research? What are the impacts of illicit drugs adding to existing problems? Where do we obtain this information? Personal accounts, perhaps, and there is no shortage of these; the literature is full of protests against unjustified detention, but little or nothing about their criminality. Autobiographies tend to be written by the gifted, artistic or creative, whose criminality, when it occurred, was a side issue rather than central to their lives – although there have been notable exceptions. Clinical impressions perhaps; they have certainly made significant contributions to the debate and will continue to do so. But there is no real substitute for good research data.

Sociologists talk of 'unpacking the question' – not the most elegant phrase, but one that conveys its meaning. However, in this case 'unpacking' often means adding to the packaging; the first piece of unpacking involves considering mental disorder and crime as affected by substance abuse.

Mental disorder, crime and substance abuse

The increase in substance abuse has changed the criminological landscape, and this is as true of mental disorder and crime as in other areas (Gordon 1990). Heroin and cocaine use is now widespread, alongside other drugs such as ecstasy (MDMA), and the likely extended use of crystal methamphetamine or 'ice'. Illicit substance use is now embedded into our national criminal culture. The use of licit substances such as benzodiazepines is also widespread; they create their own problems but are not closely linked to crime – they tend to be taken by a different age group. At one level all who are mentally disordered as a result of illicit substance misuse are criminal since those substances were by definition obtained illegally. Yet this is not the debate; the discussion here is about the impact of the drugs, including the social milieu in which the users live.

We are concerned with how mental disorder leads to drug abuse, which leads to crime. Too often this is almost impossible to determine; there are too many variables, too many sequences of events, and too many unknown quantities to be certain of the outcome. The best that can be done is to show when selected variables were present, and how one might interact with the other. Even then there is more guesswork than science, with the conclusions forever tentative and suspect. Is it worth doing? Well, yes, if only to see where it takes us.

We can begin with research that shows the mentally disordered as substance abusers. Some studies show that about half of those who were substance abusers had a mental disorder at some stage in their lives (Regier *et al.* 1990); others put the figure much higher (see Seivewright *et al.* 2004). Small-scale studies using clinically based ratings have found that at least 50 per cent, and sometimes up to 90 per cent of drug users have psychiatric conditions as a lifetime prevalence figure, and some at the time of interview (Seivewright *et al.* 2004: 124). In a study of women prisoners the lifetime prevalence of mental disorder for the whole sample of prisoners was 221 out of 394 (68 per cent) but when a diagnosis of drug or alcohol dependence was included the number of women with a lifetime disorder rose to 311 (81 per cent) (Parsons *et al.* 2001: 196). As always with this type of study, whether for men or women, methodological problems reappear. Sometimes the studies show lifetime prevalence, others give point prevalence. Some are content to point to a history of psychiatric disorder, others to more specific conditions. If the samples or populations are taken from a psychiatric treatment ward then results will show a high level of mental disorder, if taken from street heroin users results will show high levels of criminality and substance abuse; but if taken from middle-aged, middle-class cocaine users then less criminality is evident. Nonetheless, the results show a high prevalence, especially a high life-time prevalence.

One of the most important studies linking the various morbidities – tying mental disorder and substance abuse to crime – has been the ECA study (Swanson 1996: 101–36). The general conclusions are that while serious mental illness without substance abuse by itself is quite rare in the community, mentally disordered individuals with substance abuse were significantly more likely to be violent than those with mental disorder alone. The study concentrates on violence offences, with the conclusions stark and clear. It fits with other studies on comorbidity for it confirms that the risk of violence associated with mental disorder dramatically increases when substance abuse is added to the equation. Few studies have been able to provide this level of methodological rigour as the ECA study, and their findings offer a major conclusion.

Philip Connell (1958) in his seminal paper on amphetamine psychosis did not use the term 'dual diagnosis', nor did he consider the details and complexities of the treatment process. He was more concerned to draw attention to diagnostic matters. One wonders what he would have said of the modern dually diagnosed patient. These patients typically have shorter stays in treatment with poorer treatment outcomes. They pose problems much greater than those Connell grappled with. He did not need to consider the complexities of treatment: should it run parallel, be sequential or integrated, that is, should it take place in different organisations concurrently or sequentially (substance abuse first, mental disorder later or *vice versa*), or all together and preferably in the same organisation? Had he considered this he would have found, then as now, that the solution is often decided on practical and financial grounds; patients receive treatment depending on what is available, the severity of the disorder and who is prepared to take them on. He would certainly be surprised to note the extent of treatment tensions, now endemic between the various treatment providers, partly due to their different ideological backgrounds. Those with a substance abuse background will often promote stricter treatment policies, usually involving abstinence, adopting a confrontational approach, while those from a mental health tradition will emphasise something more akin to psychotherapy. Differences occur too in the interpretation of the underlying causes of the psychiatric symptoms, those involved in substance abuse holding a less sympathetic position. These differences are made worse by variations in qualifications and training (Grella 2003). Such differences as existed in the late 1950s are much greater 50 years on.

Self-medication adds another dimension, whether through licit or illicit drugs, prescribed or otherwise. It happens in various forms; sometimes paradoxically, non-compliant patients do not take the drugs prescribed but take others they prefer. Non-compliance sometimes means taking more drugs, not fewer, whether of the prescribed or of those not prescribed; or it sometimes means taking none that were prescribed, and only taking those that were not. The combinations are endless given the range and quantities of drugs available. It is not surprising that diagnosis is difficult when a patient is admitted for treatment, and misdiagnosis common – one condition may mask or mimic the other. Where self-medication is aimed at offsetting the impact of official medication or damping down an existing condition, the drug of choice seems to be heroin. For some inexplicable reason, however, schizophrenic patients often choose cocaine, which has the opposite effect – it heightens awareness and livens things up. There is much speculation as to why this should be so. The most plausible suggestion is that schizophrenia produces a cold, detached feeling whereas cocaine produces the opposite, creating the impression of once more being an active participant in human affairs.

Anecdotal evidence suggests that the patients who most often self-medicate are found among the more socially deprived populations with long-term mental disorders, but non-compliance in all psychiatric populations is common. Those who regularly self-medicate, if they use illicit drugs, are typically found living in hostels in inner-city areas; they have poorly developed social skills and a poor, sometimes non-existent work record. They may also be on high doses of prescribed medication, perhaps heavy tranquillisers, and have a poor psychiatric prognosis. Whether so or not, self-medication produces social as well as personal consequences. For some mentally disordered – the awkward, shy, lonely and friendless – it permits entry and acceptance into a new social world. These mentally disordered may find themselves accepted within the drugs community in ways they had not experienced elsewhere – as deviants but equals. Acceptance, however, is likely to be superficial; more likely they will be exploited, being asked to do lowly but risky jobs for the dealers – 'stashing' and 'running', or holding and delivering drugs that carry a high risk of prosecution.

Few clinicians and researchers are interested in this area; most psychiatrists tend to feel uncomfortable moving into the world of substance abuse. A few have become specialists in dual diagnosis, linking substance abuse to mental disorder and by implication to crime, and these have been responsible for most of the data. The research that has been undertaken shows that dual diagnosis patients are a heterogeneous group with multiple impairments. The most frequent comorbid diagnosis with opioid dependence are major depressive and anxiety disorders, the former running from 16 per cent to 56 per cent and the latter 8 per cent to 55 per cent. These figures are about eight times higher than found in non-patient groups (see Bizzarri *et al.* 2005). With ecstasy the most frequent disorders are anxiety and cognitive disorders (Thomasius *et al.* 2005). Studies that take their samples from treatment groups tend to show high rates of disorder, but it is not known whether these rates are hugely inflated, there being little else with which to compare.

Together with these mental health problems there are physical health problems such as HIV and hepatitis, all requiring treatment. 'Dual diagnosis' is not an appropriate term here: 'multiple diagnosis' is a better description. In the UK the Royal College of Psychiatrists defined treatment as being 'the prevention and reduction of harm resulting from the use of drugs'. It included social, psychological or physical harm adding that treatment may involve medical, social or educational interventions, including prevention and harm reduction

(Royal College of Psychiatrists 2000: 155). This is an inclusive definition: it recognises the social, mental and medical (physical) health of the drug user.

Irrespective of the types of drugs taken or the extent of use, there will always be a health risk of some sort, such as through overdose, or a psychotic episode (see Institute of Medicine 1996 for a list of the likely health problems drug users face). Some conditions may be mild, such as respiratory irregularities or dental hygiene – methadone has high sugar levels which damage teeth – but some may be severe, such as excessive weight loss, or muscle-wasting, alongside other diseases related to a chaotic lifestyle and poor and erratic nutrition. Some drug users will contract hepatitis B or C. At the very worst some will die, usually through an overdose, perhaps having first contacted HIV and AIDS. There are implications too for those in drug treatment agencies. The study by Bizzarri *et al.* (2005) shows that among patients in treatment for opioid addiction those with psychiatric disorders have poorer 'quality of life' assessments, underscoring the importance of performing a psychiatric assessment of patients presenting for treatment at addiction services. The authors argue for an integrated mental health and substance use treatment for patients with dual disorders (2005: 1771).

Women face the same health problems as men – the same risks of infection and the same dangers from chaotic lifestyles – but some women face other risks: the lifestyle associated with crack/cocaine dependence often includes physical abuse and outright violence. Medical complications may go undetected or untreated, especially among prostitutes who risk contracting cervical cancer with a history of sexually transmitted diseases (Inciardi *et al.* 1993: 142). Most women drug users are of child-bearing age. Incidentally it is not known how many pregnant women substance abusers seek termination. A study by Murphy and Rosenbaum in the USA (1999) showed how for a variety of reasons these women drug users did not always practise birth control; they did not think they could conceive, as long-term drug use and an erratic lifestyle meant menstrual cessation. When they did conceive it was some time before they recognised it. Morning sickness was often attributed to drug withdrawal.

Pregnant women risk transferring their health problems to the unborn child. In an ECCAS study by Baldacchino *et al.* (2003) the point was made that maternal drug abuse may affect the child at every stage of its development; the utero-ovarian environment may not be optimal, the neo-natal period may be complicated by a drug withdrawal syndrome, and if substance abuse continues the child's physical and emotional development may be adversely affected by growing up in a drug-taking environment (2003: p.v). As part of that ECCAS study John Corkery reports (2003: 98) that there is no routinely collected data on the number of pregnant drug users in the UK, the transmission of infection, or the damage to the foetus or neonate from drug effects. This type of data can only be obtained from detailed studies of medical case notes.

In one of the few studies on the general health of drug users nearly two-thirds (64 per cent) reported physical health issues and 50 per cent mental health issues in addition to drug misuse (ISD 2003). Small-scale surveys on drug users living on the streets, usually begging (or 'panhandling' to use the American terminology), report even higher rates. They show users to have severe health problems and a poor prognosis; over the years their major organs will have suffered and their immune systems will be damaged. If they inject, and almost all street drug users do, they will be at risk of other conditions resulting from the use of non-sterile needles, including HIV/AIDS, or hepatitis.

If the results from the above 2003 survey are representative of drug users generally then the numbers requiring treatment for health problems are huge (see also Bean 2005). Add to these those with mental health disorders, and this gives some idea of the extent of the problem. In the UK, as elsewhere, treatment facilities for drug users with mental health problems have not kept pace with demand, nor are likely to. How much worse then will this be for their physical health? Add the myriad other matters requiring resolution – homelessness, poor employment prospects, crime (about 70 per cent of all male treatment referrals in England and Wales come through criminal justice, women tend to come through a different route) – and the demands for treatment are daunting. Simply providing sufficient facilities for dealing with substance abuse is difficult enough; how much more for physical and mental health matters.

Given what we know of mental illness (including physical illness), chemical abuse and crime, is it possible to point to any direct links? Probably yes, but not always in a straightforward linear sense, or rather where links exist they are extremely difficult to determine with precision. In some cases there will have been criminality prior to drug use, and the mental illness will be reciprocal (the two disorders arise from the same risk factors), and any criminality arising after the onset of mental disorder will be a continuation of that earlier process, but that is only one among many. All we can say with certainty is that some drug users have a cluster of morbidities, typically found in street heroin users, or crack/cocaine users. These have high levels of substance abuse, chronic physical disorders, and are persistent criminals, usually involving property offences many of which are aimed at feeding their habit. They will almost certainly have been the subject of psychiatric investigation if not treatment. With such an erratic lifestyle and desperately poor prognosis, determining which precedes which is an impossible task. Keeping them alive is about as much as one can hope for.

All discussion surrounding mental disorder and crime must now include substance abuse, whether the discussion is about treatment – where the prognosis is made worse by the additional presence of substance abuse in psychotic patients (Seivewright *et al.* 2004: 129) – or about the links with crime. If there is any doubt it should be dispelled by the research by Steadman *et al.* (1998). They compared violence among patients and others in the neighbourhood, and found no statistical difference between these groups. However when substance abuse was added to the equation things changed immediately and levels of violence increased. The point is well made here:

> Among those who reported symptoms of substance abuse, the prevalence of violence among patients was significantly higher than the prevalence of violence among others in the neighbourhood … The patient sample was also significantly more likely to report such symptoms of substance abuse than was the community sample. (1998: 400)

Mental disorder as a means of reducing crime
The next piece of unpacking is about mental disorder as a means of reducing crime, a rarely considered question. Paul Goldstein raised it in another context when he described how drug use could have a reverse psychopharmacological effect by being able to ameliorate violent tendencies (Goldstein 1995: 256). Heroin, for example, damps down violent impulses as it produces a soporific effect, making committing offences less likely. Other drugs such as cannabis make criminality difficult. This being so, the same question may usefully be asked for mental disorder: how much does mental disorder reduce crime? The question can be split into two; first, to see if the disorder itself reduces criminality, and second, to see if the treatment of the disorder reduces criminality.

First, there are many examples where a depression, catatonic condition or debilitating compulsive disorder might reduce the patient's capacity to cope with everyday affairs. Under such conditions normal social life is suspended. But what if that normal social life involved criminality? Would that also be suspended? It seems plausible enough, although I know of no research evidence to support this. Or perhaps the mentally disordered offender turns out to be a less effective offender during the periods of disorder, not just committing fewer offences but being less successful. Much interest in the 1960s focused on middle-class women who were caught shoplifting. The explanation offered was that they were depressed. Might it be that their depression led to their being caught because they were less alert shoplifters than when they were well?

It would not be impossible to construct a research project along these lines, with the null hypothesis that the presence of mental disorder reduces criminality, but it would be mightily difficult to do well. The impact of treatment would need to be disaggregated, and changes in lifestyle resulting from the disorder assessed; there would also need to be an assessment of criminal behaviour and the changes if any that might occur during the history of the disorder. It might also be worth noting whether criminality was affected by different stages of the disorder; for example Link and Stueve (1998) report that people with mental disorder have an elevated risk of violence, and that risk is highest in the acute phase of their condition. It is possible that the opposite might occur for other forms of criminality, so, other than for violence, crimes involving property offences would be reduced during the acute phase. A lengthy ethnographic study along these lines might yield interesting results.

Second, the idea of the treatment leading to a reduction in opportunities to commit crime is easier to accept and with obvious examples. Offenders, persistent and otherwise, have reduced opportunities to offend while in detention – at least we presume they do. They may continue to commit some crime while in prison or hospital, as many do, but that criminality will be absorbed by the organisation: the police are rarely called (Brown 2006). Violence against staff is not uncommon, nor is theft against patients, and drug use is rampant, but we can safely assume that there will be some reduction in the more serious criminality. Patients in the community have more opportunities, but treatment may still reduce the risk. Strong tranquillisers and other treatments will be expected to dampen violent and other criminal impulses. But do they? No one seems to know, but it is another interesting hypothesis crying out for an imaginative research design.

*Mental disorder leading to crime: the case of the
mentally disordered as victims*

The third piece of unpacking concerns what Goldstein (1995) calls
'victim precipitated psychopharmacological crime', where drug use
alters a person's behaviour in such a manner as to bring about
victimisation. So, the drugged man may have his possessions stolen,
become a victim of a dangerous driver, or leave property unattended
to encourage or assist the burglar. And if drug use can promote levels
of victimisation, so might mental disorder. Except that with mental
disorder matters are slightly more complicated.

The term victimisation can be interpreted in two respects: first, the
mentally disordered person can be a direct victim of a crime while
being mentally disordered; second, the crime can produce a subsequent
reaction (often referred to as post-traumatic stress) or some other
consequence that appears in later life. The first is straightforward
enough; it links the mental disorder with being the victim of a crime
– the person may be subject to violence, or perhaps taken advantage
of by predatory criminals. The second is more tenuous; the person
who is mentally disordered has been the victim of an earlier crime,
and that crime has led to the particular mental disorder.

The first type of offence may take place in the street – a 'mugging',
for instance – or in the home, where relatives or others may fraudulently
take the person's life savings. Where the mentally disordered are
vulnerable they may attract unwanted attention, leading to abuse or
physical harm; in this way the incompetent or inadequate become
the butt of all sorts of unpleasantries. Traditionally the mad have
been taunted and reviled, and not much has changed in that respect.
But how many are victims of this type of crime? No data seems to be
available; again, it would be interesting to know more.

The second interpretation – having been a victim and becoming
mentally disordered as a result – can involve being sexually abused
as a child, being the victim of domestic violence, or the recipient
of unpleasantness leading to subsequent stress. It is often called a
syndrome (post-traumatic stress) in its own right, however distant
that affliction may have been. Being sexually abused, the victim of
incest, or violently abused domestically clearly fall into the criminal
victim category; but other experiences that also lead to post-traumatic
stress syndrome, say, from military combat, would not. And this is
where matters get complicated.

Gunn and Taylor (1993) argue that many patients are victims and that being a victim promotes or makes worse their criminality. Case histories from mentally disordered offenders often reveal levels of sexual abuse – or claimed sexual abuse; it is not always possible to verify the statements – that have a permanent and deleterious effect on subsequent behaviour, let alone self-image and personal esteem. They reveal a litany of damaged relationships starting from childhood and continuing throughout adulthood. (It is estimated that about 30 per cent of the male prison population have been in care as children with all the subsequent problems of personal relationships that brings.) These earlier traumatic experiences become incorporated and interpreted into an explanation of crime. This is the point where Jill Peay asks how correlation and causation can be so readily disentangled? (Peay 1997: 688). Correlations with earlier stress are clear, but are they the cause of the subsequent mental disorder? If so, which, and in what way?

Including such matters in an explanation of mental disorder easily plays into the offender's desire for self-pity, and extends the domain of psychiatry into an unnecessarily complex arena. For explanation read medicalisation. Peay believes that some offenders are all too easily prepared to see themselves as victims, and psychiatrists, being dependent on what they are told, are equally too willing to 'restructure experiences as explanations or excuses' (1997: 688). Peay asserts, without evidence, that the mentally disordered as victim is an index of social failure, not a measure of criminogenic predisposition, and ought not to be included in the psychiatric equation.

In one sense the point is made. Mentally disordered offenders are by definition the stuff of psychiatry. It is all too easy to extend the psychiatric domain beyond specific psychiatric conditions to include almost everything else in the offender's background and make-up. Once criminologists start on this path, says Peay, where will it all end? Will not all crimes be open to the same psychiatric scrutiny, with the same level of psychiatric intensity? That would reduce criminology to a subsection of psychiatry, to no one's advantage.

There seems little doubt that many in the mentally disordered offending population have been victims. And being an offender, especially a young male violent offender, and also a drug user, is highly correlated with being a victim, whether of an earlier form of abuse or while being a drug user – being an offender and victim are often interchangeable in criminological terms. But many are not victims, the more so if they are not young, male and working class. What is needed is evidence that shows that there is something about being mentally disordered, which if not directly promoting victimisation, or specific crimes, at least is indirectly attributable to them. Frankly, the evidence is not forthcoming. We need more than statements from offenders who see themselves as 'damaged' and are eager to have their behaviour reassessed. There are however other reported examples of the mentally disordered as victims who get less attention; the demented elderly losing their savings to unscrupulous conmen, fake builders, crooked investors or the like. Or of abuse in old people's homes, where the mentally disordered are unable to defend themselves or have their complaints treated seriously. If we were to concentrate on these, rather than the more esoteric links between disorder and early victimisation, we might be better served.

Mental disorder leading to crime: the case of economic necessity
Another piece of unpacking is about mental disorder and crimes of economic necessity. Sixty per cent of all reported crime involves property offences – invariably theft, but including burglary and robbery. How many of these offences are committed by the mentally disordered, and to what extent does mental disorder promote property crime? Prins (1995) gives examples of property offences committed by persons of otherwise good character against a background of a mild depressive illness, accompanied by absentmindedness (1995: 98, 100). As do Bluglass and Bowden (1990), who draw heavily on the early research of Gibbens and Prince in 1962, who defined four groups of shoplifters, one being middle-aged women of good character, alongside professional, general delinquents and repetitive thieves with a compulsion to steal (Bluglass and Bowden 1990: 789). These women of 'good character' include the stereotypical middle-class, menopausal housewife, who steals without thought for future consequences, and without need of the goods she steals. These offenders, often the subject of media interest at the time, had their cause promoted, and fostered by a number of high-profile celebrities caught shoplifting where the explanation offered was of a depressive condition. This somehow explained the crime, but it was never clear why this type of depression should reside in middle-class women, or whether it was to do with the menopause. Nowadays there seems less interest in this type of offender, or of offering this type of explanation, but it was an interesting example of the way the solution to a puzzle was to be found in a psychiatric explanation. As these types of women do not steal, and are wealthy enough to afford to buy the goods anyway, the explanation must be of some sort of psychological disturbance.

This example offers a curious interpretation of shoplifting that turns economic necessity on its head. A more up-to-date interpretation is that shoplifting is what it always was: a Swedish study of 'repetitive shoplifting' – being caught three or more times in a given year (there were 377 persons caught 1,802 times) – showed that 50 per cent were unemployed, with less than 10 per cent classified as in full-time employment. There was a high percentage of early retired pensioners who had lost their jobs, or had become chronically ill; less than 25 per cent were women (Sarasalo *et al.* 1998). The peak period of arrests was September to October – coincidentally the peak period for depression, but that was about all the authors conceded to the depression lobby. They even doubted that shoplifting was a way of alleviating depression, given the mood changes that result before, during and after the excitement about the event, and self-congratulation when not caught.

In tune with the Swedish research, a study by Parsons *et al.* (2001) of mental disorder in two female prisons shows that the most common crime was dishonesty. A significantly higher proportion of women diagnosed as suffering from a mental disorder were charged with an offence of violence, 27 per cent compared with 18 per cent (where $p = <0.01$), while a higher proportion of those without a mental disorder were charged with dishonesty: 79 per cent without a mental disorder, compared with 66 per cent who were diagnosed with a mental disorder. Little attention, however, was given to those who were charged with dishonesty. Most research singles out violence offences for attention, and this I fear is the mindset; violence dominates the thinking, and dishonesty comes a long way down the order, yet dishonesty was more common.

Clearly some mentally disordered are dishonest, committing crime for the same economic reasons as substance abusers, but it is hard to find data on them. Prins (1995) asserts that sufferers from schizophrenia may demonstrate a steady diminution of social functioning accompanied by withdrawal from social life leading to offences such as breach of the peace or vandalism. Do they also commit property offences? Patients detained under Section 136 are often homeless, usually as a result of the fractured relationships brought about by their mental condition. The police may choose not to prosecute, and families and neighbours may withdraw their complaint once the police are involved – the complaint usually follows a disturbance, fear of violence, or threats against passers-by. It often involves aggressive begging. From the police perspective it is easier to detain under Section 136 than prosecute, the latter invariably leading to a short period in a police station, release on bail, and back on the streets ending with another complaint. But in doing so this will mask relatively large numbers of property crimes; while most of them are petty, some may not be.

There is no doubt that a Section 136 order reduces recorded criminality in the mentally disordered. These patients typically come from homeless populations, have high rates of unemployment, and their prognosis and economic prospects are poor. They have few opportunities for full-time employment and petty criminality is an obvious result. But what of the more serious property offenders such as involving burglary, armed robbery or kidnapping? Are the mad too incompetent to commit such offences, or so competent that they don't get caught? In their evaluation of Grendon Underwood prison Gunn and Robertson (1982) noted that 91 per cent of their population had convictions for property offences, including burglary. Although these offenders were classified as suffering from a range of psychiatric disorders they were not overtly mad; but they were of a sufficient disposition to be recommended for therapy. Unfortunately, again, little was said of their property offence.

Yet in a study by Graham Robertson (1982) comparing differences between the various groups of persons committed under the then 1959 Mental Health Act he found that there had been a reduction in use of restriction orders for mentally disordered property offenders. How many property offences were committed prior to or during periods of mental disorder? This again was not recorded. We get something near to it however, in an almost throw-away line, when Robertson says that the mentally handicapped (as they were then called) group moved from juvenile theft to a more sophisticated type of acquisitive offending such as breaking and entering. On the other hand the mental illness group were rarely juvenile property offenders, and the development of their criminality seemed to reflect a general social deterioration following chronic illness (1982: 256). This interesting conclusion suggests that the mentally impaired have a different criminal trajectory from that of those with mental illness.

Mental disorder and sex offending

Moving on to sexual deviation, some will argue that this is always symptomatic of some other psychological disturbance (Gunn and Taylor 1993: 553). Necrophilia (or corpse fetishism), auto-erotic sexual asphyxia, and sado-masochism are clearly bizarre activities. Of themselves most are not criminal, although they can be, especially when things go wrong, auto-erotic sexual asphyxia being an obvious example. According to Gunn and Taylor, sexual behaviours, bizarre or otherwise, are rooted in the norms and values of society, and differ according to various social norms. Cultural relativism apart, this is a way of emphasising that unusual sexual behaviours, and any resulting offences, are normative, with their roots in a value system that regulates gender behaviour. In that sense it is not a psychiatric matter but a social and criminological one.

However, for some people, recognising that they are sexually different creates its own set of psychological problems. Donald West, in a thoughtful account of what he calls 'problematic sexuality' talks of two contrasting groups: the dysfunctional and the deviant. The primary feature of the former is libido loss; of the latter, being sexually aroused by inappropriate stimuli (1993: 529). Guilt, anxiety and paranoid delusions may surround problematic sexuality, and in some cases this may lead to a serious mental disorder, but often the problems are the existing neurotic conditions rather than the sexual behaviour itself (West 1990: 773). Bizarre sexual behaviour may be found in some psychotic patients but is said to be quite rare.

The range of sexual offences is wide, covering the mildest form of sexual contact to the most vicious sadistic rape. Some sex offences are masked, such as where the offence leads to something more serious – a rape that develops into a homicide, for instance. If we single out three sex offences for attention, indecent exposure, incest and rape it seems that serious mental disorders are again quite rare. Where they occur, as with indecent exposure, they cover the whole range of psychotic conditions, including schizophrenia as well as manic depression. So too with incest, where 'very rarely incestuous relations develop because of intellectual impairment or psychotic illness in either or both of the parties' (Prins 1995: 211). In rape psychoses are also 'comparatively rare'. This implies two things; first, that madness only rarely leads to sex offences, and second, that most sex offenders are not mad, though they may have personal problems, and some may be psychopathic. What is infinitely more worrying is the impact the offences have on their victims. Numerous studies report long-term psychological distress, occasionally leading to severe mental disorder; this is especially true of rape and incest, childhood sexual abuse being a violation of a child's basic right to protection, rape being, *inter alia*, a violation of a basic right to community safety.

There is little doubt that sexual excess is common among the mentally disordered. There is evidence to suggest that compared with the general population they have a larger number of partners, are more likely to engage in risky sexual behaviours and so more likely to contract sexually transmitted diseases (Thornicroft 2006: 31). It remains unclear which precedes the other, the excess or the disorder, or the impact one has on the other. Does being mentally disordered lead to or promote sexual excess or is it the other way round? Many psychiatric treatments limit sexual feelings; this can become the reason for not taking medication. What is more worrying is what Thornicroft describes as 'the ethical and legal minefield' surrounding enforced contraception of the mentally disordered (2006: 32). He notes 'tragic examples of psychiatric patients being subject to involuntary sterilisation or worse enforced on eugenic grounds' (2006: 32). Yet there are clearly times when effective contraception may be justified and the patient does not have the capacity to make that decision. Thornicroft says that there are some countries in Eastern Europe where people with mental illness are registered as 'incapable'. 'One consequence is that women can be given a method of contraception such as depot injection without their consent and there is considerable concern about whether these practices are compatible with the relevant international conventions on human rights' (2006: 32).

Other crimes

There is a fragmented literature on other crimes, such as arson, kidnapping, abduction (involving child stealing) and dangerous driving (see for example Bluglass and Bowden 1990; Prins 1994), even suicide (Levey 1990). Within that literature there is a tendency to highlight psychiatric problems that may occur as leading to criminality, for example depression in some female offenders charged with child abduction, or paranoid delusions in some rapists. With arson, the aim has been to produce a typology of motives linking it to mental disorder (see Soothill 1990: 782). However, Soothill argues that revenge is the more likely motive in most arson attacks, and those with a less obvious grudge are less likely to be caught. With kidnapping and abduction, where the offender is a woman the likely psychiatric diagnosis is depression, but more kidnapping offences nowadays involve drug offenders where a relative is taken and held in order to collect drug debts. These have overtaken the more traditional forms of abduction involving women and babies (D'Orban 1990: 802).

There is little research on the link between mental disorder and motoring offences. If madness produces unpredictable behaviour then motoring offences generally and traffic accidents in particular would surely show up as a key link. But not so. What research there is suggests that there is little evidence to suggest that a functional psychotic illness increases the likelihood of having an accident', or 'the little work that has been carried out on the association between psychotic illnesses and traffic accidents has on the whole failed to show an increased incidence' (Whitlock 1990: 836). There is a suggestion that dementia may play a part but the evidence is slim and based more on assertions than otherwise (1990: 836). However, were personality disorders to be included the picture might be different. There is a wealth of information linking such disorders to road traffic accidents and motoring offences generally. Impulsive, aggressive intolerant behaviour, the hallmark of the personality disorder in young people, figure prominently in the list of characteristics of the dangerous driver, made worse of course by alcohol or other drugs (Widiger and Trull 1996). Whitlock reports that there are associations between road traffic accidents and alcoholism, paranoid thinking, depressive affect, suicidal tendencies and poorly controlled expressions of violence (1990: 836).

It is difficult to explain the low rate of the mentally disordered among motoring offenders. Whitlock says that this is due to the low rate of people who are mentally disordered who drive (1990: 836), but this cannot be the only reason. Perhaps car ownership is proportionately lower among the mad, or perhaps they realise that they are unfit to drive, being able to recognise the dangers. It would be interesting to know, and equally interesting to know how many motorists drive under the influence of psychotropic drugs, especially in the morning, these drugs affecting on arousal and cognition (Gunn and Taylor 1993: 583).

Hallucinations, delusions and crime

Hallucinations are not of themselves unique to madness, nor do they have any specific diagnostic significance. While they occur in a number of psychiatric conditions, schizophrenia and bipolar disorders being the most obvious, they occur also with certain medical conditions, with alcohol, in grief reactions, with sensory, food and water deprivation and fatigue. Hallucinations also occur with substance abuse, where cannabis and LSD are prominent. The most common are auditory, but there are hallucinations of vision, touch and taste. Estimates vary about the number of people who experience hallucinations who are not mad, some say 10 per cent to 15 per cent of the population (McNeil 1996: 184), others put it lower. A small number of people, about 1 per cent, hallucinate regularly, with no suggestion of a mental disorder.

Various attempts have been made to classify hallucinations. Link and Stueve (1996: 144) simply divide them into two categories: 'threat control' and 'others'. The former type can be dangerous; these, they say, override the internal self-control systems by inserting so-called 'external' factors into people's heads. Included are those involving a specific threat of harm, such as where thoughts direct the person to undertake a certain task, whether he wants to or not. Or he will fear someone else who he believes is gravely threatening and he believes that he will be harmed. Patients with these hallucinations claim to lose self-control, but that raises questions about the strength of such impulses; what is the difference between and an irresistible impulse an impulse not resisted? The second type, that Link and Stueve simply call 'others', is a heterogeneous group that can include equally serious hallucinations, such as taking a person's thoughts away, making him believe he is invisible or that he has special powers; many are close to implying a loss of control.

The hypothesis is that persons in the 'threat control' group are more likely to be violent than those in the 'others' group. The figures lend support to the hypothesis. Persons with 'threat control' symptoms *are* more likely to be violent than the 'others' (1996: 155). That at least exonerates those in the 'others' group, or rather suggests that we should be less fearful of them, undermining that oft-promoted view that all who hallucinate are dangerous. The threat/control group were significantly (statistically) more associated with violence than the others. Understandably, those experiencing threat/control symptoms are also likely to promote the most fear. Case histories, especially those picked up by the media, highlight the dangers. For example, in 2005 a patient who had absconded from a mental hospital killed a passing stranger in Richmond Park, London. He said at his trial that he had been controlled to act in this way.

Another example comes from over 200 years earlier. In 1796 Mary Lamb, described by all who knew her as one of the most likeable and lovable of all human beings, killed her mother (Burton 2003: 89–99). What delusions she had we shall never know; but throughout the remainder of her long life she spent periods in Hoxton asylum. What is interesting about this case is that it destroys some of the myths about the treatment of the insane in the late eighteenth century. Mary Lamb was not chained up for the rest of her life in some private madhouse; she lived most of her life with her brother Charles, who also had a psychiatric history, and she was popular with the literary circle of the time. Her case underlines the point that the mad are not mad all the time. 'Insanity was a blow afflicting by degrees in fits, coming and going, with remissions, oscillating in intensity' (2003: 94). Mary Lamb returned to live with her brother after only two and a half years of detention, on the basis 'that she posed no threat to public safety' (2003: 149), but returned regularly to the asylum when her madness reappeared. One wonders what would the media make of that nowadays?

In contrast to specific case histories such as these, threat control symptoms are not an accurate predictor of individual behaviour (Link and Stueve 196: 156). Most respondents who experienced 'threat/control' symptoms had not engaged in recent violent behaviour, although some had. The authors were led to conclude that 'Symptoms are only an "internal operational structure" that makes violence more or less likely' (1996: 156). Their conclusions were suitably tentative. Simply put, violence was 'more likely' when patients experienced these symptoms; it was no stronger than that. Other research supports this conclusion. Most patients, it seems, ignore the commands in their hallucinations; those that do not come from a specific sub-group characterised by a history of violence – sometimes reacting to command hallucinations – and a history of impulsive behaviour (McNiel 1996: 193). Accordingly, the significance of command hallucinations becomes weakened as a predictive tool; they do not lead automatically to crime, including serious offences such as homicide. Other factors need to be present. These include a history of violence, medical non-compliance, gender (mostly male), and above all situational variables, such as the setting in which violence occurs – a topic to be picked up later.

Clearly, not all mad engage in mindless violence wreaking havoc in an uncontrolled way. Link and Stueve (1996) saw threat/control symptoms as leading to intelligible behaviour, understandable even, albeit not condoned. As such they challenge the unbridled opprobrium that legitimises coercive reactions to the perpetrator. Their hope was to undermine such stereotypes and temper public responses. (1996: 157). They have a difficult task ahead. The mood in Britain sees mental patients as dangerous and a threat to public safety. It gathers apace each time the media report another case, and no amount of research seems able to obstruct it.[4] There still leaves open the question of the direction of the link with violence. Link and Stueve based their assertions on a rather convoluted argument: that there is nothing to suggest that the threat/control symptoms are caused by the violence, and so by default it is easier to believe they were not (1996: 156). Ingenious and interesting though this may be, it is not an overwhelmingly powerful proposition.

Whereas hallucinations are sensory perceptions without external stimuli of the relevant sensory organ, a delusion is a pathological belief. Definitional problems abound; Pamela Taylor is fierce in her criticisms of standard psychiatric definitions which usually describe delusion as being fixed and unshaken by any evidence to the contrary, and found within the cultural setting of the person. She is right to see this as fitting numerous political or religious organisations: and anyway, not all delusions are fixed (Taylor 1993; Taylor *et al.* 1996: 162). She is more inclined to define them as 'psychotic delusions' found where delusions are based on an absolute conviction of the proposition which is idiosyncratic, incorrigible, ego involved and often preoccupying. But calling them 'psychotic' does not solve the problem; it compounds it by its circularity, as being psychotic is what is to be determined. In many definitions of delusions, although not Pamela Taylor's, above, there is an *a priori* assumption that delusions lead to crime. In practice some do; those that create the most fear involve an assumed persecutor, where in order to seek relief the persecuted takes violent action. How frequent and how dangerous this group is is more difficult to establish.

Delusions that lead to violence, and homicide, are well described in classical literature. Shakespeare's *Othello* is the *grande example*, yet Othello is rather special. Although strictly speaking deluded this insecure man had his delusions cunningly placed by Iago. Leontes in *The Winter's Tale* offers a better example. His delusions were his own and shown to be as the play progresses. His accusations of his wife's behaviour fit the delusional form, interpreting innocent behaviour to fit the presumed action and believing against all evidence that matters have taken a certain turn. 'Is whispering nothing? Is leaning cheek to cheek? Kissing with the inside of the lip? Wishing clocks more swift; Hours minutes noon midnight? And all blind with the pin and web but theirs only'; but all is denied by everyone who knows Leontes' wife, Queen Hermione. This type of jealousy inevitably leads to a disaster, the accused partners can never produce evidence to prove their innocence.

Morbid jealousy, itself a delusion, invariably occurs with an underlying mental disorder. It involves a range of irrational thoughts and emotions together with associated unacceptable or extreme behaviour. It is thought to pose a high risk, especially to the partner and the supposed paramour – 'supposed' because by definition the condition is likely to be a delusion, and the paramour may not exist (Kingham and Gordon 2004). In their study of morbid jealousy Kingham and Gordon concluded that the presence of paranoid delusions and command hallucinations directed towards the spouse were associated with violence. They suggested that individuals with delusional jealousy who perpetrate violence may be driven directly by psychotic phenomena (2004: 11). The problem again is a methodological one; the studies cited by Kingham and Gordon involve research on the morbidly jealous who are hospital patients, or who have been convicted. We need to know how many morbidly jealous are not patients, do not commit offences, are not convicted, and whether they are violent or not.

One obvious problem is that research on delusions is about as problematic as one can get. How does one recognise a delusion and distinguish it from a fact? In the beguiling phrase of Taylor *et al.* (1996) the concept of validity of a delusion might well be considered as almost delusional in itself (1996: 167). Moreover, if the research involves direct interviews the research worker can become part of the delusional system, in the same way that any treating psychiatrist becomes incorporated. Research questions can be as threatening as any other questions, with the patient just as suspicious as he would be elsewhere. Researchers also need to disaggregate the impact of treatment, which may intensify or weaken a delusional system. Small wonder that most studies have relied on case records, but the methodology is weak; often these were prepared by professionals, psychiatrists, probation officers, usually for the courts, and primarily concerned with jurisprudential rather than research questions.

Paranoid delusions can be associated with depression as well as schizophrenia but it is the schizophrenic type that creates the most fear. In clinical terms the paranoid subtype of schizophrenia with powerful delusional symptoms is most likely to be associated with extreme forms of violence, including homicide, sometimes involving young children, and sometimes followed by suicide. Numerous case histories support this view. However, outside that clinical framework the matter is even less straightforward. For while there is some evidence of a relationship between violence and a delusional state, that relationship is far from certain; the majority of patients do not act on their delusions. Pamela Taylor found that substantial delays occur between the onset of a psychotic condition, with its corresponding delusional state, and subsequent violence (Taylor *et al.* 1996). In a study of 121 psychotic inmates in Brixton prison their illnesses and delusional systems had been present for a considerable time, with only one prisoner giving a clear description of a delusion leading rapidly to violence (1996: 179). So too with hallucinations: there is not much evidence to suggest that hallucinations immediately lead to criminality, even among those who subsequently commit offences, which is a small percentage of all those who hallucinate. Yet on the other hand Link and Stueve found that the vast amount of violent acts (86 per cent) committed by former patients occurred within the context of family and friendship networks, and that the risk of violence is highest in the period before, during and shortly after hospitalisation, when symptoms are at their worst (Link and Stueve 1988). Differences might be explained according to the populations, where some are less deluded than others.

Nor is it clear how fixed those delusions might be. We do not know, for example, whether patients who return to a psychotic state retain their delusions or acquire new ones. Or whether those who act on their delusions always do so violently; if not, we need to identify a subset that do. Taylor *et al.* (1996) believe that there is a complex relationship between thinking, feeling and acting, with external factors influencing events (1996: 177). The hypothesis is that situational factors influence actions that occur within a subculture of violence by patients with a previous violent history. These sociological features need further consideration.

Mental disorder and violence

Studies linking mental disorder to violence have dominated research. It is not clear why this should be so but perhaps it is another example of unreason explaining unreason. That is, as most crimes – such as property crimes – involve a measure of thought and planning, composure even, they lie outside the paradigm constructed for the violently mentally disordered. These violent offenders are not accorded sufficient organisational ability to be capable of planning crimes, only to be able to act spontaneously. And violence often appears spontaneous, it appears problematic, less predictable, irrational and sometimes without a utilitarian outcome or indeed an obvious explanation. So whereas drug users commit property crimes to pay for a habit, and they are violent towards the opposition, no such rational motives are afforded to the violently mentally disordered. That they may also retain levels of competence, and be capable of operating and undertaking various complex tasks has only been recently considered.

The typical view of mentally disordered violence is of an unprovoked attack, probably on a stranger, and without warning. These incidents are, of course, a direct threat to public safety, and policies are required to provide appropriate protection. They cannot be dismissed as 'sensationalism' or simply products of the media's insatiable interest in the macabre. The public fear of madness leading to violence, especially unprovoked and gratuitous, remains a driving force. Single events can change public policy: the case of Christopher Clunis, who killed a member of the public, being an example. Looking back on this I think it was one of those defining moments that promote a new view of the mentally disordered. Gone was the earlier world-view of the mad as victims of their condition; this was replaced by the mad as predators. Community care, or rather the decarceration movement, was said to be the cause of the problem, allowing some patients to slip through the net and be involved in serious incidents. The Ritchie Report on the Clunis case was a beacon for the community safety lobby; it demanded, and received, new controls aimed at protecting us against violent mentally disordered patients placed in the community without adequate restraint (Bean 2001; Exworthy 1995; Ritchie *et al.* 1994).

The literature on madness and violence is extensive; no single review can come close to covering it. Yet the conclusions are few and the policy options limited. Beginning with some straightforward socio-demographic data, serious mental disorders are quite rare; at a rough guess less than 1 per cent of the population are at any given moment under psychiatric treatment, although this figure is higher, of course, if one includes those patients being prescribed minor tranquillisers by GPs for mild depression or the like. Moving on to criminological data only a few of that 1 per cent under psychiatric treatment will commit violent acts even though violence includes a wide range of actions, from minor assaults to homicide. Most violent acts, serious or otherwise, are not committed by the mentally disordered; at a guess about 3 per cent of the population are violent over a one-year period, but double that if domestic violence is included, with higher levels again in the USA (Swanson 1996). Serial killers are rare; some will be mentally disordered, although where their killings are followed by suicide the diagnosis remains in doubt. About one-third of all murders in Britain are followed by suicide; some of these offenders will be mentally disordered whose actions were a direct result of their mental condition. How many we do not know. A small number of offenders claim one of the mental insanity defences – the M'Naughton Rules, diminished responsibility, infanticide, being unfit to plead – where again their offence is presumably directly attributable to their mental condition (see Prins 1995 for a discussion on these defences, also Bucknill 1884). The most serious mentally disordered offenders will be sent to high-security hospitals; if not, they receive the longest possible prison sentences, thus reflecting contemporary views about violence.

What is of great interest is that the violent mental patient has a profile almost identical to that of the violent non-mental patient. It seems that the two have much in common (Taylor 1982: 276). Education, intelligence and occupational status hardly differ. The sex of the perpetrator is almost always male, and the victim female; violence is common in the lives of both groups, that is, in the family, and, most important, in both groups there is invariably a history of violence (1982: 276). The similarities are so striking that it has led some commentators to conclude that the best predictors of violence, whether in the mentally disordered group or not, is a history of violence (this is also added to by a history of substance abuse and access to firearms, see below), suggesting that the mental disordered dimension is exaggerated. That is, the mad are violent because they are violent and not because they are mad. Not everyone fits the mould – a few who are mad are violent because they are mad. But the theory that 'the violent are violent because they are violent' comes mightily close to being a general overview.

What this amounts to is that the best predictors of violent behaviour are not mental disorders *per se* but a history of violence, plus a series of socio-demographic factors such as being male, young (under 30), of low socio-economic status, and with access to firearms. Add to these a history of substance abuse, and social isolation, and we have a potent criminological cocktail. Being mentally disordered, with command hallucinations, adds to the risk but not significantly so; equally important is being non-compliant with therapy.

However, a study by Robertson (1987) showed a curious anomaly. In a 23-year follow-up of mentally disordered offenders, including the personality disordered and the psychopaths, there was evidence of a very high risk of 'unnatural death' – accidents, suicides or homicides. At the age of 40 when violent death accounts for only about 12 per cent of deaths in the general population, it accounted for 50 per cent in this group. Suicide, for example, was five times more common than in the general population (Gunn and Taylor 1993: 397). This is odd, but we should not base too much emphasis on one study, although it would perhaps be a useful avenue to explore.

Research on violence has rarely linked the psychiatric disorders to specific forms of violence. Monahan and Steadman underlined this point when they wrote of risk assessment research that a recurring problem was the lack of precision created by failing to disaggregate criterion violence into meaningful subtypes (1996: 10). Violence is not a unified phenomenon it differs legally as well as situationally, and environmentally. Violence within the family is qualitatively different from that in a hospital ward, not just in its situation, but as a structural form of dominance. And again, the violence of the schizophrenic is of a different order from that of violence of the depressed patient, and the impact of delusions may differ from hallucinations. Street violence is different again; it need not be directed at a particular person, and the subject can and often is randomly selected – 'the first white man I see', said the schizophrenic in Richmond Park – and the violence of the mad religious fanatic is directed at anyone who happens to be nearby.

What does all this amount to in terms of mental disorder leading to crime? Well, in so far as one can summarise from such a range of evidence, the general conclusions seem to be these. Mental disorder poses a threat and the mentally disordered are sometimes violent, and when serious violence occurs it carries a very high human and social cost (Thornicroft 2006: 140). There is a specific form of violence that occurs within a small group of schizophrenic patients, especially those experiencing command hallucinations, but not in the early stage of their condition. For others the greatest threat comes from those with a history of violence, and with a history of substance abuse. Beyond that I think we cannot go.

Crime leads to mental disorder

There is very little research on the way crime leads to mental disorder. Clinicians rarely consider it, and researchers likewise. Yet the practical considerations are interesting, for as said before, if crime leads to mental disorder there will be no reduction in criminality if the mental disorder is treated. That said there are numerous methodological problems that make it difficult to establish a uni-directional outcome. Self-report studies are as methodologically limited as hitherto, as are victim reports. Determining the way a crime might lead to a mental disorder is difficult; the interactions of life events, and relational and psychosocial features are hard to separate. There is nothing simple like a linear cause/effect relation between the two.

The psychiatric literature may be sparse but the classical literature is certainly not. From Dostoevsky to Shakespeare we find examples of crimes leading to madness. Lady Macbeth was *'troubled with thick coming fancies, That keep her from her rest,'* with Macbeth himself asking the doctor to *'cure her of that. Can'st though not minister to a mind diseased?'* Lady Macbeth's attempts to wash it away proved illusory. *'Will these hands ne'er be clean?'* Apparently not, for *'all the perfumes of sweet Arabia will not sweeten this little hand'*.

One wonders why psychiatrists have given so little consideration to this idea of crime leading to mental disorder. The psychoanalytic literature is full of examples of guilt found in patients, even if it is not as a result of criminality. The impact of guilt on subsequent behaviour is well understood in those circles. Yet little has been said outside psychoanalysis about whether guilt might lead to madness; few see it as a risk factor in mental disorder. I suspect that clinicians have acknowledged the patient's remorse, accepting this as a demonstration of integrated moral standards, but not considered whether that remorse might leave patients vulnerable to the effects of crimes. As one clinician said (Georg Hoyer, personal communication)[5] if there is only a slight truth in this analysis, the need to address the question how crimes lead to mental disorders is long overdue.

Consider the case where the driver a car, through negligence, kills a child. The resulting guilt could be sufficiently powerful for the driver's life to be impaired, possibly tipping him into insanity. During treatment, clinicians may interpret the offender's guilt as a positive sign; that is, remorse as an indicator of salvation, and of the offender being basically a moral human being. Guilt then becomes a path in the direction of psychic health. Yet it could equally be a sign of weakness that may lead to madness. It might mean that the offender/patient is so tortured by guilt as to become overwhelmed by it. Guilt and remorse might lead to salvation; but it could just as easily lead to mental disorder. Or consider a concentration camp guard. How does he live with himself afterwards? Either he retains the original justification, that those he guarded were sub-human, for example, or he admits he was wrong. If the former, and he retains his original belief and political stance, he is in denial, and that is a dangerous position to be in. If the latter then he is consumed with guilt. Both conditions are close to madness, but being consumed with guilt may be the most difficult to handle in the short term.

Within criminal populations it seems entirely plausible that there will be cases where the persistence and repetition of criminality will so degrade and deprave that it leads to a degeneration into mental disorder. Pamela Taylor reports on a US study of mentally abnormal homicides where 27 per cent were said to have become insane after the killing (Taylor 1982: 273). Hegel thought that the offender had a right to punishment for without an expiation of guilt there could be no moral advance. We do not have to be Hegelian to see how some persistent offenders end up depressed and alone. Their social situation is also a mediating influence; social isolation and stigma are powerful instruments of madness. These cases appear infrequently, clinically that is, but may be more common but undocumented. In violent crimes the perpetrators, often in close contact with the victim, witness horrifying scenes, even if they have orchestrated them. All who witness disasters run the same risk. We rightly provide assistance to these victims; might the same clinical conditions appear with offenders?

Crime leading to mental disorder as a result of a penal sanction

It is not just that crime can lead to mental disorder, more that mental disorder may arise as a result of the penal sanction, i.e. when offenders get caught. This is a qualitatively different kind of link; it is not about a sense of guilt – though it might be – but about the pains of imprisonment. In an obvious sense all offenders are likely to be depressed (that is, have a depressed mood, rather than be ill) when arrested and this may be more so if sentenced to custody. Custodial sentences were never intended to be pleasant; the purpose is to impart suffering. Most offenders appear to cope with imprisonment, and some seem remarkably unaffected by it, functioning with little or no apparent detriment to their personality or mental health. (Or indeed their physical health. The physical health of long-term prisoners is probably better than a control group of non-offenders, matched for age and social class. In prison, while access to them may not be unhindered, health and dental services are available. Prison cuisine may not be wonderful but it provides a balanced diet.)

Other prisoners fare less well. Women offenders are often deeply affected by the loss of liberty, especially being separated from home life and extended social relationships. Men seem to cope better in this respect. Some prisoners, however, men and women, cannot cope at all, those with long sentences being among the most vulnerable, especially in the early part, with suicides common. 'Stir crazy' is the colloquial term; it defines a condition created by the detrimental effect of incarceration on a prisoner's psychological functioning. Again, we do not know how many offenders experience this condition? In fact too little is known of the impact of sentences generally, let alone of these extremes.

Substance abuse leading to mental disorder and to crime

It has been said above that substance abuse is a potent link with mental disorder. Here, we are concerned with chemical abuse leading to mental illness (CAMI). (There is another term in use where chemical abuse is a result of the mental illness – MICA). Stimulants such as amphetamines, cocaine and ecstasy (MDMA) are the substances most likely to produce mental disorder. Typically they produce paranoid states, and the classical drug-induced psychosis, the latter being indistinguishable from schizophrenia. Philip Connell (1958) pointed out that amphetamine psychoses were relatively short-lived. As a rule of thumb, and in order to determine whether the psychosis was drug-induced or not, Connell thought that the physician should treat the patient as if it was a functional psychosis, and only if the psychosis persisted was it likely to be a mental disorder (Connell 1958).

LSD produces a short-lived psychotic experience but rarely leads to a chronic psychotic condition. With cannabis, there has been a long running debate about whether it can cause a psychotic episode. There is evidence that suggests it can, with additional evidence showing that it produces brief psychotic symptoms and exacerbates existing psychotic conditions producing schizophrenic-type symptoms (Seivewright *et al.* 2004: 126). Other research shows how cannabis acts as a predisposition to a psychosis (*The Times*, 18 December 2006). That is to say, if the patient takes even a small amount, if they are genetically predisposed or susceptible to schizophrenia, cannabis will bring on or hasten that condition. Generally speaking drug-induced psychotic conditions disappear when drug use stops, but treatment is ineffective if drug use continues. Withdrawal from drugs such as heroin may produce agitation, perhaps depression, but not a psychosis; whereas withdrawal from alcohol or the barbiturates certainly will. Withdrawal from the benzodiazepines also produces a condition similar to a psychosis.

While chemical abuse can lead to mental illness, does it also lead to crime? One can see how it might, not just because possession itself may be illegal but because the drug has within it certain criminogenic properties. Cocaine use can lead to excitement, which can spill over, perhaps, into violence, the so-called 'hyper' condition. (In a research study undertaken in Nottingham in 1985 we were told by one 'pimp' that he had given up cocaine, because it made him violent and he 'beat up the girls which was bad for business'.) The so-called 'Happy Slappy' attacks found in street violence, invariably videoed by those involved, takes place under the influence of crack/cocaine. Phencyclidine (PCP or Angel Dust) is rarely used in the UK, (the notorious Charles Manson was a user) it produces feelings of superhuman strength leading to outrageous and sometimes criminal actions. 'Ice' or 'crystal methamphetamine' does likewise.

As always the morbidities will have become so entangled that determining which is which, and which preceded which, is altogether impossible. Nor do we have the ethnographic data from long-term studies to sift through the sequence of events. Nonetheless there are ample reports to suggest that CAMIs will be society's physical and psychological casualties; there will not be much hope for the future where substance abuse has added to problems or made them worse. In whatever way the equation is presented, the presence of substance abuse exacerbates and ultimately adds to the criminogenic make-up. For whether leading to, or following mental disorder, substance abuse provides that extra dimension. Not all who take illicit substances and are mentally disordered are, or will be, criminal, but some are, and some will be, and that adds to any existing problem.

Mental disorder and crime have a common aetiology

To say that mental disorder and crime have a common aetiology involves no presumption about the relationship, or of any presupposed theoretical connection. It merely suggests that any comorbidity constitutes the beginning not the end of the research endeavour, and is of interest only because it raises important questions about underlying mechanisms. It is easy to accept Michael Rutter's version that comorbidity does not reflect any single process and its presence provides no basis for theoretical development, but is simply a description of an empirical statistical phenomenon that has no meaning in itself (Rutter 1997: 268). Comorbidity 'has no conceptual unity or aetiological homogeneity' (1997: 268). Research involves collecting data on separate phenomena.

For some such as John Gunn (1977) the comorbidity model provides the most appropriate explanation of the link with crime. Gunn says that the main problem in discussing any relationship between criminal behaviour and mental disorder is that the two concepts are largely unrelated. Part of the problem seems to be the difficulty defining the main concepts, and the lack of available data on the criminality of psychiatric populations. (1977: 317). It is also that he sees mental disorder as a 'biological entity', meaning a complex mixture of diverse conditions – some organic, some functional, some inherited, some learned, some acquired, some curable and others unremitting. He cannot see how such a melange of conditions has a clear-cut relationship with any social parameter, especially one so arbitrarily determined by legislation (1977: 317). It is an odd argument, for the obvious retort is, why not? We try to explain addiction, a similar set of diverse conditions, with crime. His solution, however, is to concentrate on specific behaviour problems caused by specific disorders, and avoid generalisations about anything else (1977: 328).

One can see why Gunn might say this. At that time, research workers were playing down connections between madness and crime, or rather saying that where madness and violence coexist the link was confined to a few individuals, schizophrenics mainly, and the overall risk was low (Monahan and Steadman 1983 quoted in Monahan 1993a: 287). The relationship between crime and mental disorder, such as existed, was explained by demographic and historical characteristics. Over the next ten years the position changed and Monahan later wrote, with much candour and not a little honesty: 'I now believe that this conclusion is premature and may well be wrong for two reasons' (1993: 287). One was that the methodology was seen as problematic – he controlled for social class and previous institutionalisation, a standard statistical technique at the time, but social class and previous institionalisation masks any relationship with crime. Second, new research, not available to John Gunn at the time, shows a consistent, albeit modest relationship between mental disorder and violent behaviour (1993: 287).

No one doubts any more that a 'consistent modest relationship' exists, whether for women or for men; it seems to follow the same patterns for both groups (Steadman *et al.* 1993: 54). Yet we still know too little of the characteristics of many patients. Gunn made the point some time ago that lack of data was a serious omission in our understanding of the population being treated by psychiatrists. He doubted if many psychiatrists knew how many of their patients were offenders; he was certain that mental hospitals had large numbers with a criminal record. Nowadays there would be more, particularly among the younger group. It is not clear whether their criminality, especially levels of violence, is more amenable to treatment than hitherto (Taylor 1982: 280). If not, then things really are bleak.

From this short overview we can examine a number of propositions that arise from the general proposition about comorbidity stated above. When broken down further comorbidity – in this case that mental disorder and crime have a common aetiology – produces at least four subsidiary questions.

1 Spurious or comorbid: To what extent are mental disorder and crime simply two unconnected features of a person's life?
2 Alternatively there is the reciprocal, or bi-directional question: If crime and mental disorder are causally linked, then to what extent are those links mutually reinforcing – does mental disorder lead to homelessness which leads to petty criminality?

3 Then there is the policy question: To what extent do shifts in policy alter or change the assessment or collective view of mental disorder, which then takes on a different hue or character in relation to crime?
4 Finally, concerning common cause or origin: To what extent does mental disorder and crime emerge from the same contextual milieu, that is, share the same variables such as poverty?

The first, the spurious model centres on the proposition that mental disorder and crime are simply two features of a person's life; they may be connected but there is no empirical or theoretical reason to believe this to be so. This model retains the essential elements of that described by Gunn above, which asserts that there is no connection between the morbidities concerned. So, where the phenomena are clustered together it will be coincidental, perhaps as a result of behaviours learned during adolescence, or in extreme cases as a result of cerebral dysfunctions (Taylor 1982: 277–80). The most powerful evidence for spurious comorbidity is found in the antecedents of violent offenders, mentally disordered or otherwise. As reported above the violent mentally disordered share the same social and criminological characteristics as the non-mentally disordered (Taylor 1982: 276). However, drunkenness was more often a trigger to aggression in the normal than in the mentally disordered. Nonetheless, the assertion remains: that these morbidities are unconnected; madness does not lead to violence, or violence to madness.

Similar assertions are made in the drugs/crime field. It could be that using drugs has no impact on crime, at least in the initial stages of use, there may be a major impact later as the cost of a habit on a homeless youngster increases. But how to tell? On what basis can one decide the morbidities are unconnected? Through clinical accounts? Hardly. Through research? But how? Through accounts by the offenders themselves? Perhaps not. Drug users are often keen to blame their criminality on their drug use; drug use is often seen as exonerating their illegality, in the way that similar howls of protest have come from the mentally disordered about the evils of compulsion. Tracing the sequence of events might help, but sequences say little about connections. A major strength of this model is that it engenders scepticism, which is an enormous attribute; we are too eager to promote views linking morbidities with little or no evidence to support them. In the drugs field, for example, there is an anchored perception within the media, eagerly and regularly promoted, that drugs always lead to crime, when the evidence is simply not there. These so-called common-sense truths can be harmful when determining policy, and may well distort it. So, yes, retain the scepticism and force those who assert a connection to bring out the evidence.

Second, the reciprocal, or bi-directional model sees any possible link as mutually reinforcing, so, for example, mental disorder leads to homelessness which then leads to petty criminality. Here a more direct link with criminality is posited. Critics of the community care programmes would say that there is ample anecdotal evidence to support this model; community care has had negative implications for many patients. In the early stages it meant pushing the patients out of hospital into third-rate bed-and-breakfast accommodation (see Bean and Mounser 1993). Community care in its most fashionable forms was an ideology that assumed it was desirable for mental patients to live independently, take responsibility for themselves, and adapt to the demands and rigours of life outside the mental hospital. In its purist form it meant keeping psychiatric patients out of institutions, with expanding community services available to help patients remain in the community. Closing the mental hospitals and replacing them with a system of community care seemed wonderfully progressive at the time; the reality was invariably different. Many patients could not cope, and those that could often found themselves in inferior accommodation receiving a substandard psychiatric service. Community care seemed more a way of saving money than providing psychiatric treatment.

As a result patients often found themselves in bed-and-breakfast accommodation, in inner-city areas plagued with crime and disorder. There is little research evidence to suggest that they resorted to crime, but it would not be surprising if they did. In the study by Rogers *et al.* (1993) very few in their sample were fully employed, in only 16 per cent did their job income provide the main source of income. Poverty remained a problem; social security benefits only ever covered the bare essentials (1993: 94). Yet if a return to something approximating reality is to be effected, patients need more than pills and potions; they need to be valued and given opportunities to break out of the plight of a welfare dependency culture that is oriented towards ghetto, inner-city living, with all the deprivations so entailed. And what of the actions of the psychiatrists and those formulating policy? How does their world-view influence things? (Mechanic 1989: 187). Might those patients confined to inner-city areas be seen in a different light from those from the middle-class stockbroker belt? Does a different form of rationing of services occur where these offender populations pay the price for being the 'unloving, unloved and unlovable'? Is the location in which patients live a factor determining the type of services received? Given the constraints on resources, are these all plausible, if unproven, hypotheses.

This leads neatly to the third question, the policy question; to what extent do shifts in policy change assessments of mental disorder, which then takes on a different hue in relation to another morbidity, say, crime? I have said throughout that demands for community safety have had a deleterious effect on the image of the mentally disordered, producing changes in the quality of services. The public mood, if one can use such terms, is not on the side of the mentally disordered, the message is that the mad are to be feared, not pitied. It is not difficult to see how such ideas grew out of the failings of community care; and after a number of dramatic failures involving indiscriminate violence, followed by the growth of a small number of highly vocal pressure groups, the government has had to show itself acting decisively. And that meant introducing measures that filled that lacuna left by the closure of the mental hospitals, with the aim of bridging the gap between care in the community and in-patient compulsion. The likely hypothesis derived from the current climate and in line with the policy model suggests that more mentally disordered will be prosecuted, and less consideration will be given to treating their mental disorder. There are sufficient straws in the wind to suggest that the hypothesis might be accepted.

Finally, what of the common cause or origin; to what extent does mental disorder and crime emerge from the same contextual milieu, sharing the same variables? This is slightly different from the spurious or comorbid model in that it presupposes a link, albeit small, between the morbidities. Consider the context in which much mental disorder arises. There is little doubt that the single most consistent finding in the epidemiological literature is the relationship between low social class and schizophrenia. The question exercising many commentators is whether there is something within lower-class life that helps produce the condition – the poverty, financial insecurity, for instance? Do the mentally disordered become hampered in their social life and employment prospects and so drift downwards socially? Do substance abusers, like the mentally disordered, fall prey to drift? This asserts that long-term use (and psychiatric treatment) leaves in its wake a downward trend in status and social class, with decreasing job possibilities, a set of fractured social relations and a loss of personal esteem. Often, sometimes after long periods of use, the drug user finds himself in a lower-class, inner-city area, with poor accommodation, on public welfare, and resorting to petty crime; or if female, to prostitution. It is the same for the mentally disordered.

Mechanic supports the drift hypothesis (1989); I have a different view. I am sceptical because I doubt the evidence is there to support it. Some patients may drift downwards but many were at the bottom to begin with; the most one can say is that their disorder and substance abuse prevented them rising to more acceptable levels. In an earlier study of compulsory admissions under the 1959 Mental Health Act I found over 50 per cent of all admissions came from social classes 4 and 5 – in contrast to the national picture where only 30 per cent of the population generally inhabited social classes 4 and 5 (Bean 1980: 110). This overrepresentation could not be explained by drift. It might be an artefact of selection; that is, middle-class patients managed their condition better – they sought help earlier and were less disruptive accordingly. In contrast, working-class patients were kept at home longer, their condition was correspondingly more severe, and they were more disruptive, leading to higher rates of compulsion. This is a possible explanation especially when linked to other factors. Employment prospects were 'severely and irreversibly damaged by entering the role of psychiatric patient' (Rogers *et al.* 1993: 93). Apparently employers discriminate against those known to have had earlier mental health problems.

Yet how to explain this overrepresentation in working-class culture? Is there something within working-class life that promotes madness – if so, what is it? Our Victorian forebears thought that there was; the working classes were left behind on the road to progress, and lust, hard drinking and intoxication made matters worse. Nowadays poverty is emphasised, alongside squalor and loneliness. Brown and Harris (1978), in their study of depression, linked it to stressful events, social supports and coping mechanisms. When these patterns were linked to low social class they became a potent cocktail. Graham Thornicroft (2006) does not talk of 'class' but describes patterns that closely resemble a working-class way of life and its links with poverty, social marginalisation, unemployment and the lack of social esteem associated with such defects. Yet not everyone with similar life events and social class position reacts in the same way. Mechanic (1989: 58) thinks that it is not remarkable that people to succumb to specific events; what is more remarkable is that some people do not.

One ex-patient, Mary Barnes, wrote an account of madness and summed things up nicely: she said that in order to have a career in schizophrenia you need a patient and a psychiatrist; the patient to be ill, the psychiatrist to hand out the label (Porter 1991: 397). Perhaps, after all, that is what matters. But how did this or that person come to be the patient? That is still the interesting question.

Comments on future research

Before adding some concluding thoughts I want to look at some research questions, or rather questions about research (see also Shah 1993). Much criticism has been made throughout about the paucity or quality of research into mental disorder and crime, but what of the future? I want to take as the theme the question posed by John Monahan (1994): 'How do you do research that significantly advances knowledge about people who commit crime, people who have mental disorder, or both?' Research, he says, has to approach the topic from three levels: methodological, legal and ethical, and political.

First the methodological. Monahan argues that the era of small-scale, single-site, bivariate, record-based research on mental disorder and crime may be passing. This is to be replaced by research using large sample sizes, from multiple sites, choosing predictor variables from several domains, and assessing the criterion in several domains (1994: 69). He is right, of course: small samples reduce statistical power; violence is multifaceted, as is mental disorder; official records are inadequate; and single sites produce single social contexts. Much of the research quoted above is subject to these criticisms, made worse by an increasing fashion for smaller and smaller sample sizes. Few would quarrel with the proposition for large-scale projects, except to add that there are only a few research centres able to call on sufficiently large research funds to do the research.

What place, then, for the smaller projects? The answer must be that they should ask different questions than hitherto. There is little more to be achieved with studies of mental patients in criminal justice institutions being asked about their history of violence or criminality. There is, however, something to be learned from research that concentrates on social situations where offending takes place, where the mentally disordered self-medicate with illegal substances or engage in prostitution. If there is to be research on criminal justice institutions then let it be about the manner in which the mentally disordered are dealt with – as with the use or lack of appropriate adults. We know enough about the way in which the mentally disordered are unnecessarily detained in special hospitals. What we need is research that shows how best to get them out.

Second, the legal and ethical. Monahan cites the case of *Tarasoff v Regents of the University of California* where it was held that psychotherapists have a duty to take whatever steps are reasonably necessary to protect identifiable potential victims from their patient's violence. He believes this judgement also applies to research studies. Can the grant-holder or research worker withhold information if he believes he has identified a potential victim at risk from a respondent's personal violence? That must always be a matter of judgement, there is no simple sliding scale to help here. It is not just the 'duty to protect others' that is important, there is also the duty of the research team leader to protect the research workers. Back in the 1960s or 1970s there were no such problems. Criminological research, in all its forms and sub-specialisms, was a relatively safe affair. Unpleasant incidents, such as there were, arose infrequently, and rarely involved violence to the researcher. Not any more. Researchers involved in most forms of ethnographic research or detailed interviewing are at risk from attack – in the same way that NHS staff, or other community workers are at risk. Grant-holders and universities have been slow to adapt to the new climate and have invariably failed to produce adequate levels of protection, including improved insurance cover. Research in inner-city areas, whether or not on the mentally disordered, who may also be substance abusers, is no longer a safe activity.

Then there are problems with disclosure of data. Friends, family or the courts may demand to see the data if they believe a serious risk exists, or if it will assist with litigation, or be called as evidence. There may be a legal requirement if the court insists the data be disclosed, and it would be a stalwart researcher who denied that request. Requests from friends or family for various reasons are a different matter. Ethical considerations arise, but to accede to such requests cuts across the accepted standard research guarantee of anonymity given to all respondents. Monahan describes this 'as the central tension' (1994: 70) which he says has to be confronted whenever there exists a risk to others. Confidentiality has long been claimed within the classical doctor/patient relationship, and with the priest as confidant. Anonymity is always claimed within the research community but largely without thought; research workers blithely gave guarantees of anonymity without the slightest expectation that they would ever be brought to account. This may now happen; the problem is emerging within most criminological research, posing new questions, yet few researchers are seemingly prepared for it.

The solution suggested by Monahan is to add caveats to the consent form such as 'confidentiality will be preserved except in emergencies', an altogether more honest approach even if it remains unclear as to what constitutes an 'emergency'. He defines it as 'where the lives of subjects or third parties are endangered', which again, all depends on what one means by 'endangered' (relatively minor physical violence perhaps – although to the recipient it may not appear minor – or a conspiracy to commit a serious fraud?). He also suggests a chain of command where the field research worker can make a decision to abandon the research if the threat is imminent; or in other cases refer to senior staff. Often in criminological research, whether on mental patients or others, the fieldwork is undertaken by young research workers, often female. They need protection but also training on how best, and where, to refer respondents who pose or are subject to a threat. More often than not the researchers must make the decision; they must know the dangers. In Monahan's view written documentation should be provided with guidelines for dealing with duties to protect staff (1994: 71). They should also be endorsed and underwritten by the university or other body that has the ultimate duty of care.

Third, the political. There has always been a political dimension to criminological research, sometimes in the politics and interests of the grant-giving authority, sometimes the researcher's motives: the hope is that the results will be used in ways that are acceptable to the researcher. Monahan gives an example where the International Committee Against Racism objected to the 'Violence Initiative' on the grounds that the US authorities were relying on it 'to convince older workers and middle class people, particularly white professionals to tame black and Latin youth for all the evils of the capitalist system'. It said 'The Violence Initiative is one of the main vehicles for this fascist agenda. It must be stopped' (quoted in Monahan 1994: 71). This view sees criminological research as one-dimensional, and it has never been that. Clearly, it has been used to man the control machinery, and help the state be more efficient when dealing with its deviants, but so too has it been able to frustrate the activities of the powerful, readjust the images of the media and represent the interests of those otherwise not represented. To its credit research has also tried to be apolitical; on those occasions when it has taken a political stance it has failed to convince, and opened itself to ridicule and accusations of bias.

Yet how to achieve a non-political stance when the subject matter lends itself to instant and extreme political interpretations? Madness and crime can 'reaffirm public fears and provide unwitting support to regressive public policies' (Monahan 1994: 72). For those with a political agenda extreme statements come easily. How much do criminologists play into this with their own political bias? This important question is often avoided. Monahan's solution is rather less convincing. He produced what he called a 'consensus statement' directed at balancing the images of sensationalism produced by the media reporting, and the popular misuse of psychiatric terms (he lists 'psychopath' and 'psychotic', but could add others including 'depression'). He said misconceptions about the extent of violence among the mentally disordered should be corrected, and better-quality treatments should be provided (1994: 72).

This simply swaps one political statement for another. When Monahan writes 'the experience of people with psychiatric conditions and of their family members paints a picture dramatically different from the stereotype', or 'Mental disorders – in sharp contrast to alcohol and drug abuse – account for a miniscule portion of the violence that afflicts American society', he is playing another political game that is not likely to convince anybody. We are entering choppy waters here. Accusations by extremists are not made in order to enter a dialogue, but to restate their political points. So, when the Violence Research Initiative is accused of distracting attention from the real problems and rearranging them as public health concerns when more properly the problems should be seen as those of racism, poverty, decay of the schools, or lack of health care (quoted in Monahan 1994: 71), what should be the response? (Incidentally a psychiatrist made the accusation!) Only in terms of the merit and quality of the research, for as long as the research meets the requirements of methodological competency and rigour, that is sufficient. It should speak for itself. To enter a political slanging match is counterproductive. What people make of the research is up to them.

Summary and conclusion

Trawling the research literature on madness and crime leads to the inescapable conclusion that researchers are primarily – sometimes exclusively – interested in the links with violence, and then only madness in its more severe forms; preferably in the links with schizophrenia, about which there are countless studies. Of most other crimes there is often a stony silence. There is nothing substantial on burglary, a little more on rape, but almost nothing on shoplifting, fraud, criminal damage and dishonestly handling stolen property, let alone motoring offences. True, there is a developing literature on substance abuse, with an additional conclusion that substance abuse as comorbidity with mental disorder has changed the criminological landscape, whether due to the reluctance to treat such patients, or the deleterious effects they have on the wards. Or in the obvious way that mental disorder and substance abuse has cranked up the crime link. But this is an exception.

Such studies where they exist owe more to the literature on substance abuse than that on madness. The model used throughout has shown up many gaps, exposed areas of weakness in our knowledge base, and identified major fault lines – but also shown where lies the excess. We know much about mental disorder leading to violent crime but not much else. To produce a more balanced literature we need a greater level of interest from criminologists, especially sociologists able to promote studies dealing with the mentally disordered in the community, including the impact of criminal justice programmes on mental disorder. Moreover, we have a surfeit of studies of the mentally disordered in special hospitals and prisons but too few on their experiences in the police station or on probation, and on those living in inner-city areas where criminality is rife. This is where I believe the research challenge lies. As I have said elsewhere, the term 'mentally abnormal offender' is a misnomer; it is better to talk of 'offenders who are mentally disordered'. That places the emphasis on the criminality where it should belong, and where the research should be directed. If we can fill some of the gaps identified here we will know more about the links between madness and crime, and perhaps, who knows, we may produce a more rational set of policy objectives.

Notes

1 Contained within terms such as 'link' are expectations of something direct; a causal explanation perhaps. The language suggests that one will lead directly to the other. Yet to use language in this way creates a certain impression, such as of those claiming the M'Naughton Rules, that the person is trapped in a psychiatric condition that means he can do no other than commit that crime, i.e. that there was a direct causal connection. If so then this requires a level of explanation over and above the usual way in which social science operates. For to establish a cause, or to say an event has a cause, is to invoke a universal law that, along with statements about initial conditions prevailing at a time, will, when taken together, allow a prediction to be made. So, to take an obvious example, when the temperature drops below zero, we can

predict that water will freeze. Here we have a typical causal relationship where a condition, which can be regarded as sufficient, can explain the event (Benn and Peters 1975: 199; see also Bolton and Hill 1996). Social scientists have rarely been able to establish 'cause' in the manner of the natural scientists.

2 A glance at the legal definition as stated in Section 1(2) of the 1983 Mental Health Act supports my contention. 'Psychopathic disorder means a persistent disorder or disability of mind (whether or not including significant impairement of intelligence) which results in abnormally aggressive or seriously irresponsible conduct on the part of the persons concerned.' Richard Jones quotes Nolan: 'No doubt whether the conduct is the result of the disorder … is a medical question. Whether it amounts to seriously irresponsible or abnormally aggressive behaviour seems to me … to raise questions other than of a purely clinical nature (Jones 2003: 15).

3 The role of the police surgeon is underrated. In an unpublished study of the way the Leicestershire Police operated Section 136 of the Mental Health Act it was clear that the police surgeon was called for a medical opinion before anyone else was approached, and that includes GPs, psychiatrists or Appropriate Adults. In fact the police looked to the police surgeon to advise them on whether others should be called. Accordingly, their influence was greater than was required in legislation. For example the decision to call an Appropriate Adult is not down to the police surgeon, nor is it a medical matter. The decision is that of the custody officer (Bean 2000).

4 Typical of the comments are these by a journalist (*Sunday Times*, 19 March 2006), who wrote after an episode in which a serial killer was sentenced to life in prison, 'The public needs protection. In the end we don't care whether dangerous people are mad or bad or abused in childhood. We just want them kept away from us – rehabilitated if possible, but locked up.' The reference to childhood abuse was presumably a swipe at those who draw attention to the background deficiencies of so many persistent offenders.

5 Indeed, if one wishes to medicalise it then why not call it PTSD (post-traumatic stress disorder)? Placing it here is no less unreasonable than in other contexts. PTSD is an example of another so-called new diagnosis, while in fact the symptoms comprising PTSD may be nothing more than a natural reaction to traumatic experiences. Many authors have criticised PTSD on exactly that basis, for when studies report that over 90 per cent of a population living in war zones suffer from PTSD, is it right to name the symptoms of the individuals of such populations as a mental disorder? Might it be nothing more than a further attempt at medicalising reactions? (I am grateful to Dr. Georg Hoyer for comments on this section.)

References

Baldacchino, A., Riglietta, A. and Corkery, J. (2003) *Maternal Health and Drug Abuse*, ECCAS Monograph Series No. 3. London: European Centre for Addiction Studies.

Baxter, H., Duggan, C., Larkin, E., Cordess, C. and Page, K. (2001) 'Mentally disordered parricide and stranger killers admitted to high security care', *Journal of Forensic Psychiatry*, 12(2) (Sept): 287–99.

Bean, P.T. (1980) *Compulsory Admissions to Mental Hospitals*. Chichester: John Wiley.

Bean P.T. (2000) *Section 136: An Evaluation of Procedures*, Report to Leicestershire Constabulary (Mimeo).

Bean, P.T. (2001) *Mental Disorder and Community Safety*. London: Palgrave.

Bean, P.T. (2004) *Drugs and Crime*, 2nd edn. Cullompton: Willan Publishing.

Bean, P.T. (2005) 'The Health of Drug Users', in J. Goethals, F. Hutsebaut and G. Vervaeke (eds) *Gerechtelijke geestelijke gezondheidszorg: wetenschap, beleid en praktijk*. University of Leuven, 57–68.

Bean, P.T. and Mounser, P. (1993) *Discharged from Mental Hospitals*. London: Macmillan.

Bean, P.T. and Nemitz, T. (1994) *Out of Depth and Out of Sight*. Report to MENCAP.

Bean, P.T. and Nemitz, T. (2000) *Report to the Youth Justice Board on the American Juvenile Drug Court and Family Drug Court* (Mimeo).

Benn, S. and Peters, R. (1959) *Social Principles and the Democratic State*. London: George Allen and Unwin.

Bizzarri, J., Rocci, P., Vallotta, A., Girelli, M., Scandolari, A., Zerbetto, E., Sbrana, A., Iagher, C. and Dellantonio, E. (2005) 'Dual diagnosis and quality of life in patients in treatment for opioid dependence', *Substance Use and Misuse*, 40(12): 1765–76.

Bluglass, R. and Bowden, P. (eds) (1990) *Principles and Practice of Forensic Psychiatry*. London: Churchill Livingstone.

Bolton, D. and Hill, J. (1996) *Mind, Meaning and Mental Disorder: The Nature of Causal Explanation in Psychology and Psychiatry*. Oxford: Oxford University Press.

Brown, A. (2006) 'Prosecuting psychiatric inpatients: Where is the thin blue line?', *Medicine Science and the Law*, 46(1): 7–12.

Brown, G. and Harris, T. (1978) *Social Origins of Depression: A Study of Psychiatric Disorder*. London: Tavistock.

Bucknill, J.C. (1884) Lecture on the relation of madness to crime, delivered at the London Institution, 28 February 1884, reprinted in *British Medical Journal*, 15 and 22 March 1884.

Burton, S. (2002) *A Double Life: A Biography of Charles and Mary Lamb*. London: Penguin Viking.

Connell, P.H. (1958) *Amphetamine Psychosis*, Maudsley Monograph No. 5. Oxford: Oxford University Press.

Cope, R. (1993) 'A survey of forensic psychiatrists' views on psychopathic disorder', *Journal of Forensic Psychiatry*, 4(2): 215–35.

Corkery, J. (2003) *The Nature and Extent of Drug use in the UK*. Official Statistics Surveys and Studies (Mimeo).

Department of Health (1992) *Review of Health and Social Services for Mentally Disordered Offenders and Others Requiring Similar Services: Final Summary Report* (Reed Report), Cm 2088. London: HMSO.

D'Orban, P. (1990) 'Kidnapping, Abduction and Child Stealing', in R. Bluglass and P. Bowden (eds) *Principles and Practice of Forensic Psychiatry*. London: Churchill Livingstone, 797–803.

Exworthy, T. (1995) 'Compulsory care in the community: A review of the proposals for compulsory supervision and treatment of the mentally ill in the community', *Criminal Behaviour and Mental Health*, 5: 218–41.

Exworthy, T. (1998) 'Institutions and services in forensic psychiatry', *Journal of Forensic Psychiatry*, 9(2): 395–412.

Farrington, D. (1992) 'Editorial', *Criminal Behaviour and Mental Health*, 2(4): iii–v.

Goldstein, P. (1995) 'The Drugs–Violence Nexus: A Tripartite Framework', in J. Inciardi and K. McElrath (eds) *The American Drug Scene*. New Carolina: Roxbury.

Gordon, A. (1990) 'Drugs and Criminal Behaviour', in R. Bluglass and P. Bowden (eds) *Principles and Practice of Forensic Psychiatry*. London: Churchill Livingstone, 897–902.

Grella, C.E. (2003) 'Contrasting the views of substance abuse, mental health treatment providers on treating the dually diagnosed', *Substance Use and Misuse*, 38(10): 1433–46.

Grisso, T. and Appelbaum, P. (1998) *Assessing Competence to Consent to Treatment*. Oxford: Oxford University Press.

Gunn, J. (1977) 'Criminal behaviour and mental disorder', *British Journal of Psychiatry*, 130: 217.

Gunn, J. and Robertson, G. (1982) 'An Evaluation of Grendon Prison', in J. Gunn and D. Farrington (eds) *Abnormal Offenders Delinquency and the Criminal Justice System*. Chichester: John Wiley, 285–306.

Gunn, J. and Taylor, P. (1993) (eds) *Forensic Psychiatry: Clinical, Legal and Ethical Issues*. London: Butterworth Heinemann.

Gunn J., Maden, A. and Swinton, M. (1991a) *Mentally Disordered Prisoners*. London: Home Office.

Gunn, J., Maden, A. and Swinton, J. (1991b) 'Treatment needs of prisoners with psychiatric disorders', *British Medical Journal*, 303: 338–41.

Halleck, S.L. (1987) *The Mentally Disordered Offender*. American Psychiatric Press.

Inciardi, J., Lockwood, D. and Pottieger, A. (1993) *Women and Crack-Cocaine*. New York: Macmillan.

Institute of Medicine (1996) *Pathways of Addiction: Opportunities in Drug Abuse Research*. Washington: National Academy Press.

ISD (Institute for Statistical Development) (2003) *Drug Misuse Statistics for Scotland 2002*. Edinburgh: ISD.

Jones, J., Thomas-Peter, B. Warren, S. and Leadbeater, C. (1998) 'An investigation of the personality characteristics of mentally disordered offenders detained under the Mental Health Act', *Journal of Forensic Psychiatry*, 9(1) (May): 58–93.

Jones, R. (2003) *Mental Health Act Manual*, 8th edn. London: Sweet and Maxwell.

Kingham, M. and Gordon, H. (2004) 'Aspects of morbid jealousy', *Advances in Psychiatric Treatment*, 10: 207–15.

Levey, S. (1990) 'Suicide', in R. Bluglass and P. Bowden (eds) *Principles and Practice of Forensic Psychiatry*. London: Churchill Livingstone, 597–610.

Link, B.G. and Stueve, A. (1996) 'Psychotic Symptoms and Behaviour', in J. Monaghan and H.J. Steadman (eds) *Violence and Mental Disorder: Developments and Risk Assessment*. University of Chicago Press, 137–60.

Maughan, B. (1993) 'Childhood Precursers of Aggressive Offending in Personality Disordered Adults', in S. Hodgins (ed.) *Mental Disorder and Crime*. California: Sage, 119–39.

McNiel, D.E. (1996) 'Hallucinations and Violence', in J. Monaghan and H.J. Steadman (eds) *Violence and Mental Disorder: Developments and Risk Assessment*. University of Chicago Press, 183–202.

Mechanic, D. (1989) *Mental Health and Social Policy*. New Jersey: Prentice-Hall.

Monahan, J. (1992) 'Mental disorder and violent behaviour: Attitudes and evidence', *American Psychologist*, 47: 511–21.

Monahan, J. (1993a) 'Mental Disorder and Violence: Another Look', in S. Hodgins (ed.) *Mental Disorder and Crime*. California: Sage, pp. 287–302.

Monahan J. (1993b) 'A View from the United States of America', in J. Gunn and P. Taylor (eds) *Forensic Psychiatry: Clinical, Legal and Ethical Issues*. London: Butterworth Heinemann, 641–5.

Monahan, J. (1994) 'People with mental disorder and people who offend: Collecting valid data', *Criminal Behaviour and Mental Health*, 4: 68–73.

Monahan, J. and Steadman, H.J. (eds) (1996) *Violence and Mental Disorder: Developments and Risk Assessment*. University of Chicago Press.

Murphy, S. and Rosenbaum, M. (1994) *Pregnant Women on Drugs*. New Jersey: Rutgers University Press.

Parsons, S., Walker, L. and Grubin, D. (2001) 'Prevalence of mental disorder in female remand prisons', *Journal of Forensic Psychiatry*, 12(1) (April): 194–202.

Peay, J. (1997) 'Mentally Disordered Offenders', in M. Maguire, R. Morgan and R. Reiner (eds) *The Oxford Handbook of Criminology*. Oxford: Oxford University Press, 661–702.

Penrose, L. (1939) 'Mental disease and crime', *British Journal of Medical Psychology*, 18.

Porter, R. (1991) *The Faber Book of Madness*. London: Faber and Faber.

Prins, H. (1994) *Fire Raising: Its Motivation and Management*. London: Routledge.

Prins, H. (1995) *Offenders Deviants or Patients? An Introduction to the Study of Socio-forensic Problems*, 2nd edn. London: Routledge (1st edn 1980: Tavistock).

Pritchard, C. and Bagley, C. (2001) 'Suicide and murder in child murderers and child sexual abusers', *Journal of Forensic Psychiatry*, 12(2): 313–29.

Regier, D., Farmer, M., Rae, D., Locke, B., Keith, S., Judd, L. and Goodwin, F. (1990) 'Comorbidity of mental disorders with alcohol and other drug abuse', *Journal of the American Medical Association*, 264(2): 511–18.

Ritchie, J., Dick, D. and Lingham, R. (1994) *Report of the Inquiry into the Care and Treatment of Christopher Clunis* (Ritchie Report). London: HMSO.

Robertson, G. (1982) 'The 1959 Mental Health Act of England and Wales: Changes in the Use of its Criminal Provisions', in J. Gunn and D. Farrington (eds) *Abnormal Offenders Delinquency and the Criminal Justice System*, Vol. 1. Chichester: John Wiley, 245–68.

Robertson, G. (1987) 'Mentally abnormal offenders: Manner of death', *British Medical Journal*, 295: 632–4.

Rogers, A., Pilgrim, D. and Lacey, R. (1993) *Experiencing Psychiatry: Users' Views of Services*. London: Macmillan.

Rollin, H. (1969) *The Mentally Abnormal Offender and the Law*. London: Pergamon.

Royal College of Psychiatrists (2000) *Drugs Dilemmas and Choices*. London: Gaskell.

Rutter, M. (1997) 'Comorbidity, concepts claims and choices', *Criminal Behaviour and Mental Health*, 7: 265–86.

Sarasalo, E., Bergman, B. and Toth, T. (1998) 'Repetitive shoplifting in Stockholm Sweden: A register study of 1,802 cases', *Criminal Behaviour and Mental Health*, 8: 256–65.

Scott, P.D. (1970) 'Punishment or treatment: Prison or hospital', *British Medical Journal* (18 April): 167–9.

Shah, S. (1993) 'Recent Research on Crime and Mental Disorder: Some Implications for Programs and Policies', in S. Hodgins (ed.) *Mental Disorder and Crime*. California: Sage, 303–16.

Seivewright, N., Iqbal, M.Z. and Bourne, H. (2004) 'Treating Patients with Comorbidities', in P.T. Bean and T. Nemitz (eds) *Drug Treatment: What Works?* London: Routledge, 123–41.

Soothill, K. (1990) 'Arson', in R. Bluglass and P. Bowden (eds) *Principles and Practice of Forensic Psychiatry*. London: Churchill Livingstone, 779–86.

Steadman, H. and Cocozza, J. (1974) *Careers of the Criminally Insane*. Maryland: Lexington.

Steadman, H., Monahan, J., Robbins, P., Appelbaum, P., Grisso, T., Klassen, D., Mulvey, E. and Roth, L. (1993) 'From Dangerousness to Risk Assessment: Implications for Appropriate Research Strategies', in S. Hodgins (ed.) *Mental Disorder and Crime*. California: Sage, 23–9.

Steadman, H., Mulvey, E., Monahan, J., Robbins, P., Appelbaum, P., Grisso, T., Roth, L. and Silver, E. (1998) 'Violence by people discharged from acute psychiatric inpatient facilities and by others in the same neighbourhoods', *Archives of General Psychiatry*, 55: 393–401.

Swanson, J.W. (1996) 'Mental Disorder, Substance Abuse and Community Violence: An Epidemiological Approach', in J. Monaghan and H.J. Steadman (eds) *Violence and Mental Disorder: Developments and Risk Assessment*. University of Chicago Press, 101–36.

Swanson, J.W., Holzer, C.E., Ganju, V.K. and Jono, R.T. (1990) 'Violence and psychiatric disorder in the community: Evidence from the Epidemiological Catchment Area Surveys', *Hospital and Community Psychiatry*, 41: 761–70.

Taylor, P. (1982) 'Schizophrenia and Violence', in J. Gunn and D. Farrington (eds) *Abnormal Offenders Delinquency and the Criminal Justice System*. Chichester: John Wiley, 269–84.

Taylor, P. (1993) 'Schizophrenia and Crime: Distinctive Patterns in Association', in S. Hodgins (ed.) *Mental Disorder and Crime*. California: Sage, 63–85.

Taylor, P., Garety, P., Buchanan, A., Reed, A., Wessely, S., Ray, K., Dunn, G. and Grubin, D. (1996) 'Delusions and Violence', in J. Monaghan and H.J. Steadman (eds) *Violence and Mental Disorder: Developments and Risk Assessment*. University of Chicago Press, 161–82.

Thomasius, R., Petersen, K.U., Zapletalova, P. Wartberg, L., Zeichner, D. and Schmoldt, A. (2005) 'Mental disorders in current and former heavy ecstasy (MDMS) users', *Addiction*, 100(9): 1310–19.

Thornicroft, G. (2006) *Shunned: Discrimination Against People with Mental Illness*. Oxford: Oxford University Press.

West, D.J. (1990) 'Treatment', in R. Bluglass and P. Bowden (eds) *Principles and Practice of Forensic Psychiatry*. London: Churchill Livingstone, 767–76.

West, D.J. (1993) 'Disordered and Offensive Sexual Behaviour', in J. Gunn and P. Taylor (eds) *Forensic Psychiatry: Clinical, Legal and Ethical Issues*. London: Butterworth Heinemann, 522–66.

Whitlock, A. (1990) 'Mental Disorder and Dangerous Driving', in R. Bluglass and P. Bowden (eds) *Principles and Practice of Forensic Psychiatry*. London: Churchill Livingstone, 835–9.

Widiger, T.A. and Trull, T.J. 'Personality Disorders and Violence', in J. Monaghan and H.J. Steadman (eds) *Violence and Mental Disorder: Developments and Risk Assessment*. University of Chicago Press, 203–26.

Subject Index

appeal, against compulsion 113–114
appropriate adults 135, 179
approved social worker 97–100,
    135–136
Approved Mental Health
    Professional 100
art, as therapy in relation to
    madness 48

Bournewood Judgement 71, 73

Cartesian dualism 7–8
cognitive model (*see* empirical)
    21–24
community treatment orders, also
    community supervision orders 74
Connelly, J. 51, 59
compulsion, impact of 93–96
creativity and madness 55–59
Cressey, Donald 27–28
crime and madness Section 4 *passim*
criminal; justice and madness
    see crime and madness and
    psychiatric services
crime leads to mental disorder
    164–168

dangerous *see* harm to self and others
Darwin Charles 3, 50
Declaration of Hawaii 67
delusions and crime 156–161
detention of patients *de jure* 68–77
detention of patients *de facto* 68–77
detention under section 5(2) of 1993
    Act 103–104, 115
detention under section 5(4) of the
    1983 Act 71 104–105, 115, 117
detention under section 136 of
    the 1983 Act, *see* police and
    compulsion
depression 40
diagnostic creep 179
differential association, theory of,
    24–25
disease model of madness (also
    medical model) 4, 5–11, 38

emergency order under 1983 Mental
    Health Act 97, 103
emotional theory of madness 17,
    31–36
empirical model (*see also* cognitive)
    21–24, 35–39

genius and madness Section 2
passim

hallucinations and crime 156–161
harm to self and others 90–93
Haslam, John 3
Human Rights Act 1998 66
Hunter and Macalpine 9, 38

Independent Decision Maker 85–86,
102
Infanticide Act 1938 34–35
informal patients *see* voluntary

Johnson, Dr. Samuel 3, 14–16, 36–37,
51
juveniles in the criminal justice
system 138

Lamb, Charles and Mary in Hoxton
Asylum 51, 93
law, therapeutic law 82–86
types of law compared 82–86
Lear, King 2–3, 5, 39
legalism (also new legalism) 63–65
liberty, negative, defined 77–82
Locke John and empiricism 11–15,
20–23, 37

Mad Lucas 62–63, 110
madness, caused by grief 3
caused by multiple sources 4
defined, 17, 19–21
medical model of madness
(*see* disease model) 6
medical recommendations 97,
101–105
mental capacity *see also* Mental
Capacity Act 2005, 90
Mental Capacity Act 2005 73–74,
84–90
mental disorder leads to crime
140–164
mental disorder and crime, a
common aetiology 168–173

mental disorder crime and
substance abuse 141–147, 166–168
mental disorder and economic
necessity 151–153
mental disorder reducing crime
147–151
mental disorder and victims 149–151
mental disorder and violence
161–164
Mental Health Act 1983, 63, 66, 179
Mental Health Act Commission
68–71, 76, 90, 100–105
Mental Health Bill 2006 66, 74, 82,
83, 86 *passim* 89–90, 104, 116–117
mind-brain theory 6–8
Mental Health (Nurses) Order 1998
117
moral treatment 16
Morbid jealousy 159–160
motoring offences and mental
disorder, 155
multi-dimensional model 4–5

nearest relative 100–101
NICE 22–23
normality *see* sanity

Parens patriae 105–108
paternalism against autonomy
105–108
personality disorder, *see*
psychopathy
police and compulsion (includes
Section 136 of the 1983 Act)
70–71, 105, 133–134, 152, 179
Police and Criminal Evidence Act
1984 (PACE) 135–136
Police surgeon (also called Forensic
Medical Examiner) 135–136, 179
Prison Medical Services 137–138
prison, mentally disordered in 76–77
psychiatric services and criminal
justice 131–139
psychopathy Also personality
disorder 6, 9, 36, 127–128, 179

psychoanalysis and Freud 17, 48

religion and insanity 19
Romantics in relation to madness 48

sanity (also normality) 3, 20
scholastics 12–13
Sex offences, and mental disorder 153
shell shock during WW1, 17
shoplifting and mental disorder
      151–152
statistical theory of madness, 25–30

Szasz, T. 6, 39, 68, 86, 87

tabula rasa 11, 12

victims *see* mental disorder and
      victims
violence and mental disorder 161
Voltaire 4, 26
voluntary patients, see *de facto and
      de jure* admissions

Willis Francis 17

Author Index

Adserballe, H. 94
Ashmore, R. 105
Audini, B. (and Lelliott, P.) 69, 71

Baldacchino, A. (and Reglietta, A., and Corkery, J.) 145
Bass, C. (and Halligan, P.W.) 43
Baxter, H. *et al.* 123
Bean, P.T. 40, 63, 71 *passim*
Bean, P.T. and Mounser, P. 104, 171
Bean, P.T. and Nemitz, T. 135, 138
Benn, S. and Peters, R. 78, 91, 92, 179
Bentall, R.P. 10–11, 13, 38
Berlin, I. 79
Bindman, J. 70
Bindman, J., (and Maingay, S. and Szmukler, G.) 66
Bizzarri, J., *et al* (there are 9 authors to this paper) 144, 145
Bluglass, R. (and Bowden, P.) 151
Bolton, D. (and Hill, J.) 9, 40, 178
Boswell, J. 15
Bowen, P. 76
Brown, A. 206
Brown, G. (and Harris, T.) 173
Brun, B. 94

Buchanan, A. 109
Bucknill, 162
Burton, S. 51, 93, 156, 157

Carter, R.B. 7
Casey, T. 108
Chadwick, P.K. 2, 24
Churchill, R. (and Wall, S., Hotopf, M., Buchanan, A. and Wessely) 62, 69, 72, 94
Clare, A. 64, 68, 107
Claridge, G. 5
Clarke, I. 6, 7, 21
Connell, P.H. 142, 167
Cope, R. 128
Corkery, J. 146

D'Orban, P. 154
Damasio, A.R. 30
Darcy, P.T. 94
Davidson, D. 10
Department of Health (includes Percy Commission 1957) 64, 66 74, 83, 87, 89, 94, 100, 132
Dixon, M. (and Oyebode, F. and Brannigan, C.) 110
Donnelly, M. 16

Eastman, N. (and Peay, J.) 84, 85, 98, 102
Ellis, H. 53, 56, 57
Expert Committee (Richardson Committee) 64, 65, 75, 83, 84, 85, 89, 90, 100
Exworthy, T. 133, 134, 136, 162

Farrington, D. 126
Feinberg, J. and Gross, H. 78–82 passim, 91
Foucault, M. 1, 37–38

Galton, F. 53
Gelder, M. (Harrison, P. and Cowen, P.) 21–22, 23, 24
Glover, J. 7
Goldstein, P. 139, 147, 148–149
Gordon, A. 141
Greenland, C. 63
Grella, C.E. 143
Grisso, T. and Appelbaum, P. 89
Gunn, J. and Robertson, G. 153
Gunn, J. and Taylor, P. 128, 150, 153, 163
Gunn, J. et al. 133, 136
Gunn, J. 124, 125, 128, 135, 168–169
Gunn, J., Maden, T. and Swinton, M. 136

Hall, A.D. (and Puri, B.K., Stewart, T. and Graham, P.S.) 104
Halleck, S.L. 123
Hargreaves, R. 97, 100
Hobbes, T. 26, 30, 31–36
Hodgson, J. 71
Hoggett, B. 35, 87–88, 89, 90
House of Lords 66, 73, 83
Hoyer, G. 90, 165, 179
Humphrey, M.S. 113

Inciardi, J. (and Lockwood, D. and Pottieger, A.) 145
Ingleby, D. 6

Institute of Medicine ISD (Institute for Statistical Development) 145
International Classification of Mental and Behavioural Disorders WHO 32, 40

Jacob, C. and Freer, T. 104
Jacobson, K.G. (and Lynoe, N., Kohn, R. and Levan, I.) 101, 112
Jamison, K.R. 2
Jensen, K. and Pedersen, B. 95
Jones, K. 63
Jones, R. 71, 74, 83, 84, 91, 179
Jones, J. (and Thomas-Peter, B. Warren, S. and Leadbeater, C.) 123

Kingham, M (and Gordon, H.) 159–160
Kinton, M. 76, 116
Kittrie, N.N. 106
Kmietowicz, Z. 69

Lamb, C. 51–52
Levey, S. 154–155
Liddle, P.T. 30
Link, B.G. and Stueve, A. 124, 126, 127, 157–158, 161, 206
Locke, J. 4, 11–39 passim
Lombroso, C. 47, 50, 51, 53

Maudsley, H. 47, 49
Maughan, B. 138
McNiel, D.E. 156, 158
McPherson, A. and Jones, R.G. 69
Mechanic, D. 171–172
Mill, J.S. 78–82 passim
Minto, A. 64
Monahan, J. 123, 140, 168, 173–177
Monahan, J. and Steadman, H. 163, 168
Morison, A.P. 22
Moss, K. and Prins, H. 116, 117
Murphy, S. and Rosenbaum, M. 145

Nemitz, T. and Bean, P.T. 70, 71

Nicolson, H. 52–53, 54–55, 56–57, 59–60

Nisbet, J.F. 48, 50, 51, 53, 55

Parsons, S. (and Walker, L. and Grubin, D.) 137, 142, 152

Peay, J. 63, 66, 81, 95, 98, 129–130, 150

Penrose, L. 131

Pickering, G. 55, 56, 58

Porter, R. 1, 3, 4, 5, 8, 9, 11, 15, 26, 36, 47, 48, 49, 52, 55, 57, 58, 61–62, 93, 174

Post, F. 53

Priebe, S. et al (there are 8 Authors for this paper) 69

Prins, H. 29, 35, 128, 137, 132, 151, 152, 154, 155, 162

Pritchard, C. and Bagley, C. 138

Quinton A. 17–21, 28, 30, 32, 33

Rapaport, A. 100

Read, J. (Mosher, L. and Bentall, R.) 6

Regier, D. (there are 6 other authors) 142

Richardson, G. and Thorold, O. 99, 114

Ritchie, J. (and Dick, D. and Linghham, R.) 162

Robertson, G. 153, 163

Rogers, A. (and Pilgrim, D. and Lacey, R.) 95, 96, 142, 171, 173

Rollin, H. 135

Roth, J. (and Kroll, J.) 1, 79, 80, 87

Royal College of Psychiatrists 144

Russell, B. 14, 55

Rutter, M. 168

Salib, E. and Iparragirre, B. 70

Sarasalo, E. (and Bergman, B. and Toth, T.) 152

Scott, P.D. 132

Screech, M. 19, 47

Scull, A. 1, 52, 56, 61

Seivewright, N. (and Iqbal, M.Z. and Bourne, H.) 142, 147, 167

Shah, S. 174

Soothill, K. 155

Steadman, H. and Cocozza, J. 130

Steadman, H. et al (there are 9 authors for this paper) 147, 169

Swanson, J.W. (and Holzer, C.E., Ganju, V.K. and Jono, R.T.) 124, 125

Swanson, J.W. 125, 142, 162

Taylor, P. 158–159, 163, 165, 169, 170

Taylor, et al. 159, 160, 161

The Stationery Office 146

Thomasius, R. et al 144

Thornicroft, G. 72, 73, 155, 164, 173

Tyrer, P. (and Steinberg, D.) 6, 7, 8, 22

Vold, G.B. (Bernard, T.J. and Snipes, J.F.) 25

Webb, T.E. 17

Webber, M. and Huxley, P. 69

West, D.J. 154

Whitlock, A. 156

Widiger, T.A. (and Trull, T.J.) 156

Williamson, T. 128–129

Wootton, B. 27, 29

Yolton, J.W. 11